Living in the Long Shadow

Living in the Long Shadow

Surviving a Legacy of Mental Illness

SUZANNE SHERMAN

SWP
SHE WRITES PRESS

Published in 2026 by
She Writes Press, an imprint of The Stable Book Group

1569 Solano Ave #546
Berkeley, CA 94707
https://shewritespress.com
Library of Congress Control Number: 2026909780
ISBN: 979-8-89636-158-9
eISBN: 979-8-89636-159-6

Interior Designer: Brynn Warriner

Printed in the United States

Names and identifying characteristics have been changed to protect the privacy of certain individuals.

For my mother
who deserved to sing longer

Marilyn Friedman, 19

Everything has its wonders, even darkness.

—Helen Keller

Chapter 1

My father never called my mother's mental illness by name but he says it started the night they saw a hypnotist on stage on Pico. It was Los Angeles, the summer of 1964, and she was thirty. They had hired a babysitter to stay with their three kids—we were two, four, and six years old. "Our seat was way in the back," he would tell me years later, indignant about the apparent illogic of it. My father was a lawyer. Logic could have been his middle name. Fifteen years after that night, my mother would decide she couldn't walk in the house of horrors anymore. She had schizophrenia, a mental illness without a cure.

I had no sense of time at four years old, and my grasp of language didn't help me make sense of what was happening around me. But I was watching.

One night my father came home from his office, suit coat draped over an arm. He closed the front door behind him, set his briefcase down, and took in the scene in the living room with a frown. My red plastic cash register sat on a card table beside a bunch of rubbery green grapes. Play dollar bills lay scattered on the carpet around it. The TV droned in an empty family room. Little David stood in his playpen wearing a full diaper and holding onto the railing with a joyful smile—*Daddy's home!* Lynne was probably in our bedroom, door shut.

"Marilyn?" My father headed for their bedroom at the back of the house.

"What's wrong with Mommy?" I asked, following.

He shooed me away with a hand. "She's sick. Don't come in."

Why was Mommy still sick? I always got better after a few days when I was sick.

The next thing I knew my mother was leaving her bedroom for the kitchen, patting her bun into place and straightening her skirt on her way through the living room. She looked lopsided.

I stood in the kitchen doorway, watching her unwrap a slab of meat. She laid it on a broiler pan, then opened a can of lima beans and poured them into a pot. I loved lima beans! But I wasn't about to say that right then.

FOR YEARS I ACCEPTED A FOGGY TRUTH ABOUT THIS time, letting perception act like fact, never tracking the sequence of events in my early life or trying to understand the impressions that shaped me. It wouldn't be until forty years after my mother's suicide that I would finally feel ready to examine the murky waters I had managed to survive without knowing how to swim. Doing it, I took a chance on either getting irrevocably lost in sorrow or finding a new peace.

To uncover how long my mother's illness lasted this first time it came, I waded deep into the waters of my earliest memories. Verifiable dates gave shape to images I had never known where to place, letting me connect the dots.

I found date-stamped Kodak slides in an old box recovered from a storage unit that some of her things went into after she died. Pictures of the General Sherman Tree at Sequoia National Park started the set. August 1964. Maybe my father took his family there hoping the beauty of the forest would bring my mother back. Growing up in New York, the neighborhood woods had been a refuge for her.

Now I had a date for a memory that for years had stayed in my mind without a place in time.

In that memory, it was morning. My mother took my hand and led me out of the cabin where the family was staying to walk into the woods nearby. My father stayed back with my sister and brother, lying sprawled on his back on the bed, exhausted from too little sleep. A squirrel had come into the cabin through a window in the night, a surprising event my sister was still giggling about.

My mother and I crunched along a dirt path leading to the trees. She seemed to know where we were going.

Suddenly—magically, it seemed—we left the morning sun for a shady, secret forest paradise. Amazed by the grandeur of this great shelter, I gazed into a world of trees so tall they touched the sky.

My mother stopped where we were, still holding my hand in hers. "Listen."

I looked up at her, not sure what she could mean. Her eyes sparkled. She inhaled the earthy scents around us with deep breaths and smiled at the beauty of the sunbeams slanting through trees, turning her head this way and that.

"What should I listen to?" I asked.

"The forest."

Birds chattered with a muted *chirr*, a *tuk tuk tuk tuk*, a sharp *yeep!* Branches waved like giant green hands petting the air. My mother was showing all of this to me. It was a soul moment I would always remember.

The next date appeared on a newspaper clipping I found in her photo album. It was September 25, 1964, a month after that trip to Sequoia (connecting the dots). The *Los Angeles Times* published a photo of her with David in the playground at Mar Vista Park with a front-page article in the Westside section of the paper about mothers using baby talk with their children. Two other photos showed mothers with their own toddlers, and a quote by each of them appeared in the captions.

In my mother's photo, her wavy brown hair was twisted into a bun at the back of her head. She wore a sleeveless, round-necked blouse and a checkered pencil skirt that hugged her hips in a shapely curve. She offered the camera a faint smile, a hand hanging limply at her side, the other resting on the climbing bars where her blue-eyed two-year-old posed with a fetching smile. Her smudged black eyeliner was the only giveaway that something wasn't right. The caption read, "Going Backwards: Mrs. Roger Sherman plays with son David. She believes the world would go backwards if adults continued to use baby talk."

The day I found that clipping I read the caption twice. Didn't the newspaper editors realize my mother's words made no sense? *The world would go backwards?* Why did they publish that?

A few of these early memories had no dated photograph to place them. But one memory must have occurred a week after that photo in the park, because there were five candles on a birthday cake. I was turning five. My friends were gathered around a picnic table in Palms Park to sing "Happy Birthday" to me and eat a special cake I'd gone with my dad to pick up that morning at Grace Pastries. I had never had a cake like this one before, with plastic zoo animals perched on top.

When the song was done and I blew out the candles on

the cake, my mother picked up a long knife to cut pieces for everyone, my father by her side. And that's when she froze, knife in midair.

"Cut the cake, Marilyn." My father sounded annoyed.

She didn't move, staring past the knife with wide, frightened eyes.

"Cut the cake!" he repeated.

I felt myself shrinking inside, hoping my friends wouldn't notice that my father was mad and my mother was acting strange. When she still wouldn't move, he snatched the knife from her and cut the cake himself, sending the plastic tiger, monkey, and pink flamingo with spindly legs tumbling into the pink cardboard box. He shoveled cake onto paper plates and handed them around the table while my mother stood with her hand in the air like she was still holding the knife, like the cake was still in front of her, staring into space.

I didn't want any cake. I didn't want to be at my party anymore. But I played along.

MEMORIES OF THAT FIRST TIME MY MOTHER'S ILLness came are like color snapshots emerging from a whorl of black. How long did it last? Weeks? Months? Years? Now that I was looking, I wanted to know. In those days it seemed everything was happening all at once—her loving attention, her vacant zombie stare, her long disappearances into her bedroom with the door shut.

In one of those color snapshots, my brother was playing with a toy dump truck in the living room when I came out of my room looking for my mother. She was sitting at the dining table, both hands pressed flat on it, and staring in front of her at the curtained window to the street.

I paused at the doorway. "Mommy?"

I took a step closer.

"*Mommy.*"

After another time or two of this, she turned to face me with terror in her eyes. Her look scared me and I burst out crying. She reached for me then, her expression gentled by love, or apology. I let her draw me close and wrap her arms around me.

It must have been willpower that walked my mother to my brother's room to change his diapers and feed him out of a Gerber baby food jar after my dad left for work Monday through Saturday. Willpower must have been what got her out of the house to run errands with two kids playing chin puppets in the back seat. Lynne was in first grade now, but David and I went with her to the bank, where there were sugar cubes on a coffee tray, and to Hughes Market or the dry cleaners to drop off or pick up my dad's suits. Finally, we got to go to Mar Vista Park to play. The swings there were a favorite, but I liked the spinning wheel too. You could hang onto a metal bar and stay in place while the floor under you and everything around you spun.

MY MOTHER KEPT HER ILLNESS TO HERSELF AS MUCH as she could, but in that year, glimpses of it slipped through. One rainy day, Mrs. Haberman took me and her son Doug to the matinee to see *The Sound of Music*. Doug was in my kindergarten carpool.

When Mrs. Haberman arrived that day, she let herself into the house and went to my mother's bedroom. I never opened her door during the day, but Mrs. Haberman did. Coming out, she said, "Do you have a jacket? We're going to the movies," and she walked me across the lawn to her car at the curb, holding a big umbrella over our heads.

I climbed into the back seat next to Doug, feeling a strange weight in my chest. I caught his mother's worried eye in the rearview mirror as we started up the street. She seemed to know something I didn't, something bad. The windshield wipers slashed back and forth—clouding, clearing, clouding, clearing.

MUSIC WAS IMPORTANT TO MY MOTHER. SHE PLAYED piano and had a trained singing voice, but she didn't have her own piano yet, only a Martin guitar her father had given her.

I found another photo of my mother in the *Los Angeles Times*'s Westside section, published in October 1965. "Mrs. Roger Sherman, a PTA member, wrote a catchy song she will perform at a Western-themed carnival to be held at the local elementary school on Saturday," the article read. My mother looked beautiful wearing a polka-dotted cowgirl dress with short puffed sleeves and trimmed with eyelet lace. Her black eyeliner was neatly drawn. A ribbon of dark hair twirled down her neck from a high bun at the back. She was singing a song she'd written, a song that would become the theme song for this carnival for years to come.

I had to wonder how she did it.

The final date marker from this time was also a picture of my mother and her music. This one was a glossy, black-and-white 8x10 I found in a box of mementoes she kept. Her writing on the back of it read, "Spring 1966, Brahms' Requiem, Los Angeles Choir, Channel 9 TV." She was in a row of singers holding a music book, her painted lips open in song.

I knew the vacant look I saw in her eyes, the haunting black smudges under them. But these were new details. All I knew at the time was that she was going to be on TV singing with a professional choir. My memory of the night was of the babysitter sending me to bed too early to see my mother on TV. That woman had no idea why I cried so hard. My mother was special that night, and I was going to miss it.

Bad dreams started, recurring ones. In the underwear dream I'd forgotten to wear underpants to school. I was terrified the kids in my class would see under my dress and make fun of me. I was especially worried about two girls in class, the Jodies. They always looked perfect, with ponytails and cardigans that matched their skirts.

My other recurring dream was the one I thought of as the walking-to-school-on-a-holiday dream. In that one the sidewalks were empty, I was the only kid out. I realized there was no school today and my mother either didn't know or had forgotten to tell me. This nightmare woke me up every time.

I WAS AFRAID OF BEING FORGOTTEN. I TOOK THAT fear with me to the movies, to birthday parties, anywhere my mother had to pick me up.

Once, I didn't wait for her.

It was first grade and I was in a posture class I hated. Once a week, before school, my mother would drop me off at Clover Avenue School, about a mile from home, to walk on a balance beam and do the "chicken exercise" to correct a forward chin, then she would bring me home to get ready for school.

After class one day I waited with the other kids for our rides home. Cars pulled up outside the building and kids climbed in and drove away with their mothers. I stood watching with a sinking stomach. No sign of my mother. I ran back to the classroom to tell the teacher she had forgotten to pick me up, and found the room empty.

The entrance to the school was on a residential street a half block off National Boulevard. We drove that street to run errands and to get to this class. I didn't know my address, but I was going to do this. I was going to walk home.

It must have been about eight thirty in the morning, and

the street was busy with drivers on their way to work and school. Feeling nervous but determined, I crossed at street corners and kept walking until at last I saw the sign for Sav-on Drugs. We had been there before.

I hurried through the noisy shade of a freeway overpass and past Arnie's toy store on the other side of it. After Chris & Pitt's Barbecue, I took a chance turning at the corner and two blocks later found myself at my street. My street! I ran all the way home.

I flung the front door open, out of breath and panting. "Mommy?!"

No one home.

There was a phone in her bedroom and I went to it to call Marla, the girl I walked to school with. Maybe she hadn't left yet.

Turning the pages of my mother's phone book, I scanned for my friend's number—which, I later realized, I never would have found, since I didn't know her last name and couldn't have spelled it if I had.

Just then, I heard the front door open. *Mommy!* I dropped her phone book and ran out to surprise her. She would be so proud of me for finding my way home by myself.

At the sight of me, my mother fell to her knees, her purse clattering to the floor. "Suzy!" she sobbed. She scooped me into her arms and held me so close I could feel her heart pounding. "How did you get here?"

"I walked!"

She buried her face in the crook of my neck, rocking me. "Suzy. Suzy." She looked deeply into my eyes. "Never leave when I'm coming to get you. Understand? I will always come to get you."

I promised I would always wait.

June 5, 1978, is my mother's forty-fifth birthday. I don't know yet she didn't expect to be here on this day. She didn't know the gun store in Hollywood would put an eleven-day hold on the .38 she's trying to buy.

The same day my mother went gun shopping, the Tuesday after Memorial Day, I was in downtown Santa Barbara looking for a birthday gift to send her. After long deliberations in a bookstore, I gave up and chose a birthday card instead of a book. She doesn't read anymore. With the medication she's on, she can't concentrate.

David is saving to buy her a bike. He wants her to get out of the house for some exercise and fresh air. I know that's as likely to happen as her reading a book.

Tonight, the night of her birthday, a rosy glow lights the western sky as I walk from my off-campus dorm with my boyfriend, William, to his ramshackle house in Isla Vista to spend the night. William and I have been together since the summer before my last year in high school, a year and a half.

Evening shadows are long as we pass a closed corner store with a pay phone in the empty parking lot. "I want to call my mom and wish her a happy birthday," I tell him. "It won't take long."

He holds up the latest fat novel he's reading. "Take your time."

While sweet William waits outside the phone booth, I drop my dime into the coin slot and dial "0" to call collect. My mother accepts the charges.

Her voice sounds flat. "Hi, honey."

"Happy birthday, Mom!"

"Thanks for calling."

"Did you get the card I sent?"

"It came yesterday. It was very nice."

I'm not sure what to say next. I know it was a quiet day for her; there is no sense asking about it. She doesn't go out except to run errands or go to therapy. She has no friends.

I decide it's a good time to tell her my news. It's something I've been putting off doing for a while. I'll be going to Santa Cruz for six weeks this summer to see if I want to transfer to the university there in September. UC Santa Cruz is farther from LA than UC Santa Barbara, where I'm about to finish my freshman year.

In response to this news, she murmurs something like, "Ummm, sounds nice," so quietly that I can hardly hear her.

I change the subject. "I'll be in LA before I leave for Santa Cruz. I want to take you out to lunch for your birthday. School's out in two weeks."

A moment passes, a soundless sigh. "That would be good." Then she adds, "I love you."

I repeat those three words to her, never guessing they will be our last.

William snaps his book shut when I hang up the phone. He takes my hand as we cross the parking lot. Feeling unfinished and unsettled, I glance over my shoulder at the phone booth. "I should have sent her a book."

"I thought she doesn't read anymore."

"She doesn't. But I still should have sent her a book."

Chapter 2

Two years after the hallucinations and voices in her head started, my mother was back. She never saw a doctor during that time. Doctors put people like her away in mental institutions or gave them electric shock treatment. Besides, why would my father take her to a doctor? He didn't believe she had a problem. She was his beautiful, smart, educated, talented wife.

It was 1966, and my father made partner at his law firm that spring. To me, this turn of events he'd been working toward looked like a new car—a shiny blue four-door Dodge Dart convertible that replaced his old powder blue VW bug. My mother, meanwhile, got a roomy white Rambler station wagon. She also bought a secondhand upright piano and brought her thick music books—Beethoven, Brahms, and Mozart—down from the attic, their pages almost black with a language I had no idea she knew and knew well. My bedroom shared a wall with her piano, and the vibrations went into the wall by my bed when she played at night. With my hand on the wall, I could take a magic carpet ride on her music into sleep.

Four years earlier, my parents had bought their first home. From Westdale, in the suburbs of West LA, my dad's office in Beverly Hills was an easy commute by car and everything my mother could need as a housewife and mother was nearby—stores, schools, a park. Santa Monica Beach was so close you could smell the red tide when it came in.

Somehow, I remember the day of the move. I was almost three, my sister was four and a half, my brother was a few months old. My father pulled into the driveway in his VW and cut the engine.

"Here we are, kids! Our new house."

I clapped my hands and, the second the driver's door swung open, bolted out of the car and up to the front door. There were small windows in the door, and if I jumped high enough I could see through them into a big, empty room.

I could hear my mother back at the car, coaxing Lynne out of the back seat. She was holding the baby in her arms, swaddled in blankets. The next thing I knew, my father was beside me, jingling a set of keys in his hand. He opened the door wide and I ran in, calling out, "Hello! Hello!" to hear the echo.

My sister hated change. But she wasn't about to miss out on something her little sister was getting to do. At the sight of me going inside she was out of the car and into the house, crying out, "Let's go see our room!"

We ran to the front corner bedroom our parents had said would be ours. Lynne chose her side (the wall side, giving me the door side), and we ran out to explore our first backyard.

In the new house, David would have his own room and bathroom at the end of our hall. Two doors led to his room; one of them had a big window in it. In two years, he would take a running leap and crash through that window, surprised to discover that glass shatters. That accident would scare our mother, who must have known how much higher a price her negligence could have brought than a few cuts on her toddler's forehead and hands.

For now, though, she was well again and it was time for a house remodel.

THE WIFE OF ONE OF MY DAD'S LAW PARTNERS WAS an interior decorator. She came in with a clipboard and a lot of plans for us. The gloomy pine tree towering over the front walk came out first, and the murky pink exterior was repainted white, with black shutters added. Inside, the half wall dividing the living room came out, and eggshell-white, wall-to-wall shag carpet was laid.

The day before that happened, my mother called us to the playroom on the other side of that half wall. "Today you can draw on the floor," she said, holding out a shoebox filled with loose crayons.

What great news! We were forbidden from drawing on the walls with crayons, and now we had the go-ahead to draw on the floor! But the best part was that she got down on the floor with us to draw pictures and break the rules.

For the most part, though, I didn't like what the decorator was doing to our house. The bathroom I shared with my sister was too fancy, with a gold-framed mirror and black and gold towels hung on gold towel rings. The two gold velour couches in the living room, with a round glass coffee table between them, made that room look like a magazine photo, not like our house.

Thankfully, my bedroom was off-limits to her. My mother cut a big circle from a shag carpet scrap, crocheted pink and green fringe around it, and put it between my sister's bed and mine. She made three big yellow-and-white daisies out of sheets of felt and attached them to the walls in my corner of the room, adding decorative white wire fencing to make a flower garden for me to sleep in. My sister thought it was stupid. I loved it.

When he got a little bigger, my brother became my pal, my playmate, my buddy. His bedroom door was down the hall, in direct line of sight from my bed. We were Hansel and Gretel, abandoned in a forest and dropping breadcrumbs to find our way home. We were fishing friends on early weekend mornings, catching cardboard fish with a clothes hanger over the back of the couch. We played "tickle bee" on the front lawn until we collapsed in hysterics.

Butterflies came to the rose garden in the backyard, and caterpillars and cocoons had a story I wanted my mother to tell me again and again. She showed me how to sniff the sweet scent of blossoms on the lemon bush she planted and she promised I would see lemons grow there soon. The deep purple tresses of a princess flower draped over the top of the garden gate, and a new peach tree grew in the center of the yard, near the place where a jungle gym would go soon.

But it was the birds that were the most captivating part of the world my mother was showing me at the new house. She called us to the living room window one day to watch a bird build its nest in the corner of the trellis over the flagstone patio. Later, we saw the mother bird fly in to sit on her eggs and keep them warm.

The day the eggs finally hatched, my mother called us to the window to see tiny beaks chip away at the shells. Featherless, scrawny baby birds emerged and we cried out with delight.

"Quietly," my mother cautioned as we pressed our faces to the window to see better.

After that, I got to see the mama bird deliver worms to her babies' hungry, open beaks.

My mother sang folk songs for us, using our names to make us the stars of the songs. "Davey will be the engineer, oh yes . . ." And there were dancing songs, like "Dem Bones" ("the foot bone is connected to the ankle bone . . .") and "All Around the Kitchen" ("cock-a-doodle-doodle-doo!"). She stirred up bowls of salty Play-Doh and helped us make shapes with it. She taught us papier-mâché using balloons, glue, and colored tissue paper, and she painted pictures on paper plates with glue, letting us sprinkle split peas and yellow lentils over the glue to see the images take shape.

She could do anything. She could color inside the lines in my coloring books.

Some days she took us to play in the shallow waters at Marina del Rey. At home again, she washed our hair and helped us into clean clothes. When we laid down to nap, she read us poems: "We had sand in the eyes and the ears and the nose / And sand in the hair, and sand-between-the-toes . . ."

MY SISTER MAY HAVE BEEN BORN ANGRY. EVERY DAY I heard her shout, "Don't touch me!" when either of our parents dared to put a loving hand on her shoulder. She had no friends. She hated school. Reading was hard. Math was impossible.

On school-day mornings, my sister would show up at the kitchen door to pick up the lunch my mother made her, sullen and gangly, with knee socks pulled up to her skirt hem. I followed at my mother's heels as she walked Lynne to the sidewalk to send her off to school. After a failed attempt at a kiss on her cheek ("Don't touch me!"), my mother would say, "I'll see you after school," and Lynne would start her crawl up the street.

Two houses up, she would stop to examine the roses curling around a fence.

"Dawdling," my mother would say with a sigh. "Go on, honey!" she'd call out. "School starts in half an hour."

While Lynne was at school, I got to have time with my mother. Her new king-size bed was my playground while she showered. Her purple beaded necklace went sailing over the waves of blankets. The scarab beetle bracelet her father had given her went sailing too.

Once, I picked up a sheet of plastic attached to one of the hangers from my father's dry cleaning box on the bed.

"Don't put that over your head," my mother warned. "You could suffocate."

I asked what the word meant, and she explained.

As soon as she was in the shower I dropped the plastic over my head just for a second, just to see what would happen.

The best part of the morning routine with my mother came next. She toweled off and got dressed in side-zip pedal pushers and a blouse, then took a seat in front of the bedside mirror and began her makeup routine. After the eyelash curler came black eyeliner and a dash of blush, then the lipstick and a smack of her freshly painted lips on a piece of tissue to blot them. Seeing that half-kiss mark on both sides of the tissue was the moment I waited for.

ON OUR BIRTHDAYS MY MOTHER BAKED SHEET CAKES and cut them into fanciful shapes to decorate with colored icings and candies. For my sister's fifth birthday, she made a cake cut in the shape of the United States. Tiny paper flags glued to toothpicks showed where Lynne had lived—Connecticut, her birthplace, and California, her home. In a rare home video filmed on that birthday, my sister smiled awkwardly and clasped her hands over her ears when the family sang "Happy Birthday" to her. She looked rattled at the same time she sparkled like a star.

David didn't concern Lynne. It was her sister who was the problem. Lynne raised a fist when my mother brought me home from the hospital, my father told me. He grabbed her hand to hold her back. It's not unusual for a first child to resent having to share her parents' attention, but the trouble didn't stop there. A crack ran up the length of our bedroom door from her slamming it during temper tantrums.

Lynne was unpredictable. I was always ready for a game of tag or a slug hunt in the yard with anyone I could get to play. Sweeping the back patio could entertain me. Whatever I was doing, everything could be going along fine, and then my sister would show up and do something to throw me off—like punch me in the stomach, laughing when I doubled over or fell to the ground, the wind knocked out of me; or grab my bare arm and twist the skin hard in opposite directions, hooting when I screamed. An hour later, she might ask me to play again, and I usually would.

Once we were sent to our room for some child offense, like bringing a wagon full of mud into the house. We sat on our beds, giggling about our silly crime—until suddenly, unprovoked, she came over and slapped me hard on the bare thigh.

"Why did you do that?" I rubbed the redness that appeared where she had struck me.

"I didn't know fat hurts!"

MY MOTHER WAS ON HER OWN WITH ALL OF THIS. IF my father was around for scenes with Lynne, he would duck out, leaving his wife to handle their daughter's rages. I stayed out of the ruckus too, but the yelling matches were around me all the time. He had his office to go to; I was trapped. My mother would ask my sister about her day at school and get yelled at—"Leave me alone!" Then Lynne would run to our room or lock herself in the hall bathroom. Once, we picked her up from a birthday party and she screamed at my mother all the way home while I cowered in the back seat of the car.

Lynne's math tutor in Malibu wasn't much of a help. They also tried a psychiatrist for her. It was useless.

My mother had been a third-grade teacher for a couple of years before she had kids. At dinner one night, to help Lynne, she suggested we all go around the table saying the multiplication tables, each person adding a set of numbers as we made the rounds. My father looked skeptical but he took his turn.

I saw my sister's expression soften from suspicious to amused as we circled the table, taking turns:

"Six times six is thirty-six."

"Six times eight is forty-eight."

Maybe she could see we were on her side. But the game went sour when Lynne couldn't get the numbers right on her turn. "You can't make me do this!" she screamed, and she ran out of the room.

DAVID WAS THE OPPOSITE OF LYNNE. HE GLIDED through the days without obstacles. He loved books. His teachers were amazed that he already knew how to read when he started school. Pretty quickly, they realized he *wasn't* reading. He had simply memorized all the words after hearing the same books read to him over and over.

One of my brother's favorite books was *The Little Engine That Could*. He would chime in as my mother read to him about the determined little train climbing a tall mountain—"I think I can! I think I can!"

Another favorite book of his was *Are You My Mother?* She could be sitting on the couch, smoking Pall Malls and staring into space, and he would come up, set a book in her lap, and climb up to cuddle while she read to him. "Again!" he'd cry when the last page came, and my mother would start over at page one, reading aloud.

"Are you my mother?" the lost little bird would ask a tree. "Are you my mother?" the lost little bird would ask a boulder. "Are you my mother?" the lost little bird would ask a tractor parked in a construction site.

The happy ending went over well every time.

It's Sunday, June 11, 1978. My French final is Thursday. I've studied all I can for it, which means I have time this weekend to work on my application to the creative writing major at UC Santa Cruz. I need three short stories to apply. I may want to write a YA novel someday, something like Judy Blume's Are You There God? It's Me, Margaret. *I've tagged about twenty-five journal entries from the seven notebooks I've kept since I was ten in case I can use any of the material. Half of those entries have been typed.*

William is reading on my bed while I type up a tagged entry from a spiral-bound notebook with a big wish weed on the cover. The journal is from 1974, when I was fourteen. It was a big year. I moved out of my mother's house in search of anything better the same month my dad remarried.

I'm typing some of that story when the phone rings.

"Maybe it's my dad," I say, turning off the typewriter. He's coming up Saturday to help me move out of the dorm. I can't wait.

And it is my dad.

"Hi, Sue." His tone sounds ominous.

"Dad!"

"Mom died."

I double over. William is up and wrapping his arms around me from behind, burying his face in my hair. He doesn't even know what's happened but he can tell it isn't good.

I manage a word. "How?"

"Suicide."

"When?"

William squeezes me tighter.

"Today at four."

I'm trembling. It's six now. "How did she do it?"

He almost whispers the answer. "With a gun."

There's a story my mother used to read to us called "Chicken Little." An acorn falls on Chicken Little's head and the chicken takes it as a sign the world is coming to an end. She flutters about squawking, "The sky is falling! The sky is falling!" Mass hysteria all around as she spreads the news.

This time it's really happening. The sky is *falling.*

"Where's David?" I want to talk to my brother.

"He's right here." My dad hands David the phone.

I don't know yet that David is the one who opened her bedroom door and saw blood. He ran to the kitchen to call our father, then waited for him for what felt like an eternity by the dining room window. Two police officers arrived first. They went to her bedroom and came back to ask David whether his mother was right- or left-handed. When my dad arrived minutes later, the police escorted him to the bedroom to identify his ex-wife's body.

David is on the line now. I hear his grief through the phone line, silent tears. Words crowd my brain, but there are none I want to speak. Dear David, oh David, what now, David? I've expected this call for years, yet nothing I can think of seems right to say.

"It was inevitable," I finally blurt.

My brother drops the phone.

Chapter 3

I wanted the few years I had two parents at home to be part of my story. I wanted the glimpses I got from those days to be 3D. I wanted vague memory to become vivid. But sand was running through an hourglass I didn't know about.

At breakfast, my father read the newspaper spread open between his face and a bowl of cornflakes with canned peach halves on top. Red bits of tissue dotted his cheeks where he'd cut himself shaving. When it was time to go, he'd give my mother a quick kiss and head for the door, with me following behind for the goodbye. I'd get a gentle tug of my nose between two knuckles. "I'm takin' your schnoz with me!" Watching from the front door, I'd see him climb into his car to disappear up the street.

Evenings with him were short. He'd change out of his suit, pour a Scotch, look through the mail, and eat dinner. Afterwards, if I was lucky, he might put on a record in the living room and dance the box step with me, my bare feet on top of his slippers so I could follow his lead.

Late in the afternoon on Sundays, I often found him in their bedroom speaking into a microphone attached to a Dictaphone, the clunky recording device of the day. These were letters his secretary would type in the morning from ribbons of turquoise reel-to-reel tape. I sat at his feet, entranced, mostly for the chance to hear him say "period" and "new paragraph" in such a serious tone.

Now and then my father came in to say goodnight to me in bed. He had a few good stories. One was about the time in college when he'd spent weeks typing a term paper, and then set it on the roof of his car when he was getting in. The paper scattered like snowflakes when he took off. We groaned every time he got to that part.

I also liked hearing about the piece of lead in his palm, from a sharp pencil in college.

When he came in wearing pajama pants and an undershirt, I would ask about the red freckles on his chest. I got the same answer every time—and every time I would cry out, "Ew! You have *blood* freckles?" After that it was "G'night, Suzie Q" and a kiss on the cheek.

IN 1967, BOB DYLAN'S HIT SONG "THE TIMES THEY Are A-Changin'" nailed it. Times were a-changing, and fast. At my house, the changes started at the dinner table one spring night just after my sister stood up to leave the table.

"Don't go yet, Lynne," my mother said. "We have something important to tell you kids."

Lynne dropped into her seat with a frown. "What?"

My father's voice sounded steady, even as he spoke words I would guess later had been practiced. "Your mother and I still love each other, but we aren't going to be married anymore. We're separating."

I looked at my mother. Separating? What did that mean?

Her gaze stayed fixed on my father, at the head of the table opposite from where she sat. "Your father is moving out this Saturday. He found an apartment in Westwood."

I burst into tears, dropping my face into my folded arms on the table. He was leaving us? I didn't know you could leave your family.

From inside that dark cave of my folded arms, I could hear David whimpering across the table. Lynne sat quietly at my side. Over a forearm, I peeked at my father. "Will you still be my daddy?"

He reached out to squeeze my hand. "I will always be your daddy."

More tears.

In bed that night, I lay awake wondering how long they had kept this secret from us. My dad had an apartment. He would be gone on Saturday, in four days. Father-daughter night at school was Friday night. I couldn't go without him.

THE LAST NIGHTS AT HOME WITH DAD WENT FAST. On one of those nights, he asked what I was reading. He never normally asked. The book was *From the Mixed-Up Files of Mrs. Basil E. Frankweiler*, a story about a brother and sister in New York City who ran away to hide in the Metropolitan Museum of Art and got locked in overnight. He grew up in New York and he knew that museum. He asked me to read to him before bed. I ran to change into my nightgown and sat next to him on their bed, starting the book over again and reading one chapter after the next out loud to him. He never once interrupted to say it was time for me to go to bed.

On Friday night I was ironing a shirt in the living room when he got home from work. He came over to see what I was doing—not usual. Briefcase in hand, he watched me pull a shirt sleeve tight and press a crease into its sides with the hot iron.

"Mom showed me how to make a line like that," I told him.

He nodded and walked off to his room—to finish packing, I imagine. At the time, I thought I had bored him. Now I wonder if he felt sad thinking I was growing up and he was going to miss it.

On Saturday, my mom took us to Fosters Freeze for soft-serve cones, chocolate dipped, and after that we went to see *The Jungle Book* at the Picwood Theater. By the time we got home, our dad was gone.

Bettina, my best friend, came over the next day, and so did Debbie, my friend from up the street. I told them my parents were separating.

"What does that mean?" Bettina asked.

"They're getting divorced." Debbie was almost ten. She knew these things.

I was quick to correct her. "They're not getting divorced. They're getting separated." I repeated what my father had told us when he gave us the news. "They love each other, they just can't be married anymore."

Debbie smirked. Bettina looked worried.

I didn't want my friends thinking this was something bad, so I quickly defended it. "It's okay. My dad's going to take us out to dinner every Wednesday, and we get to go somewhere fun with him on Sundays. I'm going to see him more than usual."

My friends weren't impressed.

At seven—and for years to come—I was sure my father was the one who had ended their marriage. Wasn't that obvious? He was the one with a life; my mom was the one tumbling down a mountainside. I didn't get that his refusal to believe she had a mental illness and his lack of support of her in those scary times was a deal-breaker for her, even though she told me as much soon after he moved out. She said he had never believed she had been hearing voices and having hallucinations. When the voices and hallucinations went away and she was well again, she wasn't sure she could stay with him any longer because he hadn't believed they were real to her. She needed her husband to believe her.

I HAD CLUES ABOUT MY MOTHER'S UNHAPPINESS with her marriage, but for many years I didn't connect the dots that would lead to my understanding. When I was nine years old, we were in the car driving somewhere together when I told her about a strange dream I'd had the night before—or was it a memory? I was in a small space I didn't recognize, hanging a little red-and-white polka-dotted dress on a cord. It might have been a doll's dress. A nice woman I didn't know was helping us. There was a curved ceiling and a row of windows on both sides of this strange cylinder we were inside.

My mother gasped. "You remember that?! You weren't even two years old!"

Incredulous, she told me the story. We were flying to New York to stay with her parents. A glass of water had spilled down the front of my red-and-white polka-dotted dress and a stewardess helped us by hanging a cord near the cockpit so we could put the dress over it to dry. That was *my* dress, not a doll's dress.

A few years after my mother died, I visited my aunt and grandmother on the East Coast. My grandmother told me about my parents' wedding. My mother wasn't sure about marrying Roger, she said. Grandma would say my mother had been unhappy with my father for a long time. She flew home to New York once with me and my sister when she was thinking of leaving him. I was almost two years old at the time, Lynne was four. That, I realized, was the plane flight with the polka-dotted dress.

My grandmother told me my father flew out for the weekend to try to change my mother's mind. "And it worked," she added bitterly. My mother returned with him to California, and nine months later David was born.

I would come to realize how another piece fit, too, as more random-seeming memories from the foggy reaches became clear when I let myself look at them. In 1964, two years after that plane trip east, the family went to San Diego for a weekend to stay at the Catamaran Hotel and play on the beach. After their separation a few years later, I would find out from my mother that we went on that trip so my parents could have time together to talk about her unhappiness with him in their marriage. My father was more involved with his work than he was with his family; she didn't want to do it all on her own.

An accident derailed their conversation on our last day in San Diego, when David got pulled into the ocean by a wave while they sat talking on a towel nearby. Panicked, my father jumped into the water and rescued his son.

Driving home that afternoon, I didn't understand why everyone was so glum. Wasn't David safe now? Hadn't we had fun at the beach?

Home again, my father spent time with us on Sundays, his one day off. He took us to Beverly Park to ride the merry-go-round and eat puffy clouds of pink cotton candy on sticky paper cones. We climbed giant dinosaurs at Dennis the Menace Park and lay on our backs with arms overhead to roll, screaming, down a high, grassy hill.

He gave his wife more attention too. One night they went out to dinner and a show—they wanted to see a hypnotist they'd heard was performing in a club on Pico Boulevard. Nothing would be the same after that night.

IN THE FIRST WEEKS AFTER MY FATHER LEFT, MY mother was up late at night in the living room, talking on the phone with her father. From my bedroom, I could hear her crying quietly after they hung up. Her father was dying of lung cancer. When he died, she flew to New York for his funeral, and for the next few years she lit a candle in his memory on the anniversary of his death. He had always believed in her, she said.

It was second grade, and I had a lisp, something particularly unfortunate for a girl named Suzy (Thu-thee). When the other kids went back to class after lunch, I had to go to Miss Bush's stuffy little office to learn how to speak without lisping (also an unfortunate word for someone with a lisp to have to say).

"She sells seashells down by the seashore. She sells seashells down by the seashore. She sells seashells down by the seashore." Over and over. My lisp was gone by June.

Lynne was in Campfire Girls. Every summer, they got to sell boxes of Campfire Girls candy. I tagged along with her when she went door to door in the neighborhood selling candy—when she would let me. Now and then she let me open a box of chocolate caramels to share with her. I longed to be in Campfire Girls. I was in Bluebirds, the group for younger girls. I looked forward to "flying up" one day.

It was around this time that something strange I thought of as "the echo" started happening. With the echo, the last words of sentences sometimes repeated in my head after people spoke. It could happen even with a sentence I said. The echo was like ripples in a lake when you toss a pebble in—the last word repeating, repeating, repeating, then fading away. I knew my mother had heard voices in her head when she was sick. It was happening more often lately. Was I getting what she had? The thought of that was frightening.

One week, on the day of a Bluebirds meeting, I had a dentist appointment and my mother couldn't take me there. She had her own doctor's appointment. So she called a cab to take me—not usual in my neighborhood. She assured me I would be fine in the cab. I was nervous. A strange man would be driving. What if he was a kidnapper? Or a killer? A girl in my sister's class had been murdered on her way to school one morning recently. The murderer had hidden in the bushes by a staircase she used to get down a steep hill.

I didn't tell my mother about the murderer on the staircase, but I did tell her I was afraid to go in a cab. She promised I would be okay and that she'd be home when I got back to take me to Bluebirds.

As the cab snaked its way across the city, I held tight to the armrest in the back seat, never taking my eyes off the driver. If he tried to kidnap me, I had an escape plan: I would open the door and jump out. I was relieved to see that the driver had waited in front of the dentist's office while I went in. He was there to pick me up when I came out.

After surviving the cab ride home, I changed into my Bluebirds uniform: a navy blue cotton skirt with a short-sleeved white blouse and a red tie around the neck.

I was attaching the metal bluebird pin to the front pocket when my mother peeked into my room to say, "It's time to go" (". . . time to go, time to go, time to go . . .").

Oh no! The echo again.

She waited for me at the front door, her purse hanging over an arm. She looked listless, distracted—something I'd seen before many times. I thought of telling her about the echo I was hearing, wondered if I had the guts to do it. I decided to try.

"Mommy?" I ventured. "I have to tell you something."

It was a confession, describing how words trailed off sometimes, the last one repeating a few times before the sound disappeared. I may have seen concern flash across her face as I spoke, but if I did, it was a flicker, nothing more. Her expression stayed as flat as a stagnant pond.

All she said when I finished was, "We can't be late."

I never found out what the echo was. As mysteriously as it came, it eventually disappeared for good.

The day after my father's call on June 11, the sun rises like it would on any summer day in Santa Barbara. All night I lay next to William, drifting in and out of consciousness, wishing for the vacancy of dreamless sleep. Now I have to get up and face the hopeless glow lighting the bare walls of his bedroom.

My mother is dead. My sorrow is a bottomless cavern, a hole where my heart used to be.

I tell William I don't know what to do, and he suggests we go to the beach.

It's an easy walk from his house through Isla Vista to a small cove called Sands Beach. We take towels with us—he brings a book, too—and we find a place on the sand, surrounded by rocks, to spread our towels, peel off most of our clothes, and sit unprotected in the bright morning sun.

William lies down to read while I sit looking at the world the way it is now. A few little kids are on their knees in the wet sand, eagerly digging holes with plastic shovels. A few joggers pass by them, leaving footprints for the waves to erase with a careless sweep. I watch that happen as the waves keep coming.

I look to the horizon, that straight line dividing the sky and the sea that has been my solace. She used a gun? What was she thinking? She hated guns. Ten years ago, they were war toys. She tried to get Arnie to stop carrying them in his toy store.

"Give it back!"

One of the little boys digging holes in the sand is mad at his friend.

"Give him the shovel, Tommy," his mother shouts to them from a beach blanket nearby.

It's Monday, I remind myself. Just another day.

She must have wanted to be sure no one interrupted her this time. That's why she used a gun. How long had she been planning this? When I stopped by on Memorial Day, did she know it would be the last time we saw each other? Was that the last time I talked to her? No, I talked to her on her birthday last week.

I try to conjure her voice to see if I can hear it again. I can. How long will I be able to? I have a feeling death takes voices too.

Chapter 4

My father had a one-bedroom bachelor pad in an apartment building in Westwood, near UCLA. He took us to see it one Sunday not long after he moved in.

In my West LA suburb there were no apartment buildings, just single-story houses with two-car garages and front lawns. The elevator in the lobby of my father's new building was nothing like anything I'd seen before—none of this was. Its back wall had a winding plastic plant trailing down a mottled mirror, with an ornate red metal bench attached down below.

"Don't sit on that," my father warned when he saw me eyeing it as we rode up to his floor. "The bench is supposed to be decorative."

"Really?"

He shrugged. "New Orleans style."

Inside my father's apartment, unopened cardboard boxes lined the walls, each one numbered in black marker at the top right corner so he could identify their contents on a list he'd made. The bedroom was filled with new furniture—a queen-size bed covered with a blue bedspread, a dresser holding keys and a cup of loose change on top, nightstands with white porcelain lamps. In the living room a faux fireplace had a rotating paper log lit by a red lightbulb that you could turn on and off with a switch. My father thought it was silly. I couldn't get enough of it. I also liked the counter in his kitchen, which had two bar stools that spun like the wheel on *Dialing for Dollars*.

"You have a remote control!" My sister was looking at the new color TV a client had given him. I thought a color TV was a big gift from a client, but I didn't say anything.

Outside the wall-to-wall living room window, more tree-lined neighborhoods with apartment buildings filled the view as far as I could see.

Before we left for lunch in Westwood Village, we stopped off to see the swimming pool out back. My brother and sister shouted, "Wow!" and jumped on the chaise lounges, kicking out their legs like they did this all the time.

I didn't care about a pool. I didn't like how I looked in a bathing suit and I couldn't figure out how to open my eyes underwater anyway. But I had to admit, I kind of liked my father's new bachelor pad.

IN JULY, GRANDMA FRIEDMAN, MY NEWLY WIDOWED grandmother, visited from New York. I had just come home from the hospital after twenty-one days stuck in bed in traction to set a broken elbow I got falling off a horse when I went riding for the first time at a stable in Kenter Canyon. My mother came to see me at the hospital every day, and her visits, the *Tiger Beat* and *16* magazines she brought for me, and the remote control TV mounted on the wall got me through. My father stopped by a few times after work, looking very out of place in his suit and tie. But I always felt special when he came.

And now I was home again, with Grandma staying with us for two weeks.

It didn't take long to see why she'd never been invited to visit before.

Grandma Friedman was shorter than my mom—she was only five foot two. She liked to brag about her figure, pointing out her trim waistline when she modeled another dowdy summer dress at the breakfast table.

I'd never met anyone like Grandma Friedman. She had a New York accent. Both of my parents were from New York, but they didn't have accents. Grandma called her purse a pocketbook. Pants were trousahs.

The first morning I was home from the hospital, my right arm bound in a fat, L-shaped cast, my mom rifled through my closet and dresser drawers looking for sleeveless tops that would fit me for the six weeks I had to wear the cast. "We're going to the fabric store," she announced after finding I had no shirts to wear. "I have an idea."

In the fabric store, Grandma cooed over Simplicity patterns my mother skipped over in her hunt for dress patterns in my size. I was tall at seven and I weighed over 100 pounds.

Home again from the fabric store, my mom converted the dining table into her sewing station, with her black Singer sewing machine, sewing kit, pinking shears, and basting tape set on it.

Grandma sat with us, looking dejected, as my mother busily marked up the fabric with a special pen and prepared three new dresses for me. "I can sew those for you, Marilyn," Grandma said.

My mom ignored the offer, saying, "You can do the basting and thread bobbins for me."

Grandma leaned in to tell me something like it was a secret, something confidential: "I made both of my daughters' clothes when they were your age. And I grew up sewing. I had four sisters! I made all their dresses. Oh, those dresses were so pretty." She patted her stiff cotton-candy hair, which smelled like perfumed paint thinner from the hairspray she used every morning.

Two days later, I had three new dresses. My grandmother screeched when my mother held them up for us to see. Each perfectly sewed dress had only one sleeve.

"Marilyn!" she cried. "What have you done?"

My mother gave me a big smile, letting the comment go by. "When your cast comes off, I'll sew the second sleeve!"

I thought her solution was brilliant.

My grandmother tried to be useful during her stay. She vacuumed the living room. She polished the bathroom mirror. She straightened the towels. She folded the clean clothes and set stacks of them on our beds. She emptied our new dishwasher when it was full and wiped the kitchen counters clean.

And then she went too far.

One day she and I were playing a board game called Trouble in the living room when my mom came home from therapy. She put her purse on the stereo cabinet and went into the kitchen. And that's when she screamed. "*You put the dried fruit in containers!*"

Grandma sat next to me wearing a dress, stockings, and low-heeled shoes, her ankles crossed. She looked like an alien on our saggy, gold velour couch. Now she was up and hurrying to the kitchen to explain herself. "Marilyn, I do that at home. I give them labels. Apricots, Prunes . . ."

"Never do anything like this without asking me first!" my mother shouted. "*Never!* This is *my* house!"

Later, I would hear about the time both sets of parents visited her and my dad's first home together, a Quonset hut in Delaware, when my dad was in the ROTC before law school. Grandma Friedman had walked through the house criticizing one thing after the next. She pointed to the dining set my mother had found at a yard sale—"The chairs don't match." She tugged at the curtains my mother had made for the windows—"Yellow is not for living rooms." My mother ran to her bedroom to cry.

The day my grandmother left for New York, I went to the curb with my mother to watch the cab driver load suitcases into the trunk while my grandmother took her place in the back seat.

I was the only one waving goodbye.

AT DISNEYLAND THERE'S A RIDE CALLED *IT'S A SMALL World*. In the cool dark, small boats glide on a manufactured river past singing and dancing mechanized puppets dressed in costumes representing their corner of the globe. With a light slosh of water, the boat makes a turn to view more life-size puppets, singing the same song but this time with Japanese accents and wearing kimonos. Another jostling turn of the boat and you're in the Swiss Alps, seeing blond puppets in braids and lederhosen sing about the wonderful world we all share.

I knew by that time I didn't live in a small and wonderful world filled with colorful cultures. I lived in a world where men killed people in wars, in the streets, and at home. Oceans were dangerously polluted, and so was the air. An offshore oil rig spilled in the Pacific, and photos of the damage covered the front page of the *Los Angeles Times*. At school, a film showed suffering seagulls on beaches, their oil-soaked wings weighting them to the sand. We saw a film showing rivers pouring dirty soap suds into oceans, killing fish and seabirds along the way. My mother took a poem I wrote about it to the piano and turned it into a song with this chorus: "Is there no solution to the air pollution? The birds will not fly, everything will die. Oh why, oh why, oh why."

I was troubled by this question: Were people kind or cruel? One day, waiting in the car for my mother while she picked something up from the drugstore, I turned on the radio. As Dionne Warwick sang about the world needing "love, sweet love," I lay down on the car seat feeling sad and scared for myself, sad and scared for the world.

My mom did what she could. She boycotted grapes to support farmworkers' rights. She quit shopping at a local supermarket because it had discriminatory hiring practices. She stopped taking us to the toy store because Arnie refused to stop carrying plastic rifles—"war toys." I stayed home from school for two weeks during a teachers' strike and helped my mother make protest signs. We stood in a picket line at Webster Junior High, a few blocks away. School districts across the city were divided about mandatory bussing to balance the racial makeup across the city. I didn't understand anything about it. I only knew I liked standing up for fairness with my mother.

One night she let me go with her to a candlelight peace march held in the neighborhood. I would get to walk in the street at night! My mother wore her guitar strapped across her chest to play and sing while we walked. I held a candle wrapped in aluminum foil at its base, being careful to keep it upright, like she told me to do, and not burn the hair of anyone in front of me.

The crowd was a moving river of light, filling the streets for more than two blocks at a time. We sang "We Shall Overcome" with my mother leading us, singing and playing guitar with tears in her eyes—"*We shall overcome, We shall overcome, We shall overcome, someday . . . Oh, deep in my heart, I know that I do believe, We shall overcome someday.*"

My throat became too choked up to keep singing.

EVERYONE SEEMED TO THINK THERE WAS HOPE. BUT I watched the news after school. I wasn't so sure.

A high school girl named Lory lived at the corner of my street. She babysat us sometimes and let me watch the news at night before bed. Once, we saw a pregnant girl slumped on a bathroom floor in Golden Gate Park. "Okay, that's enough," Lory said. "Time for bed." And she turned off the TV.

Another night, I couldn't sleep and I got up to see what Lory was doing. From the doorway to the den, on the TV I could see soldiers tromping through a leafy jungle, wearing army jackets and heavy boots, their rifles raised. "Are you watching a movie?" I asked.

Lory frowned. "It's the news. Go back to bed."

I was too young to be part of the counterculture, as my mother called it, but I was interested, and I watched the news for stories. I saw runaways, hippies, and speed freaks in San Francisco. I saw civil rights protests in the South. I saw white police officers bash Black men and women with metal batons. Blood spattered walls and sidewalks. Torrents of water shot out of fire hoses, making protestors run for their lives as grimacing white officers blasted Black people who were trying to stand up for their right to exist.

I watched for as long as I could stand it.

AT MY SCHOOL, RACISM SHOWED UP IN DIFFERENT ways. In October, Jewish kids were given the option to stay home from school for the Jewish High Holidays—Rosh

Hashanah and Yom Kippur—and I did, though we didn't celebrate Jewish holidays at home. When I came back to school after the break, two girls in my fourth grade class, Cathy and Cindy, came over to talk to me.

They stood by my desk like self-appointed school police, hands on their hips. Cathy flicked a lock of blonde hair over a shoulder. "Are you Jewish?"

"Yes," I admitted.

They shared a conspiratorial chuckle.

"Did you go to temple yesterday?" This was Cindy.

"No."

"So why didn't you come to school?"

I could have said I didn't come to school because I didn't have to. I could have pointed out that school was closed for Christmas and everyone stayed home whether they celebrate the holiday or not. But I didn't. I felt shamed by them for being Jewish. All I could do was shrug.

Apparently satisfied to have intimidated me into speechlessness, my tormentors turned on haughty heels and headed back to their seats across the room.

That was the last time I stayed home for the High Holidays.

IT WAS 1968 AND THE COUNTRY WAS ROCKIN' AND rollin'. Miss Winnick, my pretty fourth grade teacher, wore miniskirts and heeled sandals to class. Her false eyelashes fluttered like moths, her dark hair hung long down her back. Two short, perfect ringlets framed her face. I longed for hair like Miss Winnick's, but the most I could do was wait a few weeks between shampoos to keep it from frizzing.

As a single mother, my mom was doing what she could to manage childcare at home and do some work that was important to her. She volunteered at Planned Parenthood in Venice, counseling women about pregnancy. "Women shouldn't get pregnant unless they can afford to raise their children," she told me. She helped women get birth control, which Planned Parenthood offered for free.

My mother also volunteered at a place called Project Action, where little kids whose mothers were on welfare came for daycare while their mothers looked for work. The *Los Angeles Times* ran a story about the organization, and they ran a photo alongside it showing her seated at a table at Project Action, making dolls out of Styrofoam globes and yarn while a group of doe-eyed girls in pigtails watched. She wore a white turtleneck in the photo and looked focused as she painted eyelashes on a Styrofoam ball.

Venus was a friend of my mother's at Project Action. My mother visited her at her candle shop near the beach one summer day, and I came along with her. A sheet of stringed plastic beads hung across the doorway, where Venus greeted my mom with open arms.

"How you doin'?" she asked warmly. "Is that your little girl?"

I said a shy hello, more interested in the swinging beads than anything else.

"I'll be right back," my mother said, and she disappeared with Venus into a back room.

On my own in the shop, I explored the shelves of candles. In my bedroom I had a peace sign candle like the one on sale here—a red, white, and blue circle standing on end. Beaded earrings hung from a metal earring tree and jars were stuffed with incense sticks with names like frankincense and patchouli. I poked around, sniffing incense and trying to hear what my mother and Venus were discussing in the back room.

When she finally emerged, my mother was flanked between Venus and a tall, spindly man with a big Afro and dark sunglasses. The weight of their conversation hung heavy in the air. My mother ushered me out to the car with a *hush, hush, gotta go* feeling. I wondered if the man was a Black Panther.

THAT SPRING, A STRING OF BAD THINGS WERE HAPpening in the world around me. In April, Martin Luther King, Jr. was assassinated. The day he was killed, my mother and I sat in front of the TV watching a clip from his famous "I Have a Dream" speech. I couldn't understand why such an important man was so hated. What had looked like hope for a better world had been shot down.

Recently, my father had started spending Saturday nights at the house. I guessed my parents were trying out their marriage again, but no one explained anything and we didn't ask. On June 5, they went out to dinner for my mom's birthday. Early in the morning I woke to the sound of my father running down the hallway to my bedroom. "Bobby Kennedy's been shot!" He was crying.

I sat up in bed, shaking off sleep, and fell into his arms. I didn't know a thing about Bobby Kennedy—only that he was JFK's brother—but I started crying because my dad was.

AROUND THIS TIME THERE WAS A GIRL FROM THE next block who would sometimes ride her bike down my street wearing a patch over one eye. "Why does she have her eye covered?" I asked my mother once, after the girl passed our house on the sidewalk. "She may be blind in that eye," my mother told me, and she tried to explain blindness when I told her I didn't know what that meant. To help me understand, she went to her room for a scarf and asked me to sit on the couch.

"I'm going to tie this around your head so your eyes are covered," she said, and she did that while I sat wondering what was going to happen. "Now we're going to walk around the room. I'll be right next to you."

I had been blindfolded before, when we hit piñatas at David's birthday party once, but this was different. We were in the house.

I stood up just fine, but found I could barely take one step. "I don't know where anything is!"

"I'm here," my mother assured me, and she squeezed my hand.

Slowly, we walked through the room while I felt my way around, tracing the contours of a couch arm, bending to feel the edge of the coffee table so I could tell how far from it I was.

"Now," my mother said. "Imagine you could never take the blindfold off."

MY MOTHER WENT TO A THERAPY GROUP IN THE valley every week and she saw a therapist on her own and a marriage counselor with my dad, but those were things we didn't talk about, and nothing about it seemed strange. She took skating lessons at the ice rink in Culver City, practicing fancy moves like the Camel Spin. I got to go along and watch from the stands. I was impressed she still had her own skates from New York, a place where it snowed in winter. After dinner she played records by José Feliciano, a blind Puerto Rican guitarist she liked, and Judy Collins and Joan Baez, or she played guitar, sometimes singing in a language she didn't even speak, with "La Bamba" and "Guantanamera." On the piano, she mostly played from movie soundtrack songbooks—*The Sound of Music*, *Fiddler on the Roof*, and *West Side Story*.

On the outside, it looked like she was an involved mother. And she was. On warm weekends we went to the beach and sometimes filled a box with sand to make a sand candle mold at home. We made candles and rolled them in sparkles on sheets of newspaper before they set. On weekends, friends came over to play on the Slip 'N Slide on the front lawn at my house or to cool off with the Water Wiggle Sprinkler, a contraption that danced in the force of the water at the end of the hose. My mother bought flats of Shasta grape soda or made pitchers of Kool-Aid she poured over ice. Sometimes we had Fizzies.

Inside my house, the look of things told a different story. A mountain of laundry, clean or dirty, always waited on the washing machine. The kitchen was a disaster. My bedroom was a mess too, impossible to keep clean because my sister never made her bed or picked up her clothes from the floor on her side of the room. My brother's room was his sanctuary, door closed. It could have been messy, but I didn't know. I didn't go in there.

None of this bothered me until I started seeing how my friends lived. At Debbie's house, clear plastic runners lay across the plush white carpet in the living room and hallways. Sometimes she invited me to go with her and her parents on weekends to look at model homes. They had no plans to move; it was just a hobby of theirs to look at fancy new houses.

Bettina's house was spotless too. When I went to her home for lunch, her mother served grilled cheese sandwiches on toasted bread cut on the diagonal. I had never seen bread cut like that. Her mother traced her lips with a dark liner and filled them in with a soft, pale pink. I thought it looked stunning. Every night she chose Bettina's clothes for the next day and hung them on a hook outside her closet. My friend's birthday cakes were fancy sheet cakes topped with perfect buttercream flowers. She had a two-story dollhouse, every room in it filled with miniature figurines and furniture. On Easter she woke to an overflowing Easter basket filled with chocolate bunnies and a big, hollow, pink sugar egg the size of a small football. That sugar egg had a peephole at one of its ends. Inside were pink and green hard icing flowers. And yet Bettina couldn't have cared less about the sugar egg. She wanted to dye real eggs like the ones I made at Easter with my mom.

"You're so lucky," she whined. "My mother thinks dyeing eggs is too messy."

I couldn't believe she thought *I* was lucky. Bettina had it all.

The sea draws back from the wet sand, waves build power and crash with a loud and gorgeous violence. Inhale, exhale.

I will never see my mother again.

Seagulls ride wind currents, soaring and angling, coasting and flapping. Sitting on the sand on this terrible day, it's comforting to see. The sun is their compass. This is the order of things.

I have no compass. William sleeps on his towel next to me, his abandoned book lying face down at his side. His silky, golden hair is a flaxen puddle. His smooth, downy cheeks look so familiar amidst the strangeness my life has become. Is he here for me? Or is he just here?

I look to the undulating surface of the sea for answers. Thorazine made her numb inside. Thorazine paralyzed part of her face. Thorazine left her anxious. Thorazine stole her ability to concentrate. Her doctor wouldn't let her quit taking it. When she quit the medication anyway, hoping to feel better, she became catatonic. Schizophrenia had her locked in.

Have I ever thought the ocean was beautiful? These breaking waves seem relentless. I look up the beach one way and down the other, hoping to find a better feeling. It's nowhere, and neither is any idea about how to live anymore. This beach is simply a place for being, and being isn't simple at all.

Chapter 5

My father was not the adventurous type. Driving a motor home was the most outdoorsy thing I'd seen him do. In the summer of 1969 he rented a Winnebago, a big playhouse on wheels, to take the family camping. My bed was a dining table that converted with a few easy moves. My parents, who were still spending Saturday nights together at the house, slept at the back of the camper, behind a privacy curtain. David and Lynne shared the loft bed over the driver's cab. Two sinks had flowing water, there was a toilet and a shower, and my father heroically figured out how to fill the propane stove and use the dump station at campgrounds. We were headed to Lassen Volcanic National Park, Victoria Island, and the Trinity Alps, where Lynne and I would be dropped off to stay at a camp called Bar 717 for four weeks.

As we left the straight strip of I-5 to enter Lassen on winding mountain roads, my mother was excited. "Look at the red earth!" she cried, and she pointed out the oversized front window as hairpin curves revealed more rosy brown soil.

I knelt on the floor between their seats up front to see this new world through her eyes. "Red?" I was puzzled.

"It's called 'red,'" my father said, keeping his eyes on the curving road.

I didn't know what to make of that.

In a Lassen campsite we helped my father park level so the Winnebago's refrigerator would run. After that, it was time to go exploring.

In a meadow, my mother showed us shiny black rocks in the soil from a long-ago volcanic explosion—obsidian, she said it was called. She showed us pumice too, cream-colored volcanic rocks as light as cork. My sister and I pocketed a few of both types of stone before joining the others on a trail that led high above the valley floor.

My father took the lead. "Look how blue the sky is," he said with a wave of his hand. He seemed happier here. Maybe the great outdoors was his element—I'd never seen him in it before.

My mother followed, and we three kids trailed behind.

Forest carpeted the mountains far into the distance with greens of every hue. Switchbacks came, and the trail twisted tightly back and forth as we ascended without straining up a single steep path. I liked it here, so quiet, and with sky-filled vistas unlike anything I'd ever seen in Los Angeles.

We plodded on, and the trail climbed higher.

And then my mother stopped abruptly. She stood still, shielding her eyes from the view with both hands.

"Marilyn, it's fine, keep going," my dad said. He went to her and put a hand on her shoulder.

David, Lynne, and I waited, counting the pieces of pumice and obsidian we'd stuffed into our pockets.

After some fervent, guarded whispering between our parents, my father said, "We have to go, kids. Your mother doesn't feel well."

A sickening pitch sank my stomach. This was too like the trouble I'd seen before, though it had been a long time since it had last appeared. I watched my mother make a cautious turn on the trail and my father move ahead of her to start the trip back. She walked with her eyes cast down, gripping my father's arm like he was a life raft.

An older man striding up the trail in our direction stepped aside to let us pass. He smiled at my father sympathetically. "Fear of heights?"

My dad nodded, and we continued on.

Safely in the Winnebago again, my mother went to their bed at the back and pulled the curtain closed. The rest of us put our heads together to read the directions and stir up a pan of Hamburger Helper mix for dinner. The next day we were headed north to Vancouver, where we'd take a ferry to Victoria Island for a few days. After that, it would be on to Trinity County, back in California, and a first taste of a place that would one day be life-changing for me.

THE MOUNTAIN ROADS WERE STEEP AND NARROW ON the way to Bar 717 Ranch. For the month of August, Lynne and I would sleep in tent cabins (mine was Sluice Box), take care of barn animals (I named my sheep Samantha), make lanyard keychains in a crafts workshop, swim in a clear mountain lake every day, and sing around the campfire at night. I loved every minute of it. My sister couldn't wait to go home.

I imagine that the first night my parents were on the road without me and my sister was a good one. They probably parked at a KOA in Redding, a first stop off I-5 after navigating the winding road out of Trinity. Night would have been approaching and my parents may have opened a bottle of cold champagne as soon as David was asleep in the loft over the driver's cab. August 2, 1969, would have been their sixteenth wedding anniversary. The kitchen table in the RV was oddly intimate, with cushioned seats on either side and a curtained window facing the campground. My dad may have taken a seat across from my mother and filled two glasses with bubbly.

Where would an anniversary celebration start when you're holding tight to a broken marriage? "I remember the night we met," my mother may have said. It was 1950 and she was eighteen, an English major at Wellesley College in Massachusetts. She took a train to Connecticut one weekend to go to a dance at Yale, where her high school boyfriend, Pete, was in college. Pete introduced her to a friend of his, a handsome, dark-haired New Yorker named Roger, a freshman with intelligent hazel eyes and a warm and genuine smile. She found him charming and witty, and on top of that the boy could dance. Before she lay down to sleep that night, my mother knew her long romance with Pete was over.

Back at Wellesley, my mother was on cloud nine. She wrote her new sweetheart's name up and down the margins of her class notes, tasting its sound on her tongue. "Roger," her notes read over and over again, in small and bigger letters, and "Marilyn and Roger," with a heart drawn between their two names. My father gave up weekends at the Yale library to travel by train from Connecticut to Massachusetts and see the woman he couldn't stop thinking about. They held hands walking in the woods, recited favorite poems for each other, and sang songs together, his resonant tenor harmonizing with her silken soprano (*"Blue skies smiling at me, nothing but blue skies do I see"*). They kissed in shadowy corners of campus, both of them certain they had found "the one."

In months they were engaged to marry, and they did, with a wedding his father would give them at the Pierre Hotel in New York City the summer before their senior years.

After a honeymoon on the beaches in Bermuda, they would return to college in their separate states to graduate in June. My mother would move to Connecticut with her English degree from Wellesley to join her husband, who had been accepted to Yale Law School. They undoubtedly clinked glasses on that one.

Perhaps their next toast was for the day they moved into their first home together: a prefab building made of corrugated steel, a Quonset hut near an Air Force base in Delaware. My father had signed up for the Reserve Officer Training Corps and was notified he had to be there for two years before starting law school.

At last my mom had a home to decorate without the influence of her controlling mother. Growing up, she hadn't been allowed to help with cooking or baking, and her mother insisted she leave the housecleaning to the live-in housekeeper, her mother's badge of arrival into the middle class after growing up in the crowded Lower East Side tenements. When they moved into married student housing at Yale in 1957, my mom was pregnant with their first child.

I imagine at this point in their recollections they sat for a long time without taking another sip of champagne. At Yale, my dad was absorbed in his schoolwork, leaving my mother on her own to care for their raven-haired baby with porcelain skin and dazzling hazel eyes. My mother turned to her friends for support, other women married to men buried in law books.

It was the mid-1950s, and in the style of the times, The Yale Law Wives, as they called themselves, created a collection of recipes to use when their husbands graduated and they could launch into their American Dreams. For this recipe collection, the women typed each of their recipes five times on five index cards so that everyone in the group could have a complete set. Mrs. Harold Palmer gave up her secrets for Swedish meatballs. Mrs. Carl Perchuck offered a frozen fruit salad with canned fruit cocktail and sweetened mayonnaise. Marilyn Sherman, the only one to use her first name and not her husband's with "Mrs." before it, gave her mother's recipes for chocolate cake, brownies, and beef stroganoff. She was just learning to cook.

What could my parents have said about what came next? Early on, my mother was starting to realize she had married a man who was more closely wedded to his career goals than he was to her. Smitten as she was by him, she hadn't learned much about his background before accepting his marriage proposal. She knew he was from Yonkers, a suburb outside of Manhattan. She knew his grandparents were Eastern European Jewish immigrants who lived on the Lower East Side, like hers had. But she had no idea the man she had promised to love for the rest of her life was a workaholic, running a race without a finish line.

The roots of my father's workaholism ran deep. It started in his immigrant grandfather's stuffy little cigar shop in the Bronx. At twelve years old in 1916, my father's dad was rolling cigars in his father's cigar shop. In high school, to earn money, he set up pins at a bowling alley after school. His sights were set on studying law, but there was no money for college. He couldn't even afford to go to Cornell with a scholarship he received.

Then serendipity stepped in.

At twenty, my grandfather, the tall and handsome Isadore Barushka Asherman, was going by the more Americanized name Irving Asherman. He was a head-turner with a gift for making anyone he talked with feel at home. One day, while waiting for a friend at the friend's father's furniture store in the Bronx, he spontaneously volunteered to help a young Yiddish-speaking couple find a walnut table. He sold the table to them while his friend's father was in the back office with the door closed. That was all it took; he was offered a job in the store. Irving knew Yiddish and he was a natural salesman. A few years later he was head of sales at a department store so big it filled an entire Manhattan city block. Doormen in suits and caps stood at the store entrances.

In 1924, Irving married a graduate of Hunter College—my grandmother, Fannie. By the time their first child, my father, was born in 1932, Irving was a high-ranking executive in the furniture business. Law school was off the table. "Money in the pocket meant a lot in those days," he would tell me. He changed his name to Irving B. Sherman, because it looked more professional, and put his own dreams into dreams for his son.

And so it was that my father came into this world expected to achieve what his father hadn't been able to. He got straight A's at a prestigious prep school. He skipped weekend fishing trips to do homework. Voted most handsome in high school and most likely to succeed, he earned an undergraduate degree at Yale University and went on to graduate magna cum laude from Yale Law School at twenty-seven, with a ticket to anywhere.

It was July 1959 and my mother was six months pregnant with me when they moved to California, where my father took a job as a law clerk in San Francisco. Their rented flat was in the Sunset District, two blocks from Ocean Beach. Did they make a toast to that decision on that August night in the motor home?

San Francisco impressed my dad. Creaking cable cars rode the rails up and down impossibly steep hills, the conductor ringing a clanging bell as the cables groaned. Victorian rooftops cut a jagged silhouette against a soft blue sky, an image he admired every day as he commuted by bus to work from his home near the glittering Pacific on the west side of the city to the sparkling San Francisco Bay on the east side.

My mother had an entirely different view of their new life. In their neighborhood, two blocks from Ocean Beach, faceless flats built with no space between them filled the streets, one block after the next. Barred iron gates made uninviting entryways. Gardens grew cranky rose bushes, no one tending them with a sack of fertilizer or a pair of pruning shears when she walked past, pushing a baby carriage, her toddler at her side.

And there was the fog. Swirling clouds of fog drifted past the flat, blowing in so thick sometimes that my mother lost sight of my playpen in the backyard. When she saw that from the kitchen window, she would go out to fetch me and whisk me back to the warm indoors.

My dad didn't know about that fog. He didn't know my mother strolled the path at the edge of the sandy beach dressed in her thickest sweater while waves broke along an endless shoreline. He didn't know she stood with their toddler and baby at the top of the hill past the Cliff House restaurant, watching pelicans draw giant V's across the sky on their way to anywhere else. He had no idea she wondered how she was going to manage this lonely life with no friends nearby and a husband at the office six days a week.

It was an election year, with JFK running against Richard Nixon. When my father came home from work, in the few hours of night after the kids were put to bed, they may have sat on the couch in front of the TV news, my father dropping off to sleep with his head resting in my bored mother's lap.

THE MEMORY OF THEIR NEXT MOVE MAY HAVE INspired another champagne toast that night in the motor home. In 1961, my father was hired as a copyright attorney at an entertainment law firm in Beverly Hills, where he would represent Hollywood actors, directors, producers, and screenwriters. He had his first job in the field, and one he would keep for many years.

Hope was alive again after their new start in the City of Angels. They were in their late twenties and ready for this change. They rented a duplex in the Mid-Wilshire District, where tree-lined neighborhoods spanned miles. There were no steep hills or cable cars, just cars and buses and houses with front lawns and porches without iron grates across them. My mother liked her new home. On the backs of black-and-white Polaroids, in her neat handwriting, she recorded the look of their life in that house. The mobile hanging over my crib featured little stuffed birds. The new Formica dining table had four metal chairs with white vinyl seats. A musty-smelling Victrola played thick vinyl records.

My father's hurried script marks the back of a few of those Polaroids. In one, my mother sits on their nubby, secondhand couch holding a cocktail and looking beautiful and worn out. Her chubby-cheeked baby (me) is nestled in the crook of an arm as she offers a half smile to the camera. "Time for the bottle!" my father has written on the back.

In a rare color photo, I'm sitting in a high chair wearing a food-spattered bib. I'm blue-eyed and cherubic, with rosy cheeks and dark hair, an eighteen-month-old baby with no idea what lies beyond this moment.

At the law firm, my father had his own office and secretary. His client list included popular stars of the day—Jack Lemmon, Burt Lancaster, Robert Mitchum. Six days a week, he wrote and reviewed contracts. He went to business lunches and stayed late for dinner meetings while my mother took care of the girls. On Sundays he relaxed at the breakfast table, reading the paper in his bathrobe and laughing at the *Blondie* comics. After that, he'd light a pipe (it was Sunday, after all) and settle into a chair to go over some work.

My mother smoked too; she smoked the days away. She smoked talking on the phone, she smoked cooking dinner, she smoked lifting spoonfuls of baby food to my mouth. She smoked looking at baskets of laundry that had to be hauled to the laundromat when she could use my father's VW on Sundays. That was the day for grocery shopping, too. She washed diapers in the bathroom sink, then hung them to dry on the clothesline in the postage stamp–sized cement yard out back.

My mother may have been getting the idea that she had made a mistake in choosing the man she'd married. To appease her, my father promised her things would be better as soon as he made partner: They would buy a house and get a second car. She could hire household help.

It was a dangling carrot, but her appetite was fading.

I imagine my parents in the motor home on that August night in 1969 with a half-full bottle of champagne, and I'm left thinking of all they couldn't toast.

Less than twenty-four hours ago my mother shot herself in the head, and here I am at Sands Beach in Santa Barbara, watching surfers in wetsuits wait for the good waves they seem sure will come. They ride the pulse of these gentler waters like pieces of swaying seaweed and drop down when it's time to let whitecaps curl over their heads. The sun burns my skin as I sit watching this scene without really seeing it.

Regrets come. Why didn't I try to help her? I never held my mother close so she didn't have to feel so alone. No one gave her support for how hard she was trying. Everyone always wanted her to change. If we had done it differently, would she have chosen to stay?

Accusations come. You left home and you could have lived with her four years longer. You hurt her. How could you have been sure you'd be better off living anywhere but home? What made you think it could be enough to see her now and then? *Another voice inside comes to my defense: I had to leave to survive. There was nothing I could have done to help her or stop her.*

I'll sit through this internal argument for years to come, tangled in its sticky web. I want to press her sweet hand to my lips and tell her I'm sorry. There's no one in the world I want to be with more.

Chapter 6

After a month at summer camp in Trinity I was home again, trying to hang onto what felt like the best dream I'd ever had. Forest trails and falling stars, a sleepover with eleven other girls my age for four weeks.

Here at home, my mother's ashtrays were full to overflowing on the coffee table, windows stayed shut, the rooms smelled like stale tobacco. The bedroom I shared with my sister felt like a jail cell. Through the constant haze that was the sky at night, I could make out maybe five stars if I tried hard enough to see their light.

I was hooked on tragedies I read about in the newspaper that came to our house every morning. A boy drowned in a well. A plane was hijacked. The Manson Family, a hippie cult, savagely murdered people in a house up the street from my camp friend Abbie. I tortured myself over the gory details, like the murderers cutting the phone line before breaking into the house. The murderers stabbed Sharon Tate, an actress, right in her pregnant belly after she screamed, "Don't hurt my baby!" (She was eight-and-a-half months pregnant.)

The world looked like one big car accident, and I couldn't stop rubbernecking.

My father came over on Saturday nights. I still barely saw him. One night, after dinner, he asked me to play a game of cards with him.

"Sure!" I clapped my hands. We had never played cards together, just us two. "Meet you in the den!" I ran to get the cards.

When I came back with them my father was sitting cross-legged on the floor, waiting for me. I handed him the deck and sat down across from him.

"What do you want to play? War? Gin rummy?"

He shook the cards out of the pack. "Let's play gin." He held the deck high above our heads and looked at me with an impish twinkle. "Ready?"

"Yep."

He let go of the cards and they fluttered to the floor, scattering like dead leaves in autumn.

"Why did you do that!?" I cried.

He leaned back on his hands with a smile. "It's fifty-two pick-up!"

I burst out crying.

He reached out to me. "It's a joke, a card game. Fifty-two cards in a deck. Fifty-two pick-up?"

I jumped up and fled to my bedroom, where I dove onto my bed to cry into my pillow. This was supposed to be our time. He had spoiled it.

Moments later, he came in and sat beside me, put a hand on my shoulder. "Sunshine, I was playing. I didn't mean to upset you."

I cried harder. He didn't understand.

In December, my parents' marriage was over—again and at last. My father stopped coming over on Saturday nights and my mother stopped going out with us on Sundays to places like an apple farm south of the city or trout fishing at a stocked lake in the valley. Wednesday night dinners out with Dad were on again, but now he wanted just one kid at a time, not three of us together. He said he didn't like the arguments about which restaurant we'd go to. I didn't believe that was why. I was sure he didn't like being with all of us at once. I wasn't convinced he even wanted us at all.

And that was how the legendary year of 1969 came to an end in my world.

MY NEW YEAR'S RESOLUTION FOR 1970 IS WRITTEN on the opening page of my first diary, a book with vertical chartreuse and magenta stripes and a tiny metal key I promptly lost. "LOSE WEIGHT," I wrote in turquoise ink. Below that I wrote: "I am 10 years old and weigh 133 pounds. My favorite radio station is 93 KHJ." Priorities.

My mother was single and she didn't seem too unhappy about it. Her hair was short and she wore jeans and miniskirts with long strings of beads or African medallions. New books showed up on her shelf, books like Eldridge Cleaver's *Soul on Ice* and Hugh Prather's *Notes to Myself.*

Ojai was an artist's community in the hills outside of Santa Barbara, about two hours north. With a friend from her therapy group, on a few Sundays when we were out with our dad, Mom went there to have her own time. Before dinner, she showed off her new treasures. One time she brought home an oil painting of a ceramic pot tipped on its side that she'd bought at an outdoor art show. She came back from another day trip with a hand-painted ceramic vase, which she put on the piano with a spray of tall pussy willow branches arcing out of it. A small ceramic armadillo went in the living room—a Chia Pet. She told us it would grow hairy green sprouts when we watered it. We never watered it. But for now the new possibilities seemed promising, and Mom was excited.

The framed print of a seagull she brought home from Ojai interested me the most. It was a black-and-white image of a single seagull in flight. She told me it reminded her of Jonathan Livingston Seagull, and she took me to her bookshelf in the hall to show me the paperback by that name.

I read the first few pages of this book she liked so much. Jonathan Livingston Seagull was smaller than the other seagulls; he seemed weak. His mother didn't want him to fly high, and he wanted to. Jonathan said, "I just want to see what I can do in the air and what I can't, that's all. I just want to know." Jonathan Livingston Seagull defied the odds. He did more than hunt for food. He flew high and let the wind currents carry him upwards to the bigger view. The message in the book? *We can be more than we think we can.*

My mother hung the seagull print in her bedroom, where she could see it from bed when she woke every morning.

MIDNIGHT SCARED ME. IT FELT LIKE A DANGEROUS hour, too late to be awake. And I couldn't sleep. Lying in bed in the dark, I thought of the immense, starry universe the earth floated in. I saw the planet suspended there, covered with land masses and oceans. The land masses had cities on them, with houses filling those cities. My bed was in one of those houses. So many cities, so many houses!

Meaningless. Our lives were meaningless. Everyone's was. In the end, we meant nothing. We would die and disappear without a trace, like the fuzzy spokes of a wish weed blown off its stem. Look how many millions of people had lived and died with no one left to remember them. I tossed and turned, troubled by these thoughts.

Besides this nihilistic drama, also keeping me awake at night was my fear of prowlers. I was sure a strange man lurked outside, waiting to break in and murder my family in our beds. I was the only one who could save us, and I had a plan: At the first sound of the prowler opening the window to my room, I would jump up, run down the hall, grab a table lamp, and, wielding it like a baseball bat, club the prowler the moment his feet hit the floor.

As I lay in bed and wrestled with these worries, my mother sat in the living room musing about her own. My sister, who slept across the room from me, was oblivious to it all. When I heard the terrible click of the living room light switch—and it always came eventually, usually just before midnight—I knew my mother was going to bed.

"Mom!" I called.

In moments, my mother was there, framed in my doorway. "Can't sleep?"

"Stay with me until I fall asleep?"

The routine was always the same. I'd move closer to the wall to make space for her to lie next to me. I'd curl on my side facing her when she did, trying to fall asleep while she flicked her fingernails—*click, click, click, click*. I hated that nervous sound.

She didn't always stay until I fell asleep. If I wasn't sleeping yet when she got up, I might get up to check the front door and make sure it was locked. We'd gotten a new locking front door with a peephole after my sister punched out a glass pane on the old door during one of her temper tantrums.

MY MOTHER WAS LOOKING FOR A DATE. SHE STARTED going to singles bars on Friday nights and having Lory babysit. With David eight and me ten, twelve-year-old Lynne was not the caregiver my mother wanted for us.

I loved Lory. A senior in high school, she was seventeen, with wavy brown hair that touched the top of her hip-huggers. Her skin was olive and her eyes were olive brown too. That impressed me—but really, everything about her did. She went to rock concerts and to parties where there were lava lamps. Rock posters hung on her bedroom walls: Jimi Hendrix, The Doors, Janis Joplin. She also had a bumper sticker pinned on her bedroom wall with the number of Americans killed in Vietnam: 12,037 and counting. Over a million boys had been drafted, she told me. I worried about my brother, who would be eighteen in ten years. What if the war kept going on?

The book jacket for *Sisterhood Is Powerful* was tacked on Lory's bedroom wall, a red fist inside a circle with a cross under it. She explained that was a women's symbol and tried to explain what women's rights meant. I knew that some women were burning their bras; I'd seen a photo of it in the newspaper. But I didn't get why they were doing it. I *wanted* a bra. My mother said I was too young to get one.

In May, a month before Lory's high school graduation, my mother let her move in with us temporarily. Lory was having a hard time with her "establishment" parents.

With Lory sleeping on the couch in the den at our house, I got to hear her music all the time. She played the Turtles and Simon & Garfunkel, The Doors and Janis Joplin. She showed me her album from Woodstock, with pictures on the inside cover of hippies sliding in mud and swimming naked in a river.

While I sat daydreaming about being older and having that much fun, my mother sat smoking in the living room, lost in her thoughts. I had no idea the voices in her head were back. She was so good at hiding it, I couldn't have known even if I had been paying attention.

Cars pass beyond the ghost of my face in the dirty Greyhound bus window. She's coming to LA with me, this girl I see reflected in the window glass. Her long hair swirls around her shoulders, her eyes stare back at me. I want to put an arm around her but my hands are folded in my lap.

The glittering strip of ocean disappears from sight, leaving vacant lots, telephone poles, and uninspired storefronts in view as we pull into Ventura, the first stop south of Santa Barbara. A woman takes a seat beside me. She fiddles with a bag on her lap, and when I glance at her, she taps at her frowsy hair.

I look out the window again.

"Hello," she says.

I nod, still looking out the window. I don't want to talk to anyone.

The bus makes a deep, achy groan, returning to the highway headed south.

"Are you a student at the university?"

"Yep."

"Going home for the summer?"

I suppose I could tell her. I want somebody to know what's going on. William is the only one who knows I'm on this bus. My father and stepmother, Jill, don't even know I'm on my way home.

"I'm going to LA for my mother's funeral," I say. For effect, and because it's true, I add, "She killed herself Sunday."

The woman gasps. "Two days ago? Oh my goodness! I'm so sorry."

I steady my gaze on my ghost in the window. There. I said it. My mother is dead.

Two hours later, the Greyhound makes a sweeping turn into the Santa Monica station parking lot, three blocks from the beach. I get off the bus, collect my suitcase outside from the driver, and walk the few blocks to a bus stop on Wilshire Boulevard. The place looks familiar, but everything is different today. The sparkles in the sidewalks look surreal.

At last a city bus heaves to the curb and I get on and take a window seat near the back. The floor is black where it meets the bench seat. Decades of dirt. I close my eyes and disappear into the dark, my attempt at solitude interrupted every few blocks when the wheezing behemoth screeches to a stop.

This street I travel runs the east-west length of Los Angeles, from Santa Monica Beach to the heart of downtown. Today I'll take it to Beverly Hills, where my father, my stepmother and my stepsister, Vicki, live. I long to lie on my bed upstairs, door closed. Will I be able to? I have no idea what to expect. David is staying with them; he has nowhere else to go. One more year in high school. Lynne has her apartment near Culver City with a bunch of cats. And I'm riding a bus I don't want to be on, going somewhere I don't want to go.

I open my eyes in time to see the sign announcing the city of Beverly Hills. My father works on the fifteenth floor of one of the buildings here, north of Wilshire. Today must be like any other for him. He's at his desk, reading contracts as thick as telephone books. There's no place at work for chaos, just intellect and order, like slats on a railroad track, even spaces between them for miles. Tonight at six he'll put a stack of paperwork in his briefcase, grab his suit jacket off a hanger, and wave to the secretaries on his way to the elevator. They like my dad—he's handsome, witty, and kind. At home, he'll give Jill a kiss at the front door and go upstairs to change into sweatpants and a pullover. Downstairs, he'll pour a glass of Scotch and sort through the mail on a kitchen counter in front of the TV news until Jill says it's time for dinner.

I've seen this evening routine a thousand times. Vicki will have the table set, forks resting on two-ply, apricot-colored paper napkins, side plates to the left. Her mother will sit across from her, my dad between them at the head of the table. Jill will say, "So, Roger. How was your day?" The inquiry will sound like a statement: cold, monotone—her job. She's not really interested. He'll share a few details and she'll comment where she can while

Vicki sits out their conversation until she's excused to hightail it upstairs to her bedroom. Even now that she's in high school, she's still never part of the dinner conversation.

I pull the cord at my stop and walk the few blocks past groomed front gardens. This cannot be my life. I'm in a movie. No one has called to ask how I'm doing or tell me what's happening. I don't know how my brother and sister are. All I know is I have to get home.

When the phone in my dorm room rang last night, I hoped it was my father or Jill, someone who could understand how hard this is.

"Where the hell are you?" Jill spat.

I put a hand over the earpiece so William wouldn't hear her screeching. He had been with me all day. "I was at the beach."

She gasped. "I'm down here on my hands and knees, cleaning up your mother's blood, and you're at the beach!?"

I wanted to scream, "I don't know what I'm supposed to do!" But I didn't. I acted calm. "I have a French final on Thursday. I have to—"

"You have to get down here right away!" She slammed the phone down hard, ending the call.

At the beach that day with William I had sat numb in the sun for hours, watching seagulls soar somewhere beyond the image of my mother holding a gun to her head and pulling the trigger.

The house sits in the middle of a block south of Wilshire. The mansions are on the north side of Santa Monica Boulevard, but Jill thought it was a good idea to have bars put on the windows downstairs.

I set my suitcase down at the doorstep and knock. Nothing. I knock again. Footsteps. The deadbolt turns, the door swings open, and my stepmother is standing in front of me, tight-lipped. Artsy turquoise and silver drop earrings match the turquoise stones circling her neck. One hand glitters with stacked diamond rings. A whiff of French perfume follows her even now. I tower over her at five foot ten and am hardly the same kind of put-together—no lipstick, no jewelry, matching or not. Today I don't care.

"Well," she says with a smirk. "Finally."

I pick up my suitcase. "Can I come in?"

She steps aside to let me pass, no doubt holding onto a million comments, none of them good.

Chapter 7

Every two-page spread in my diary was devoted to a week, with three blank lines to fill for each of the seven days. That may have been why I recorded events in short, simple sentences. Or maybe I wrote so few words because I didn't have language yet for the feelings I was experiencing, though I would remember how I felt about what happened for the rest of my life.

The year I was ten, I wrote in the diary that I wanted to give my mother a Judy Collins album for her birthday but had to save more allowance first. Her birthday passed on June 5 and I didn't mention it in the diary again. A few days later I wrote, "Debbie's mom took us shopping at May Company. I got a pair of opaque tights, 2 bras, slightly cupped." For the next entry I wrote, "Fifth grade is almost over." I wrote that Debbie and I had set up a tent in the backyard to have an overnight. On the morning of June 17, I wrote, "Two days of school left." Later that day I added, "Mommy took too many pills. Went into deep sleep. Hospital. Dad's staying with us."

There was a game I liked to play when I was walking home from school. In it, I was lost and looking for my house. Every house I passed between school and my street *could* be mine—but no, not that one, keep walking.

Sometimes I was the young boy in a book I loved, *North to Freedom*. I'd escaped from a wartime concentration camp and I was making my long journey home. Other times I was the Little Match Girl in the Hans Christian Andersen fairy tale. It was winter and I was walking barefoot on a snowy night, seeing through windows into houses where families gathered around dinner tables with tall candles burning bright, a roaring fire in the fireplace. The people in these houses didn't see or care about the little girl selling matches in the street. Her wretchedness paled beside their glow. There was no seat for her at the table. I walked on, pretending the next house was a new possibility, only to decide it wasn't the house I was looking for.

On June 17 I didn't play the "I'm lost" game on the way home from school. I had to hurry. Something important was waiting for me. My mother had promised to take me to Hollywood after school to buy a leather purse, the kind with a shoulder strap and long, swinging strips. I would finally have something cool to wear without having to worry about whether it would fit.

The house was quiet when I opened the front door. "Mom?"

She wasn't in her usual afternoon seat at the dining table. She wasn't in the kitchen or the living room. Maybe she was in her bedroom.

"Mom?" I tapped lightly on her door and opened it.

The room was dark, the shades pulled down over the windows to the yard. My mother was sleeping, her head resting on a pillow, the covers pulled to her neck.

"Mom?" I whispered. I looked around for a way to make

a noise and wake her without being obvious about it. Her desk was covered with loose papers and a typewriter. An empty water glass sat at the edge of the clutter. I lifted the glass and set it down with a loud *clink*. She didn't stir. Years from now, I'll realize this was probably the last thing she touched before climbing into bed to die.

Lory's graduation was that night. The Beatles's *White Album* was playing in her room when I knocked at her door. "Something's wrong with my mom," I called to her. "She won't wake up."

Lory flung the door open and rushed past me to my mother's bedroom. I watched from her bedroom doorway as she shook Mom by the shoulder. "Marilyn! Marilyn!"

My mom didn't stir.

"I'm calling your father." Lory hurried past me to the wall phone in the kitchen.

Time is compressed here like in a movie: One event follows the next, and who knows if it happened in a second or five minutes or longer. My dad is on his way from his office. I'm trying to decide where in the house to wait for him or whether to wait outside. The next minute he's bursting through the front door and running to the back bedroom. Lory grabs my arm to keep me from following him. "Let him go." Next, he's rushing past us to the kitchen phone shouting, "Call an ambulance!" On the phone, he says, "Yes. There are three empty bottles on the bathroom sink. Two bottles of sleeping pills, one bottle of tranquilizers."

My friend Debbie is with me for the next part. Did I call her? Did she just happen to come over? No idea. We're waiting outside for the ambulance. If my brother and sister are around for this, I don't know. Years will pass and we'll never talk about it. I don't know where my father is. Maybe sitting with her.

Waiting outside for the ambulance with Debbie, I kick at piles of dead leaves in the gutter. My mother might be dying right now. The wail of a siren is getting closer.

"That's the ambulance coming for your mom!"

Debbie sounds excited by the drama of the idea. I want a trap door to open in the street and swallow me whole.

The next thing I know, an ambulance turns at the corner of my street—no siren—and comes to a stop in front of my house. How horribly out of place it looks on my street. Two men in white jump out and grab a stretcher and medical gear out of the back. They rush through the door Lory holds open wide for them.

The rest of the slide show goes like this: I'm standing in the doorway to my house. The medics hurry past to the ambulance, carrying a stretcher with my mother on it. Her face is ghostly pale, her lips look dry. I quick-study her face, committing it to memory—this could be the last time I see her. Her short pink nightgown is hiked up on one thigh. I want to pull it down for her but all I can do is watch her go by. My dad is getting into his car as the medics load the stretcher into the back of the ambulance. One climbs into the driver's seat while the other closes the back doors and jumps into the front seat. The ambulance takes off, my father's Buick Electra following close behind. I'm too young to wonder how he's feeling. The woman he fell in love with, the mother of their children, could be dying right now. Both of their futures hang in the balance.

Lory sighs when the ambulance turns the corner at the top of my street. "You kids are coming with me tonight. I have to take a shower." I hear the siren start up again as the ambulance shoots up Sawtelle to UCLA Medical Center with my mother inside on a stretcher.

The slide show pauses.

When the slide show starts again, a police car is pulling up in front of my house. An officer gets out and walks past me and Debbie on his way to the front door. I'm transfixed by the gun he's carrying in a holster at his waist. He looks all wrong walking across my front lawn.

"Anyone home?" he asks as he's walking.

"My babysitter."

Lory opens the door wearing her yellow bathrobe, her wet hair wrapped in a towel like a turban.

"There was a suicide attempt here?" says the officer.

Lory nods.

"What'd you do? Try to hang yourself in the shower?"

He thinks that's funny. I want to kick him. Lory frowns and opens the door wider to let him in. She calls cops pigs and this one is certainly acting like one.

"Let's go to my house," Debbie says.

I say okay—what else can I do?—but tell her I can't stay long.

Debbie's mother opens the door. "Oh, no," she says when she hears the news. "I'm so sorry."

I hate her pity. I don't like her House Beautiful life—her hair-sprayed "up do." I don't like her bridge games with "the ladies" in her plastic-wrapped living room. I don't even like their dog, a Dalmatian you can't touch or it will bite you. At Debbie's, the refrigerator door has an automatic ice maker that makes identical cubes in half-moon shapes. Boxes of sugar and flour are kept in plastic bags tied with twist ties. At my house, dishes may get moldy in the sink, bread can grow black hair in the bread drawer, maggots might crawl in hamburger meat in the garbage can—but I know how to live there. Debbie's house is too much for me.

"I should go," I say, and I leave my friend on the doorstep and head home.

That walk to my house down the street feels about ten miles long. Trembling, I keep my eyes fixed on the sidewalk squares so the lines dividing them can guide my steps, one after another.

In the next slide I'm in an auditorium at Lory's high school, sitting between my brother and sister. Graduates in caps and gowns cross the stage to accept their diplomas when their names are called. Numbly, I applaud with the crowd. *My mother could be dead right now. The rest of my life might be different after tonight.* I feel like a girl in a book, a girl who only had a mother until she was ten. The man sitting in front of me has a balding head and big ears. Everyone's watching the stage; no one knows what's happening with my mom.

When the applause is done, I'm swept with David and Lynne into the stream of people exiting the building. My brother and sister look as disoriented as I feel. Strangers hug, slap backs, exclaim "Congratulations!"

Lory appears from out of nowhere and says, "Follow me." She's with a friend. We walk to her car in the parking lot. On the way, she says, "God, with all that's going on I almost forgot your mom might be dead."

I keep walking.

As David and Lynne climb into the back seat of Lory's Pinto, Lory's friend gestures to the two of them and asks, "Who are they?"

"I babysit them. Her too." She points at me.

"No way." The girl looks me up and down. "She's got to be at least fourteen."

I want to shout, "I am *not* fourteen! I'm ten, and my mother might be dead right now!" I climb into the car after my brother and sister and sit with them without talking.

THAT NIGHT, MY FATHER CAME OVER WITH A SUITcase and good news to tell us. "Your mother's going to live. They pumped her stomach."

I was still taking that in when he added a detail that would haunt me for years: "The doctor said she had a half hour left if no one had found her."

A half hour left? Does that mean I saved her life?

If we hadn't had a plan to go to Hollywood after school to get a fringe leather purse for me, my mother wouldn't have made it to sundown.

I don't like numbers when they have anything to do with math, but when they're repeating and they show up in uncanny, coincidental ways, I'm interested. The repeating date in my life with my mother is June 17.

In my 1970 diary, on June 17 I wrote, "Mommy took too many pills. Went into deep sleep. Hospital." In 1977, on June 17 I graduated high school. My mother came to the ceremony and afterwards gave me a simple white card with a note on it. When I got home, I put it in a box with photos and a scrapbook of cards.

Forty years later, I will take that memorabilia box down from the attic one night to look for a photo for a book I'm writing. I'll strip the yellowed sealing tape off the box's seam, then decide to leave the photo hunt for the morning. I'll set the box on a table in the living room and go to bed. In the morning, I'll see an envelope lying on the floor a few feet from the box. There will be nothing else on the floor. Going closer, I'll see my name on the envelope, in my mother's handwriting.

Heart pounding, I'll open the envelope and read her note to me.

June 17, 1977

Dear Sue,
The world is your oyster and you are the pearl.
Much love and happiness,
Mom

And there's one more important date to note: My mother was buried on June 17, 1978.

Chapter 8

The last day of fifth grade was a Friday, two days after my mother went to the hospital and had her stomach pumped and her life saved. Lory was packed and home again. The den was back to being just a room with a couch, a TV, a lamp, and a piano. In my diary, under "Special Events" for the week, I wrote, "School's out." What else could I say?

There was nowhere to go for refuge. Basements were only in books I read, where snow sat in silent mounds outside front doors in winter. In LA, books were my basement. Books were where I went to be alone. They were my shelter when rain fell and collected in cloud-filled puddles, a stray leaf here and there.

It was June now. The skies were dry. And I read. I curled up under a tree with Bonnie in *The Wolves of Willoughby Chase* while furry, four-legged prowlers howled at the moon. In *Manchild in the Promised Land* I ran from policemen with the author, a thirteen-year-old boy making his broken way through the streets of Harlem.

And I disappeared into music. While my mother was in the hospital recovering, I hung out with Debbie and Bettina, playing record albums in my room. My dad came home at night with Mexican takeout from a place with the best burritos ever. He never had news about our mom or told us what to expect when she came home from the hospital, and we didn't ask.

I liked having my dad around. He was getting kind of hip lately. He had a beard and mustache and he listened to Blood, Sweat & Tears. (It wasn't a band I liked, but for him, it was way out.) One night, he brought one of their albums home with him and said he wanted to play it for me. He offered an arm to escort me into the living room. "Like to dance?"

The music seemed corny, but I couldn't say no. Dad wanted to dance with me.

That weekend he took us for a ride up and down the street a few times in his Dodge Dart, top down. He let me sit on top of the back seat with my arms up in the air, a first-ever "yes" I'd gotten to that request. Wearing my new powder-blue John Lennon sunglasses, I felt the sunlight flash across my closed eyelids after the shade of every tree we passed.

I couldn't begin to make sense of all this. How could I have so much fun with Dad when Mom was in the hospital? She had tried to leave us. I pulled the great cloak of coping around my shoulders, ready to wear it for the rest of my life.

FIVE DAYS AFTER I WROTE THAT "MOMMY TOOK TOO many pills," I wrote the next entry: "Mommy's home again." I didn't write that my dad went back to his apartment right away or that nothing was said about what my mother had done.

That week, I went with her to the vet—one of our cats

had an eye infection. On the way home, we picked up my developed fifth grade graduation photos at the drugstore.

"You look pretty," my mother said, admiring the brown chiffon dress she'd bought me for the occasion.

I wondered if she realized she might have never seen me in it.

I STARTED SUMMER SCHOOL, TAKING AN ART CLASS and a folk dance class. Two girls from school I barely knew invited me to their birthday parties. I imagined word had gotten out about my mother and they were asking me out of pity. I went anyway.

Two weeks after she came home, my mother left again, this time to stay at a private psychiatric hospital called the Westwood Hospital. My father seemed unhappy when he came to stay with us again, but he didn't explain anything. All I knew was that he brought takeout Mexican dinners home, he slept at our house every night, and he went to work in the morning.

According to my diary, my mother was home two weeks later, my father left, and life at home went back to normal. She gave me a pair of purple slippers she'd knitted for me at the hospital. They were too small, but I liked them anyway. She took me to the hobby shop to buy clay for my art class. She fed our cats and dog, Sam, every morning and night. Sam was a puppy she'd brought home when I was six, the year she was "well" again, and she'd named him Sam I Am, for a character in a Dr. Seuss book we liked, *Green Eggs and Ham*. One morning, for fun, she made him a dish of green scrambled eggs using food coloring.

On Sundays at eleven, my dad picked the three of us up for our weekly outing. I have no idea what my mother did when we were out; all I know is that when we got back, the living room smelled like an ashtray.

One night, after dinner, my mom called her kids back to the table right after we'd left for our rooms. "I want to talk to you."

She sat in her seat at the head of the table with one knee bent, one bare foot on the chair, and the other bare foot tucked under her. The three of us stood in the doorway.

"I'm sorry," she said.

David shifted from one foot to the other. Lynne frowned and folded her arms. I looked at the "Home Sweet Home" plaque I had made with a decoupage set and hung on the dining room wall.

I tried to make sense of my mother's apology. She was sorry she tried to die and leave us? I was sorry I lost my sister's umbrella. I was sorry I hit my brother in the head with a rake by mistake. I didn't understand this sorry.

Speaking very deliberately, she said, "I will never do that again. I love you kids."

My sister choked on a laugh. It hadn't occurred to me that our mother could do that again. But of course she could. I wanted to believe her, but I didn't know if I could. The mother I knew would never have tried to leave us.

"I don't blame you kids for being angry."

Silence.

"Is there anything you want to ask me?"

More silence.

"You can tell me how you feel." My mother looked like she'd be happy if we said anything at all. She tried to explain. "I was hearing voices again. I couldn't take it anymore. I really tried."

My sister took that as her cue. She flew out of the room, and seconds later the hallway bathroom door slammed shut—hard. David backed away, headed for his room. When he got to his door, he turned, slipped inside, and shut it behind him.

I didn't want to leave my mother alone, but this was too much for me too. "I don't want to talk about it," I said, and I fled to my room, where I threw myself face down on the bed.

The voices in her head were back? I should have noticed there was something wrong. I was old enough by now. But she made everything look so regular, like there weren't any problems. I had missed it.

MY MOTHER WENT TO DAY CARE AT THE WESTWOOD Hospital that summer, gone all day and home in time to make dinner. Sometimes she brought home an art or craft project she'd done there—a pair of moccasins, drawings in a sketchbook.

She was talented, I knew that. Once I saw a framed charcoal drawing she kept stored in a box in the attic. Graceful black curves in charcoal showed a seated woman holding an infant to her breast.

She brushed off my praise when I showed it to her to ask about it—"Oh, that was just a college art class."

"You're really good, Mom," I insisted.

She shrugged.

IN AUGUST THE THREE OF US WENT TO NEW YORK TO stay with relatives for two weeks. To me, the trip was a vacation. To those who had planned it, the trip was probably to give my mother some quiet time to get back on her feet. No one ever said a word about what had happened—not at home, and not during our visit to New York.

We started with our dad's parents on the Upper East Side. Riding from the airport to their apartment in the back of a cab, I gazed out the window open-mouthed—slanted rooftops, flat rooftops, high rooftops behind gigantic wooden water towers on high platforms. LA was a subtropical basin, filled with strip malls and tree-lined suburbs from the San Gabriel Mountains to the Pacific. This was a forest of modern glass-and-cement buildings.

At their apartment, Grandma Sherman guided us into their lobby, where a doorman carried our suitcases to a metal cage they called an elevator. We rode to the eleventh floor, where Grandpa Sherman waited for us in an armchair with a newspaper open in his lap. He probably didn't know what to do with any of this.

Grandpa Sherman left early for work, where he was an executive at the New York Furniture Exchange. In the evening he was home again, wearing a suit and tie. I liked riding "the lift," as they called it, to hear him greet the elevator operator in the man's native language. "Sveiki!" my grandfather would call out as we stepped inside. He prided himself on being able to say hello, goodbye, and thank you in any language, and the streets of New York seemed full of languages. The elfin elevator operator smiled wide, and his pointed ears tilted back when he did. He repeated the salutation with a sharp pull of the iron cage door, slamming it shut. A yank of the creaky lever and the cage lowered eleven flights to the lobby, where it landed with a loud clang.

I liked Grandma Sherman. She was unaffected and gentle, with pale skin and blue-gray eyes like mine, her graying hair brushed back from her face. She wore no makeup yet didn't look drab, though I thought the gold watch dangling on a chain around her neck made her look old. She seemed to like us, and her goodnight hugs to me and David were loving. (Lynne didn't like being hugged.)

New York City was hot and muggy. I'd never felt air so thick or seen air conditioners drip water onto sidewalks from metal boxes high above. But I liked the city. Just by raising an arm, my grandmother could get a cab to pull over out of the sea of traffic to take us places that impressed even my sister. We rode a ferry to the Statue of Liberty, watching a white trail follow us across the water while a cooling mist spritzed our skin. Over dinner my grandparents sometimes slipped into speaking Yiddish, a language they grew up with, and they refused to tell me what they were talking about. I had a feeling I knew: They had news from home.

MY MOTHER'S YOUNGER SISTER, AUNT BARBARA, WAS the next stop on our trip. A divorced mother of two, my aunt lived in a small garden apartment in a woodsy suburb outside the city.

Aunt Barbara reminded me of my mother, with her brown hair and eyes, but she wasn't beautiful in the same way. Our cousins were around my sister's and my ages, but the apartment was too small for all of us, my aunt said. We would have to stay with our grandmother, who lived in a high-rise apartment nearby. My mother had an older brother, Uncle Leonard, but he and my mother never spoke. We wouldn't be seeing him on this trip.

Grandma Friedman's apartment had views of a sprawling field and a kids' play area with swings. Her apartment was spotless. Once, I saw her pick up a strand of hair from the white carpet and carry it to the trash can under the kitchen sink. Both of those actions—seeing a hair on the carpet, depositing it in the trash can—made it onto my list of mental notes to tell my mother about for a laugh.

One afternoon, Grandma called us to come see something in her bedroom. David and Lynne were watching TV and didn't want to go, but I went, to keep our grandmother from feeling ignored.

She opened a dresser drawer and took out an envelope. "This is your mother's," she cooed, opening the envelope to show me a perfectly formed brown ringlet. "She was your age when we cut her hair."

My mother had been my age once? I reached out to touch the ringlet, but my grandmother whisked it away. "Don't touch! This is precious!" She pressed the envelope to her heart. "Your mother was such a beauty. People stopped us on the street to ask if she was Elizabeth Taylor—you know, when *National Velvet* came out. They wanted her autograph!"

The ringlet went back in the dresser drawer.

Grandma cared more about looks than anyone I knew, and she couldn't contain her dismay about my size. One morning she brought a loaf of date nut bread to the table and spread a slice with cream cheese for each of us. After that, she went back to her kitchen—a room so small you could reach the sink, stove, and refrigerator standing in one spot—to tidy up.

A few minutes later she called out, "Anyone like another piece of date nut bread?"

Lynne and David said no, they were done. I popped a last bite into my mouth and said, "Sure, I'll have another piece!" Date nut bread was a real treat—tender and sweet, with a sticky top.

Grandma Friedman brought the loaf to the table again and cut a slice for me, but as she set the slice on my plate she said, "You really shouldn't, Suzy. You need to lose weight." David and Lynne got up and left the table. I'd like to think I got up and walked away too, but chances are I ate the date nut bread first.

AUNT MARIAN WAS MY DAD'S ONLY SIBLING. SHE LIVED in Baltimore with her husband (for the time being) and their two kids, another long bus ride away, this one over interesting bridges and waterways I got to admire while my sister curled up against the window, sulking.

Aunt Marian was a psychologist, which impressed me, and I found her two-story house, with its rooms full of antique furniture and wool carpets, enchanting. I secretly longed to be one of her kids, with an upstairs bedroom in a big, clean house full of antique furniture on a street without sidewalks. My cousins didn't know how good they had it.

Aunt Marian took the five of us swimming at a public pool one afternoon and out for a crab dinner afterwards. Wearing plastic bibs the waitress gave us, we hammered crab legs with special tools we were given and sucked out what my cousins called the natural mustard. Everyone was laughing and cracking and dipping the succulent meat into bowls of melted butter, reaching for more from the pile on newspapers in the center of the table.

I had never had fun like this with my family. Aunt Marian had even gotten into the pool with us that afternoon and played Marco Polo. With her eyes closed, she'd called out "Marco?" and we'd shouted, "Polo!" She'd found us every time.

We're gathering at my father and Jill's house before the funeral. Aunt Barbara and Grandma flew in from New York sometime yesterday. I don't know my aunt too well, but I'm glad she's here. She and my mother were pretty close. Aunt Barbara stayed a week with us once when she was single and thinking of moving to California. I know she went with my mother to a singles bar one night, because my mother was doing that in those days. They came in well after midnight, even though my aunt had an early flight the next morning.

We say an uneasy hello in the foyer. My father approaches to say a somber hello and talk quietly with Grandma, and I step away to give them privacy. My aunt and grandmother must feel in shock. On top of everything, they're in my father's house. Neither of them has seen him in years. But none of that matters right now.

Jill is in the kitchen. I'm not sure why she's welcoming her husband's ex-wife's family into their home before the funeral and for a wake. It's out of character. Maybe she's doing it because she knows he's upset, or because she thinks it's her job. She's doing the right thing as my father's wife.

Aunt Barbara takes me aside and tells me in a whisper about sleeping at my mother's house last night. Grandma slept on Mom's bed—"She wanted to," Aunt Barbara says, "I couldn't stop her." She doesn't tell me the mattress is bare and blood-stained and so are the walls and carpet. She doesn't tell me about the bullet hole in the ceiling or say a word about the bathroom, where my mother was found on the floor with the gun after the second shot. I'll never go into that room again.

"My mom put on one of your mother's nightgowns and cried herself to sleep," my aunt tells me. She glances around to make sure no one is listening. No one is. "I covered her with an afghan she found in your mother's closet."

I know that Grandma knit that afghan and sent it to Mom a few years ago.

Leonard, the mystery uncle, knocks at the door around nine, after catching a red-eye from Boston. I'm meeting Mom's older brother for the first time, the Harvard-educated psychiatrist my mother didn't speak with for most of my life with her. She never said why. Maybe it was because he was the Do No Wrong First-born Son when they were growing up. Or it may have had some-thing to do with a conflict they had at their father's funeral. I knew he had called her last year hoping to reconnect, and they did. He came out to stay with her. She was surprised to find they had a lot in common—progressive politics, divorces, problems with their mother. She liked him after all.

I put my hand out to shake hands with him and he reaches out to cradle me in a hug. Such sad conditions to meet in, we both say. I think he is nice-looking—tall and slightly balding, in a tan suit with an open shirt collar and a loosened tie. He has the Friedman features; my brother looks just like him, with his blue eyes and sandy blond hair. He seems tired and knocked off his game.

Once Leonard moves on to say hello to his mom and sister, I take my father's car to go to Conroy's Flowers. I plan to ask the funeral home to put roses in my mother's coffin, along with a note I've written to her. She'll be buried with roses and my loving words next to her heart, for whatever that means. Nothing. Everything.

Back from the florist's, I go to the kitchen for a vase to hold the roses for now. Jill is in there, assembling snack trays for a refreshments table she'll set up while we're at the funeral. She's arranging slices of cheddar and Havarti in neat rows on a platter—orange, white, orange, white. I ask for a vase and promise to bring it back.

"Did you hear?" Jill sounds almost cheerful. "The funeral parlor said your mother can have an open coffin. Isn't that great?"

Did she say "isn't that great"? Does she mean isn't it great your mother's head wasn't blown apart?

My answer comes quickly: "I don't want an open coffin."

"But isn't it good to know that you could have one if you wanted?"

Jill doesn't get it. I drop the bouquet of roses into the vase and fill it with water. I leave the vase on the counter and escape into the breakfast room to be alone.

Chapter 9

In my final stretch of something like a childhood, the casualties of the wider world were coming in closer. Starving Biafrans in the Nigerian civil war looked haunting in photos on the front page of the paper on our dining table. The Vietnam War was dragging on despite protests all over the country. On the cover of *LIFE* magazine, a boy lay face down on the asphalt in a pool of blood, one of the four college students shot dead by the National Guard at Kent State in Ohio while protesting the war. Joplin and Hendrix OD'd on heroin within weeks of each other. The Beatles broke up. Nothing could be counted on, at home or anywhere.

Summer was almost over when my father said he had a surprise for us. It was a Sunday, and we were in the car after lunch at El Torito in Fisherman's Wharf. "Kids," he said, "how would you like to go to Santa Barbara next weekend to stay in a beach hotel? It's Labor Day weekend. I have three days."

Three whole days with Dad? A beach hotel? Restaurants and cards games? And his birthday, too. I couldn't think of anything better.

Even Lynne said it sounded good.

That Saturday he picked us up for the two-hour ride up the coast highway for our beach weekend together. The car radio was tuned to my favorite station, KHJ. Riding in the back seat of the convertible with the top down, I sang along with every song that came on, the wind whipping my hair. "Good Morning, Starshine" came on, and my sister groaned.

"Come on!" she shouted at me from the front seat. "Stop singing!"

I ignored her.

Just after Malibu, my father made a turn off the highway at an exit ramp and headed into a neighborhood I had never seen before.

"Where are we going?" I asked. There were no gas stations in sight.

He pulled to a stop on a residential street without answering. "There's something I have to tell you kids."

My stomach lurched, and the sight of him fingering the car keys in his hand didn't help. He looked nervous. My sister, sitting next to him in front, rolled up her window, which made no sense to me since the convertible top was down.

"I'm dating someone," he blurted.

What? My father had a girlfriend? Why was he telling us this now?

"Her name is Jill. She has a daughter a little younger than David. Her name is Vicki." The next part was like a bomb dropping. "They'll be staying with us this weekend."

My sister shouted, "Why didn't you tell us before?! I wouldn't have come!" She burst into tears, sobbing like her heart was breaking. "I want to go home!"

I understood. My heart was breaking too. David didn't say a word.

Over the tops of houses I could see the coast highway, where we'd been just a few minutes ago, when everything was good.

My dad had a girlfriend. With a daughter. They were crashing our weekend with him. My sister was right. He should have told us before. I wouldn't have come either. It was obvious our father didn't want to be alone with us.

He turned to Lynne, who was sobbing with her face in both hands. "I'm sorry you're upset." Gently, he urged her to calm down.

I didn't cry. It wasn't my way. I wanted to disintegrate.

After a few minutes of this, my father started the car again and drove back to the highway. I was wearing shorts, and my bare thighs stuck to the vinyl seats in the hot sun.

As we drove, he told us about Jill. By the time we got to Santa Barbara I knew she was thirty years old and divorced, she was an artist, she lived near Century City, and she had an art studio in Venice Beach. She made silkscreen prints. I would find out she stored most of those prints in a metal cabinet at her studio; she didn't show them in galleries. She also made purses out of burlap water bags, he told us, which she planned to sell in boutiques.

I stared out the window while he spoke. I had never seen him admire my mother like this, like anything, really, even though my mother was a beautiful singer who played piano and guitar, who could draw and paint and dance. She could do anything.

When we pulled into the parking lot at the Miramar Hotel, I shrank from the view. We'd been sideswiped.

AFTER UNPACKING IN THE THREE-BEDROOM SUITE we would share with Jill and Vicki, we went to meet them in the hotel restaurant. Jill was small and pretty, with an icy smile and porcelain skin. She had big green eyes and red hair that fell in waves to her shoulders. She was carrying one of those burlap water bags my dad had told us about. Vicki was a skinny six-year-old with long brown hair and bangs.

Over dinner, my father's girlfriend flirted with him. "Like to spoon?" she asked, holding a spoon toward him with a flirtatious smile.

He looked like he was purring.

The next day was a beach day, but the beach was no fun. My father and Jill walked holding hands at the shoreline while my sister lay in the sun on a towel in her bathing suit, fuming, and my brother industriously built sandcastles with a pail and shovel. I went back to the hotel room and ended up playing a game called Barrel of Monkeys with Vicki, who apparently didn't want to be at the beach just then either.

"I've known your father longer than you've known my mother," she gloated, lifting a flat plastic monkey by the tail of another as we played. I could have said, *Shut up, you little brat*, but I held my tongue. She managed a third monkey in the chain before losing control of it and turning the next round over to me.

I hated the surprise of Jill, and this skinny little kid with the big brown eyes was only making things worse. I scooped up a green monkey by a red monkey's tail and strung together a chain of six plastic monkeys. Then the chain broke and the plastic monkeys scattered across the table.

Game over.

I WAS ELEVEN, FIVE FOOT ONE, AND 180 POUNDS, facts I recorded on the first page of my second diary. Under that, I listed my likes: writing poems and stories, talking on the phone, James Taylor, soft music, hard rock, all music, Cat Stevens, looking pretty, everything pure, beautiful, and happy. And my dislikes: school, cruel people, smog, bad days, cigarette smoking, weed, bad dreams, reading the newspaper, TV, shopping for clothes, being fat.

Being fat. On the schoolyard, a boy in my class called me Sherman Tank. Hilarious. A stranger riding down the street on a ten-speed bike shouted, "Mama Cass!" as he rode past.

Diets started. Three days into the Doctor's Quick Weight Loss Diet, which I followed using a booklet I bought at Thrifty drugstore, I wrote in my diary, "So far I haven't lost a thing. I expect to by tomorrow." The next day I wrote, "I lost two pounds." I also noted that I'd eaten pizza and shared a bear claw with my dad at the Rose Parade on Sunday.

That diet lasted three weeks. Having to drink eight glasses of water a day was the deal-breaker.

The low-carb diet came in a booklet listing carb grams in every imaginable food. For eight days I dutifully tracked my daily allotment of carbs and weighed myself every morning. On the third day I was down one and a quarter pounds. It must have been a fluke.

Tests came next. My thyroid was normal and I didn't have diabetes. I could have told them I didn't need those tests. I knew why I was fat. Food was my entertainment, it was my addiction. And my mother was my unwitting supplier.

It started each day at breakfast, when I filled a bowl with sugary cereal or warmed a couple of Pop-Tarts in the toaster. But most of the damage happened after school. I read a lot and watched hours of TV, and I liked to eat while doing both. *Bewitched* and *That Girl* were two of my favorite shows, but my list of favorite foods was much longer. Scooter Pies, Ding Dongs, Twinkies, Fritos, and potato chips . . . they crowded the kitchen cupboards. I would toast a slice of American cheese set on top of a piece of bologna, making the bologna curl into a bowl that held the melted cheese. I munched Oscar Mayer hot dogs straight out of the package.

If there was a box of Jell-O 1-2-3 in the cupboard, I cooked it up and filled glass bowls with it, seeing the mixture cool into three layers: creamy, foamy, and firm. And I couldn't stop eating straight out of the half gallon of ice cream in the freezer and buying Bit-O-Honey bars at the laundromat on the way home from school.

"Health food" was new, and my mother was right there for it. She starting buying whole wheat bread instead of Wonder Bread and fresh fruit instead of canned. Once, when we were out to lunch, she bought a sandwich with alfalfa sprouts on it.

"Like a taste?" She held out the horror to offer me a bite.

I recoiled. "You're eating grass! Gross!"

For years, she had made chocolate chip pancakes for David in the morning, to have with his chocolate milk. Now, carob chips and carob powder replaced the chocolate in the pancakes and the milk.

At breakfast, she sat with him and he read her highlights from the sports pages in the *Los Angeles Times*. She tried to sound interested; "Mmm-hmmm," she would murmur here and there.

I asked her about it once when David wasn't around.

"I have to try," she told me. "Your brother doesn't have a role model at home."

That was puzzling. Did I?

MY MOTHER TOOK ME TO A WEIGHT WATCHERS meeting. She wanted to lose a few pounds herself; it was something we could do together. When I weighed in the first day we went, they told me 110 pounds was the goal weight for my height.

I had seventy pounds to lose. And I was ready. Bring on the cottage cheese!

On Tuesdays I weighed in at Weight Watchers, shoes off and hopes high. The intake clerk recorded my weight with a plus or minus sign in front of it, indicating whether I'd gained or lost weight. I held my breath, watching. At home afterwards, I might write in my diary, "I weigh 178, lost a pound! I was good last week" or "I gained 1/2 pound this week. I was bad. But I'll be better."

Week after week, the scale crept up or down only a fraction when I stepped onto it. Meanwhile, my mother was dancing in front of the mirror. She had reached her goal weight. "Look at my collarbones!" she boasted, showing off without meaning to. Men in passing cars whistled when we were out together. My mother waved and smiled, calling out, "Thank you!"

"You're not supposed to say anything, Mom," I would scold.

At the drugstore, a salesgirl asked if we were sisters. Oh, ha ha.

"Sisters?" my mother repeated, laughing.

I wanted to scream. And every Tuesday I was at Weight Watchers, measuring my worth by the scale. When the numbers hit 182, two pounds higher than my starting weight, I finally quit.

THE DOCTOR PRESCRIBED DIET PILLS THREE TIMES A day, which meant sneak-taking my lunchtime pill at the drinking fountain on school days. These were amphetamines, drugs that made it hard to sleep at night. The rasp of my brother's clock radio from his room at the end of the hall kept me awake. The racket helped him sleep.

In those sleepless hours in the dark, I thought about the universe I floated in. And I thought about God. Prayer had been coming up in books I was reading, and on top of that, two of my friends had fathers who were ministers. One of them, Joanna, prayed with her hands folded on her chest when she slept over at my house. But it was what she had to say about heaven that really got my attention.

My sister's parakeet, Greenie, died; we buried it in the rose garden out back. When I told Joanna about it, she said, "That bird isn't there anymore; it flew up to heaven." We argued about that.

Later that day, I told my mother what Joanna had said. "Do you believe in God?" I asked.

She looked surprised. "I'm agnostic."

"What does that mean?"

When she told me, I said, "I'm agnostic, too." I thought there *could* be a God, but I wasn't *sure* there was.

"You're too young to know, honey." She took a sip of her coffee. "When you're older, you'll see."

I didn't want to wait. That night, when the hands on my bedside clock started their climb to midnight, I imagined God watching over me and everyone else on the planet. I saw him as an old man with white hair and a long white beard, seated on a throne above the clouds. His eyes were twinkly, his smile was loving. I felt safe and tucked in knowing he was watching over me.

In *North to Freedom*, the boy prayed on his long journey home after escaping a concentration camp. In another favorite book, Louisa May Alcott's *Little Men*, the orphaned children prayed before bed with their beloved Father Bhaer. On my quest to find out if there was a God, I created my own prayer by combining those two prayers and adding a personal message at the end, a kind of PS. For three years, I'd had a crush on a boy at school named George. He was in my class now. If I prayed for George to like me and I found out he did, I would believe in God. If it stayed like it was and he didn't pay any attention to me in class, I would give up believing in God. George's attention would be my gauge for God's existence.

I tried out the prayer in bed that night—in a whisper, to keep from waking my sister—with my hands folded on my chest. "Dear God, please forgive me and the rest of my family for our sins and let us live long, good lives. And please let George like me and let him look at me at school tomorrow. I am Suzy. Amen."

I prayed every night for weeks. I prayed for myself. I prayed for my family, since they didn't pray for themselves.

At first, it seemed to be working. George glanced at me a few times. But eventually, doubts started. I might catch George looking at me and realize I had forgotten to pray the night before. Other nights I might pray and find I was invisible to George at school the following day.

In bed one night, I decided it was time to make a decision. I either believed in God or I didn't.

I pictured God sitting on his throne in heaven, watching over me. It felt good to see him there. Then I looked at it from another angle. There was no God watching over me from his throne in heaven. I was simply lying in bed in a house in a city on a planet with thousands of cities on it. I floated in a starry universe, with no father in the sky watching to make sure I was safe. Was God imaginary? Was that what "having faith" was about?

I stopped praying to a father in the sky who made me feel safe at night. Not long after that, my mother let me quit the diet pills. I was forgetting to take them anyway.

I'm alone in the breakfast room, trying to get my bearings after Jill's "great" news. Newspapers are stacked by the phone; a framed drawing of the family dog hangs on the wall. I can hear the adults speaking in hushed voices in the living room.

No cousins are here. They had never met Aunt Marilyn, living all the way out here in California. And besides, suicide has a cloud of shame around it. It isn't the kind of death adults want their kids to think about.

My father appears in the doorway suddenly, with an envelope in his hand. "Your grandmother found this in Mom's nightstand drawer." He holds out the envelope; he wants me to take it.

Did she write a suicide note? I take the envelope from him. Our eyes meet. How strange to have good news right now—or even to think a suicide letter is good news. But it is. It's very good news.

My mother's last words. Gold in my hands.

Chapter 10

My life took a new turn when Corinna was assigned a seat at my table in sixth grade. Corinna was a new girl at my school. She was tall like me, and she was pretty, with long, silky hair the color of beach sand. She had a freckle-dusted ski-jump nose and teeth that were straight on top and crazily crooked on the bottom in a way that, on her, looked good—charming, even. She walked with confidence, like the world was on her side, and I had the feeling it was.

"Hey, can I see your radio?" she asked on our first day of class in September.

She was referring to the chartreuse transistor I had next to me on the table. I played KHJ walking to school and back and pretty much whenever I could. I handed it over.

"Nice!" She turned the radio over to admire the hot pink flower power sticker I had pasted on the back. "Would you like to have lunch today?"

The cafeteria sold 35-cent hot lunches but I didn't eat those anymore; I brought a sack lunch. Corinna hopped up on a schoolyard lunch table with hers, resting her feet on the bench, and I did the same.

She unwrapped a sandwich. "So. What's your favorite station?"

I noticed her sandwich was cut on the diagonal. Of course. "KHJ," I said.

"Cool! I love that station!"

I turned on my radio and we both sang along to the next few songs. She knew them as well as I did. We impressed each other with knowing all the words to Don McLean's "American Pie," the longest song we'd ever heard.

Nicki was in our class too, another recent transplant to LA and a neighbor of Corinna's on a street in a new neighborhood. Before the sidewalks were put in there and two-story houses went up, that area had been all hilly dirt mounds. David and I had liked to ride our bikes and go frog hunting there; we would even bring along a small box to put our captives in so we could take them home to "race" across the living room.

Nicki was a little odd; I wasn't sure about her, but she and Corinna were already friends so I gave her a chance. During class she drew cartoons starring some of our classmates and wrote funny captions under them. We laughed over them at recess.

BOYS HAD CRUSHES ON CORINNA. IF SHE CARED, SHE didn't act like it. She shrugged off their attention. It was different for me. Too often, on the schoolyard, I was Fatso. I acted like I didn't hear the name-calling, but oh, I heard it.

Corinna ignored my tormenters, except for the time a boy directed a slur at us both, laughing as we passed by—"Look! It's Laurel and Hardy!"

Corinna shot back, "Shut up, creep," and he did.

Magic followed my new best friend. A cashier at Thrifty saw us admiring a box of rice candies at the counter and offered it to us for free. At lunch we called KHJ from the school pay phone to request Santana's "Evil Ways," and it played before lunch was over. We could try on lipsticks at Thrifty after school and walk out with one in our pocket without getting caught.

But the real magic happened at her slumber party. After a group of us snuck out late to TP houses, Corinna taught us a game called levitation. In the living room, the eight of us formed a circle around a girl lying on her back at the center. Corinna took the position at the girl's head while another girl sat at her feet. The rest of us knelt at her sides. Corinna said a single, calming word like "blue" or "peace," and we went around the circle repeating that word for about ten rounds. Then we slipped two fingers of each hand under the girl on the floor and easily lifted her several feet into the air.

Everyone wanted a turn. Except me. There was no way I was going to do it.

When I was the only one left who hadn't gone, Corinna insisted, "Suzy. You have to try this."

Still, I resisted—but she kept pressing, and finally, to avoid making a scene, I resigned myself to the humiliation that was sure to come. The girls would never be able to lift me into the air.

Kneeling, Corinna took the lead position at my head. The other girls knelt at my sides and feet. The hypnotizing words began to circle me. And then the girls slipped two fingers under me and—miracle of miracles!—up I went. Weightless for a few unforgettable moments. Something new had happened, something good.

IN THIS TIME BETWEEN THE APPARENT DISAPPEARance of my mother's illness and its return, it seemed like nothing was wrong with her. She liked world cultures and she met people from other countries at Hughes Market, two blocks from home. UCLA's international student housing was nearby and everyone shopped at Hughes. My mother met an Indian woman she invited over to teach my sister's Campfire Girls group how to wrap a sari. They used bedsheets for the fabric. Afterwards, the woman taught everyone how to make curry, filling the kitchen with the fragrant scent of spices—ginger and cloves, cardamom and cumin.

At school every year, my classes studied a country for a class project. For the South Pacific in second grade, my mother helped me carve a tiki god from a bar of Dial soap. She brought a plate of rumaki to class on the last day, skewering chicken liver and water chestnuts on toothpicks and wrapping them with strips of bacon.

In sixth grade, we were studying Africa. My mother asked my teacher if she could bring a man from Ghana to come tell us about growing up in his West African village.

The day that UCLA grad student from Ghana came, he stood in front of the class, looking handsome in a blue and white dashiki, and smiled radiantly as he told us how the kids in his village chewed a root to do the equivalent of tooth brushing with toothpaste. He described neighbors playing drums and dancing right outside his house. After his talk, my mother took a seat next to him and played an African folk song on her guitar, "Cool Running Water."

I loved being able to say, "Yeah, that's my mom," when anyone asked me about her afterwards.

MY BODY WAS CHANGING. THE DAY I STARTED MY period, my mother gave me a box of sanitary pads and an elastic belt contraption with two metal clasps dangling from it to hold the pads. I was practically doubled over from the pain in my lower tummy. This was going to happen twelve times a year for the rest of my life?

I snatched the offensive tools from her. "I can do it myself, Mom."

She was happier about these changes in my body than I was. When I'd asked her if I could wear deodorant after hearing girls at school talking about it, she'd bought me a jar of blue cream called "Secret." I didn't think that was funny.

My mother was all in for these changes I was going through. She gave me Midol for my cramps and showed me her box of tampons in case I wanted to use them instead of pads. To show me how they worked, she set a glass of water on the bathroom sink, unwrapped a tampon, and dropped it into the glass. In seconds, the white cotton cylinder became a blooming white cotton flower. She waved a hand at it. "Isn't that something?"

I said I was sticking with the pads.

Corinna was different. Her mother wouldn't let her wear tampons, and she wanted to. One Saturday she came over feeling bummed because it was her "time of the month" and she couldn't go swimming with us at the public pool. My mother to the rescue!

Corinna followed her into the bathroom and they shut the door. Waiting for them was agonizing. I was embarrassed for Corinna.

Ten minutes later, Corinna came out with a big smile. "Let's go swimming!"

THE DRESS CODE AT SCHOOL CHANGED THAT SPRING. At last, girls could wear pants to school! My friends were excited. Corinna traded her skirts for Levi's 501s—straight-legged button-ups. Nicki wore hip huggers. Bettina liked pink or yellow corduroys.

I was stuck with pull-ups from Lane Bryant. My mother said Levi's didn't come in my size.

My size.

Shopping was a dreaded event. At Lane Bryant I cried in the dressing room, sinking onto the bench seat with a freakishly patterned size 16 blouse settled over my shoulders like a collapsed parachute.

"You look pretty in that color," my mother would say, tugging on a sleeve to even it out or asking me to face her so she could see how a tunic hung over the matching pants.

I hated tunics with matching pants and I hated the surly old salesladies, who looked like they wanted to say, "Can I find you something, fatty?"

At one point, my mother wrote to the store manager about a candy bowl on a table in the children's section. (Butterscotch suckies, yum.) The candy bowl disappeared; we had to keep shopping there.

Corinna wasn't having it. "Levi's come in your size," she insisted. "Ask your mother to take you to the Surprise Store in Venice. I promise you'll find something there."

My mother took me to the Surprise Store that afternoon to try. The walls were covered floor to ceiling with stacks of blue jeans. And the ceiling was high. While my mother sat outside the dressing room, I held my breath trying on a pair of 501s. So far, so good. And then every button in the five-button fly slipped right into its buttonhole.

"They fit!" I shouted.

My mother clapped her hands on the other side of the dressing room door. I had banked a turn out of my dowdy pull-ups for a gold medal win.

IN THE SUMMER OF 1972, I WENT TO THE BEACH EVery day with Corinna and Nicki. We spread our towels on the sand by the lifeguard tower at Station 24, whose occupant was the main attraction. Corinna's pink-and-white flowered bikini showed off her flat tummy and perky, teacup breasts. She slathered Bain de Soleil all over her svelte body and turned every hour to tan her front, back, and sides evenly.

Nicki had naturally browned skin. Her B-cup bust filled out her white bikini top and she painted her nails white to match.

Coppertone was the practical tanning cream my mother sent with me, and I still got sunburned. My bathing suit was a frightful one-piece skirt-suit that covered the tops of my thighs. I felt like a navy blue pot holder.

QT ("quick tan" or "cutie") seemed like a possible solution. I bought a bottle at the drugstore. The bronzer stained my legs and arms an otherworldly shade of orange. The tanning light I clipped to an open dresser drawer and lay under for hours one night didn't help either. My cupid-white skin turned pink.

And then there was the horror of my hair. I had an elaborate routine. I wrapped and clipped lengths of hair to my scalp with long bobby pins at night and unleashed the strips of hair in the morning. Who cared if the bobby pins left crease marks? They would be gone by lunchtime, and so would my straight hair.

Murmured conversations continue in the living room while I escape to my bathroom upstairs with the envelope my father has given me.

My mother wrote a letter.

Heart pounding, I close the door and carefully remove the

precious piece of paper from the envelope. In seconds, I'll know what she was thinking.

And there is her familiar, even handwriting, covering the unlined page top to bottom. When did she write this? Sunday morning? Why did she leave the letter in her nightstand drawer? No one found it for days.

She's addressed it "To my beautiful children." There is no date.

In the first sentence she writes that she is proud of us. She is proud of our accomplishments. She hopes we will understand. She hopes we can forgive her. She explains she can't live with the fears anymore. She can't hold a job. She's losing her short-term memory. Her face is getting paralyzed. She can't live with or without the medication. I read that sentence twice.

At the end of the letter, and possibly the most painful of all, is the word "Goodbye." With a period after it. Who knew a tiny dot could pack such a powerful punch?

And below that, at the bottom of the page, the words "I love you, Mom"—without a period.

I return the letter to its envelope and fold over on the pink bathroom tile. Sunlight slants through the louvered windows. I avoid my reflection in the mirror. The well of sorrow is so deep inside that by the time the sobs reach my throat, they are soundless. I was born from my mother's body. My blood spilled with hers on the bathroom floor. How am I supposed to get up and keep going?

My mother's reasoning couldn't be clearer. I know now she wasn't delusional or having scattered thinking. She couldn't live with her illness any longer. She hoped we would understand. I don't understand. She wanted us to forgive her. I don't know how to begin. I do know she didn't want to leave this life any more than most of us do. She just couldn't live any longer with this incurable illness and no hope for her future.

I need to go before someone comes up here looking for me. We have to leave soon. There's a funeral to go to.

I walk down the stairs, feeling shaky, and go back to the breakfast room. My father is there the second I arrive. He must have been watching for me. I hand him the envelope and turn away.

Chapter 11

How wide was my field of vision in those days of uncertainty? Life had seemed so wonderful at the start, with sunny mornings in the backyard with my mother. She taught me about caterpillars when we saw a fuzzy black one inching along the flagstone. She knew that little creature would build a cocoon around itself soon and emerge from it in a few weeks as a paper-light flicker of color with flapping wings. She leaned in close to my face and brushed my cheek with her long eyelashes, blinking a few times to make it tickle. "That's a butterfly kiss for you!"

There was no place anymore for wonder to live.

But I had friends. Corinna and Nicki met me every school-day morning at the corner leading to our new junior high. We were a trio, three best buddies. After collecting books at our lockers, we'd separate for homeroom. We'd pass notes to each other in the hallway between classes about boys we liked—or hated having to tolerate.

Before homeroom one morning, Corinna called us to come close and see something in her purse. It was a pack of

Marlboros. "My cousin was visiting this weekend and he left these for me. Like to try them after school?"

We were all in.

"Let's do it at Alise's house," I suggested.

Alise was a girl a year younger than us who lived near the corner of my street. Her mother was usually gone and her older brother, Mark, didn't care what she did. If he wasn't hanging out in Vincent's garage next door, he was usually holed up in his front bedroom, smoking bowls in his water pipe and staring at the globes of neon green and hot pink jelly floating in his lava lamp, or doing whatever he did in front of his black light poster of Raquel Welch in a wet T-shirt.

"Perfect," Corinna agreed. "Let's stop there on the way to your house after school."

On Alise's porch that afternoon, Corinna pulled out her pack of Marlboros. We sat cross-legged, eyes on Corinna on the front step. She pulled a cigarette out of the pack.

"First you pack down the tobacco." She tapped the filter end of a Marlboro on the step a few times, then she put the cigarette between her lips and lit it with a match. "Inhale just a little. Don't worry about the cough. It will go away." She took a deep drag and blew out the smoke in a steady stream without coughing, then gave each of us a cigarette of our own.

Alise went first and exploded in a fit of coughs as soon as she inhaled. She hit her chest with her little fist and had another hit as soon as the coughing stopped. I took a cautious puff, wincing the second the smoke seared my lungs. Nicki coughed after inhaling and then finished a whole cigarette without inhaling again.

We agreed to do this every day after school. In no time, I was buying my own packs for a couple of quarters at the gas station cigarette machine a few blocks from my house.

Buying cigarettes from a machine was easy to do—I was

tall at twelve, I looked older, and besides, no one was watching. But getting away with smoking at home was a different story. My sister found me smoking one day in the woodshed behind the garage.

"Ooo, you're going to get in trouble!" she snickered, peeking over the gate. She was thrilled the "good girl" was finally going to get it.

But she was wrong. My mother wasn't too concerned by the news. She had guessed I would smoke when I was older; I had sucked my thumb until I was seven and broke my arm horseback riding. She grounded me for the rest of the week, but that was it.

I didn't like being grounded (no friends after school, no phone calls at night), but I still found a way to smoke.

Weeks went by, and cigarettes were disappearing from my packs. Suspecting my sister, I went to my mother's room one day to tell on her. The hallway reeked. My mother was the cigarette thief!

I opened her door to find her sheepishly crushing out a cigarette in an ashtray.

"I borrowed one of your cigarettes," she said. "I hope you don't mind."

I had helped my mother quit smoking a few years before, when we learned at school about the dangers of cigarettes and were given tips on how to help our parents quit if they smoked. I'd marked a whole carton of her cigarettes at the halfway point with a felt pen so she could cut down and eventually stop entirely, like the teacher taught us. "I don't want you to die," I'd told her, and she'd let me dump out packs of filterless Pall Malls on the kitchen table and draw a line on each one before carefully returning the cigarettes to their packs. It took some time and a lot of half-smoked cigarettes, but eventually she quit.

And now here we were, both smoking.

Before long, she was buying cartons of Carltons for herself (low tar and nicotine), Kools for Lynne, and Marlboros for me. We kept the cartons in a big potato chip can in the kitchen.

MARIJUANA WAS MY NEXT SMOKING ADVENTURE. Corinna's cousin had visited again, and this time he'd left her three joints. The joints she showed us were the first I'd ever seen. "You're going to like it," she told me and Nicki.

On Saturday morning we found a curb to sit on in a quiet cul-de-sac in their neighborhood. Corinna told us to inhale deeply and hold it before letting the smoke out.

"Do you feel anything yet?" we asked each other after every exhale.

No one did.

We finished the joint, still feeling no effects.

"My cousin said we'd feel it after three joints," Corinna said, and we agreed to try it again the next two Saturdays.

After smoking the third one, we laughed until our sides split.

I DON'T REMEMBER MY MOTHER MUCH FROM THIS time. Most likely, she was in a long nowhere period—depressed, listless, not much of a presence in the house. She went to therapy, she went to the market and the bank. She put dinner on the table every night at six o'clock—something simple, like hamburger patties or lamb chops with mint jelly. She'd given up on vegetables long ago.

Dinnertime was when my family was together, and things didn't usually go well. My mother and brother limped along in a conversation about his day while my sister and I sat in stony (or stoned) silence.

Once, I tried to talk with Lynne, asking what she thought about riding the bus now that she was going to Uni High. She shot me the stink eye and pushed her chair back from the table with a loud scrape.

"Don't leave," my mother said. "Please."

Lynne scowled. "Guess I'm stuck here."

WHEN MY SISTER STARTED HIGH SCHOOL, SHE TRADED her daily uniform of an oversized orange windbreaker for a figure I'd never seen on her before. She had a bust, a waistline, and rounded hips. She moved out of our bedroom and into the den, taking her bed, her stereo, and most of her clothes with her. The only sound that came from behind her closed doors was from her records: Black Sabbath, Jethro Tull, Cat Stevens, and Neil Young.

Free of her at last, I painted my room powder blue and got my own stereo. On weekends, I liked to pretend the house was an apartment building with four apartments in it. I would sweep my apartment and take on the hall bathroom after that. After sponging the sink and polishing the mirror, I'd drop any stray items my sister had left on the counter into a crowded drawer for her to deal with. Or not.

The best part of these days came when I got to see the boy who lived at the corner of my street. Vincent was sixteen and had a car and a ten-speed bike he liked to tinker with in his garage after school, door open wide. This was his man cave, set back about twenty feet from the sidewalk. The Allman Brothers or Led Zeppelin played loud on his stereo, and he had a double bed in the garage too. Vincent was tall, with wavy golden hair that fell to his shoulders, gentle brown eyes, and a smile that lit up my sky. Alise's brother hung out in that garage a lot, along with another neighbor, Perkins. We called them the Corner Gang.

Vincent started coming out of his garage—shirtless in faded denim overalls, with his hands pushed deep in his front pockets—to say a bashful hello when Corinna and Nicki and I walked by on our way to my house after school. Corinna was the main attraction, although Vincent made it look like a casual hello to all of us.

That worked. We all had a crush on him.

Electives in seventh grade were still gender-divided in 1972, with print shop and carpentry for boys and cooking, sewing, and typing for girls. I liked those classes, but I wanted to get into print shop to make a rubber stamp with the word "Vincent" on it.

I told my mother girls weren't allowed to take print shop, sure she wouldn't like the sexist gender division of electives. And I was right. She called the school the next day.

That spring, as the only girl in print shop, I learned how to set type, but more important, I made a rubber stamp and stamped the word V-I-N-C-E-N-T in red and green ink on every inch of my denim school notebook.

Eventually, Vincent's greeting when we walked past his open garage became more obviously directed to Corinna. His casual "Hey, how ya doin'?" to all of us turned into "Hey, why don't you come in and hang out awhile?" directed to Corinna. Vincent walked her home when she left my house in time for dinner. He rode his bike there on Saturdays to make out with her in the alley behind her house.

Before Vincent, I was Corinna's best friend. Now I wasn't much more than an excuse for her to visit him. Her dad showed up at my front door a few times, demanding to see his daughter. "I have no idea where she is," I told him, and it was true. Chances were she was in Vincent's garage, but she hadn't told me so and I wasn't about to spill her secret.

My little taste of attention from Dream Boy didn't taste so good anymore. I hadn't just lost him, I'd lost Corinna too.

CORINNA HAD STORIES FOR US. NICKI AND I KNEW about second and third base before we even went to first. One day after school Corinna took us into Hughes Market, near the junior high, to see something. In the lunch meat aisle, she picked up a package of Oscar Mayer knockwurst.

"Squeeze this," she said.

We complied, giggling with her without knowing why.

"That's what it's like!" she cried.

We all collapsed in hysterics, leaning against the refrigerator case.

Another time, Corinna was ready to share more with me about her life up at bat. We were upstairs in her bedroom after school and she was telling me about French kissing. I couldn't imagine how it worked. Kissing with tongues?

She was about to demonstrate it when her mother opened the door suddenly, entering without knocking. "It's time for dinner, Corinna." She threw me a stern glance before leaving the room. I'm sure we looked interrupted.

WITH NO ONE WATCHING AND NOTHING MUCH TO DO after school, I floated into fantasyland, smoking joints and playing mind-altering music, headphones on, volume high. I had given up Carole King and Donovan for Emerson, Lake & Palmer, T. Rex, and a progressive English rock band called Yes.

When Yes played the LA Forum that spring, I went to my first rock concert with my two best friends and a handful of joints.

Nicki's dad handed us the gate key to this big experience, driving us to the Forum and dropping us off at a curb in the parking lot. Long-haired girls and boys in jeans and T-shirts streamed toward the auditorium to stand in a line that had no apparent end.

"Girls!" Nicki's dad barked, doing his best to command the attention of three excited twelve-year-olds. "Meet me right here when the concert is over. Understand? Right here!"

We hopped out of the car and linked arms. "We will!" we promised. "See you later!"

In line we passed joints that came our way, happily smoking right out there in public, a part of the crowd. When the auditorium doors finally opened, we joined the stream of concertgoers to have the experience of a lifetime.

Blaring speakers the size of small buildings flanked the stage, filling the room with throbbing electric sound. We found our seats and, awestruck, watched clouds of dry ice swirl across the stage. Bass beats vibrated in my bones and beams of green, purple, and red shot down from the ceiling, lighting the mist and playing tag with each other. Rick Wakeman, the man I referred to as God, strode onto the stage, his white toga and sheet of blond hair swaying with each measured step. The rest of the band took their places as he settled in behind a multilevel synthesizer. I was ready for my ride into the universe.

When the show ended and the house lights came on, Corinna led us through the dimly lit reefer haze to a glowing green neon exit sign. My head felt packed with cotton. Had I lost my hearing?

I shrugged it off, following Corinna into the parking lot and directly to Nicki's father's car, which was parked exactly where he had left us light years before. I realize now he probably sat there waiting for us the whole time.

At the funeral parlor, I sit alone in the lobby with no clue what I'm supposed to do. A few neighbors I know huddle near me, murmuring. I hope they won't come over. They're probably saying what they know about my mom and trading stories about me—"I heard she moved in with her father"; "She's in college now. She looks good."

Ann breaks off from her pack to walk over to me. The first years we lived in that house, Ann came over for coffee with my mom while I played with her son. Those visits ended long ago.

"I'm so sorry," she says now, in her wobbly Jell-O voice. I remember that voice and remember her shelf of a bosom. She's wearing an ugly beige housedress, like always.

I say thank you. It's all I know to say.

Ann's daring move has triggered a chain of condolences. One after the next, the group of neighbors come to me to say "I'm sorry" and "She was so young."

Was she young? Forty-five doesn't seem young to me. And her age isn't the point. They don't say, "She was your mother. I'm so sorry." They don't think of that. To them, she was probably the crazy neighbor who killed herself. End of story.

Chapter 12

Losing our virginity was a priority for my threesome in 1972, when seventh grade came to a close. In our minds it wasn't cool to be a virgin, and being cool was the primary reason for just about everything. Other girls at our school had done it.

Of the three of us, Corinna was the only one with a boyfriend. But she was thirteen, five years under the legal age to buy condoms. Vincent was underage too, and apparently wasn't interested in doing his part. Birth control was up to her.

Corinna was trying to figure out a solution when I remembered the clinic in Venice where my mother had worked a few years before.

"I know where we can get free birth control!" I said, and told them we could take a bus to Planned Parenthood.

Corinna hugged me.

Ready with fake names, we rode the bus to Venice the next day. I kept a nervous eye on the stores passing by the window on Venice Boulevard, hoping for a sign of anything familiar. At last, the clinic came into view and I pulled the cord at our stop.

Inside the clinic, mothers with toddlers clinging to their legs sat next to gloomy young women turning pages of magazines or staring blankly at the wall in front of them. Babies cried; children played on the floor.

A receptionist said, "Add your names to the sign-in sheet on that table."

"We just came for some birth control," Corinna explained, like this was something that set us apart from the others in the waiting room.

"That's fine. But you have to see a doctor first." She went back to her paperwork.

"I didn't know," I whispered.

Fortunately, my friends didn't mind. We were on a mission. We wrote our fake names on the sign-up sheet and found seats on opposite sides of the waiting room, since there were no seats together.

"Get ready to wait," the teenage girl next to me grumbled when I took the empty seat next to her. Her arms were folded across her chest, her long legs kicked out in front of her. "I've got crabs. What are you here for?"

Crabs? What was she talking about?

She sighed. "The asshole. Can you believe it? He gives me crabs. And then he breaks up with me." She turned to get a good look at me. "So what's your problem?"

"I'm here to get some birth control."

"Smart." She leaned back in her chair and pushed at her bangs. "They have everything."

I wondered what she meant by "everything" but wasn't about to ask. I was sure I didn't belong here.

By the time the teenage girl was called in, I had heard all there was to know about her venereal disease and sat through her endless cursing about her last two boyfriends.

With nothing to do in the crowded room filled with so many women and little kids, I thought about the time I first learned about pregnancy. I must have been about six when the subject came up after I saw a pair of bloody underpants soaking in my mother's bathroom sink before her shower. "I'm fine," she said, quick to reassure me. She promised to explain after her shower.

Sitting with me on the living room couch that morning, my mother explained about ovaries and fallopian tubes, eggs and sperm. I was completely lost. For the pregnancy part, to make sense of what she told me, I concluded that impregnation happened at the hospital just before the baby was born. It involved a man and woman briefly pressing the soles of their feet together, without socks.

Next came the part about giving birth. There was a painkiller shot and a cut with a scalpel to help the baby fit through the vaginal opening.

Horrors! "Didn't that *hurt*?"

"Not too bad," my mother said.

I knew that adults didn't feel pain the way kids did. Anything that hurt my mother would surely kill me. "I'll never have a baby," I vowed.

My mother kissed me on the forehead. "You may change your mind."

She told me about my own birth. She had wanted natural childbirth, she hadn't wanted a pain blocker. She'd wanted to experience giving birth. But the nurse wouldn't do it. "So I asked for a mirror so I could see my baby being born," my mother said. The nurse had never heard of that, but she agreed to do it.

I like thinking of my mother seeing my head crown as I came into the world. She never could have guessed she would miss most of my life.

"Suzy Flowers?" A woman's voice interrupted the memory.

A nurse was calling me by the name I had written on the sign-in sheet. (Steve Flowers was a crush of mine in class; today I was Suzy Flowers.) I looked to my friends for solidarity, but they were involved with the action going on around them—Corinna engrossed in a conversation with the woman next to her, Nicki scowling at a couple of toddlers playing on the floor by her feet.

I followed the nurse down a long hallway to a private exam room, where she handed me a folded paper gown. "You can put your clothes on the counter."

Was she saying I was supposed to be naked under this flimsy gown? I had never been naked in front of anyone. Even in the group shower at camp, I wore my bathing suit.

I held up the gown. "Do I *have* to wear this?"

I did.

Once I was in the paper gown, the nurse helped me turn it so the opening went in front and not in back. "Get on the table," she said, and she gestured toward a slanted board draped with butcher paper.

Metal stirrups in worn oven mitts stuck out at the bottom of the board, looking like a secret I didn't want to hear. I wanted to bolt.

The nurse patted the table. "Just lie down. You'll put your feet in the stirrups when the doctor comes in."

I lay on the table, keeping my knees pressed tight together. That was not an easy feat while dressed in a short paper robe with a slit down its center.

A doctor in a white lab coat and horn-rimmed eyeglasses came in. He frowned at me (probably thinking, *She's twelve?*) before taking a seat between my legs. When the nurse guided my feet into the padded stirrups, my knees naturally parted and my legs started to shake hard.

She put her warm hand on my arm. For the first time since I'd gotten here, she seemed kind. "This won't take long."

She steadied one of my knees as something cold touched a part of my body I barely even knew about, sending my knees knocking together uncontrollably. I felt a peculiar, vague pain somewhere deep inside—and then, in seconds, it was over. The doctor jotted a note on the clipboard and left without a word.

The nurse helped me out of the stirrups. "Are you okay?"

I hoped I was.

I dressed fast while she filled a bag with tubes and small boxes from a cupboard. "Be sure to read the directions on the box of foam," she said.

I wasn't about to ask what foam was. I thanked her and practically ran with the bag to the waiting room to find my friends.

That weekend, Corinna stayed the night at Vincent's. To her credit, this time she told me her plans before lying to her parents about spending the night at my house.

On Friday I lay awake in bed for half the night, curled up in misery. I wrote melodramatic, self-deprecating thoughts in my diary: "She is everything. I am nothing."

In the morning, Corinna came over at ten looking radiant. I felt like I'd been hit by a car.

THE NEXT WEEKEND, CORINNA WENT TO VINCENT'S house with plans to see me afterwards, no doubt to support her alibi to her parents. I watched the clock, feeling more upset every time another record ended.

It was four thirty by the time she finally knocked at my front door, looking pretty in her white peasant blouse and faded 501s and saying, "I am *so* sorry!"

"You said you'd be here at three," I complained.

"I know. Can I get a glass of water? I'll be right there."

Corinna disappeared into the kitchen and I went back to my room to wait. Five minutes later, I went to the kitchen to see what was going on. There she was, standing at the sink, rinsing dishes and stacking the dishwasher. I couldn't believe it.

"What are you doing?" I asked her.

"I'll be right there."

I went back to my room to wait. After about ten minutes I went looking for her again. She was still pulling dishes out of the chaos of the crowded sink and stacking the dishwasher.

"What are you doing?" I asked once again.

"I'm cleaning up a little." She rinsed another plate and stacked it in the dishwasher. "Give me five minutes."

In my room again, I put on headphones and played T. Rex loud, wondering why she was in my kitchen washing my family's dishes. There were always dishes to wash. If the dishes in the dishwasher were clean, plate by plate and fork by fork the machine was emptied as dishes were used. This went on until all the clean dishes in the machine were gone and the sink and counters had no space left to fill. Dirty plates and pots and pans tumbled over each other in the sink and on counters. I ignored it; the whole family did.

Twenty minutes later, I went to the kitchen again. Corinna waved me off.

The next time I saw my friend, she was at my bedroom door, buttoned up to the neck in her blue peacoat. "I promised I'd be home by six." I knew she would stop at Vincent's on the way and walk with him.

After she was gone, I went to the kitchen to see what she had done. The porcelain sink gleamed. The dishwasher hummed. Clean pots and pans were piled precariously high in the dish drainer.

I shrank inside. Someone else knew there were problems at my house.

A few weeks later, Corinna broke up with Vincent. She had dropped by without calling first and had seen him driving down the street with his arm around a girl. "I was with my friend Gordon," he told her, denying her accusations when she asked him about it.

His excuses were useless. She was done with him.

My phone rang on a Saturday morning a few weeks later. It was Corinna. In tears. "We're moving in two weeks!" Her father had found a job in San Francisco.

What dreadful news. The only light in my life was going out.

NICKI WAS HARDLY A CONSOLATION. FOR HER, CORINNA's move was a social disaster she could overcome. Nicki thought I was too serious. I thought she was shallow. But we forged ahead, hanging out together after school. We passed notes between classes, using a code we'd created for making plans to buy pot. A Doobie Brothers album was a lid, joints were 45s (singles). A note might read, "Sandy has a new 45 she wants to play for us after school."

And I liked some things about the friend I had been left with. Nicki could make me laugh. Sometimes we played made-up characters with each other, like Blanche and Mabel, two New York matrons with thick New York accents. We would improvise a story as Blanche and Mabel, and an afternoon would fly by.

"Lids" were ten-dollar ounces of marijuana we bought from a dealer on my street using cash we collected returning soda cans and bottles from our houses. In my bedroom after school, we'd get high and listen to *Tales from Topo-*

graphic Oceans by Yes or *Trilogy* by Emerson, Lake & Palmer, delivered by marijuana to a better reality, one where imagination could soar and take me away.

We were in this altered state once when a knock came at my door. It was my mother.

"Oh no!" We couldn't hide what we were doing; the room was a cloud of smoke. Evidence lay in full view on my bed—a plate littered with rolling papers, matches, a baggie of pot, a gold chamber pipe, and a second, smaller baggie of the fine powder that fell to the bottom of the most recent lid I'd bought.

With a "bring it on" twinkle in her eyes, Nicki waved a hand. "Open the door."

I took a deep breath and did it.

There stood my mother. "Can I come in and watch what you're doing?" She sounded shy asking.

Unsure what to do, I let her in. She took a seat at the foot of my single bed. Nicki sat cross-legged in the center of it. After taking a moment to let this turn of events sink in, I closed the door and went back to my place by the pillows. I knew that if I looked up I would burst into giggles, so I steadied my gaze and stayed focused as I filled the bowl of my chamber pipe.

My mother was in the room! Nicki and I shared a glance. We didn't think parents smoked pot; this made no sense.

But Nicki wasn't holding back. "Want to try some?" she asked my mother in her careless, blunt way.

I shot my friend a look. Get high with my mother? What was she thinking?

"Oh, no," my mom said. "I've tried marijuana before. It made me feel strange. I just want to watch." A few years later, she would tell me it made her feel too much like she did when she was sick.

I lit the packed chamber pipe, took a hit, and passed the pipe to Nicki.

To be helpful, my mother picked up the baggie holding what we considered the good stuff: the fine powder that had sifted its way down to the bottom of the ten-dollar bag of stemmy weed. We always saved this for last. "Would you like me to throw this out for you?"

That did it. All composure flew out the window. We fell over cracking up.

My mother left.

My mother's gravesite is on a softly sloping hill with a tree by it. The day of her funeral, four long rows of chairs are assembled there. The coffin sits suspended over a gash in the earth, her burial plot. A spray of burgundy and gold mums decorates the top of the coffin. Those are the colors I suggested when my dad asked me yesterday what color flowers I thought should go on her coffin.

"Earth tones," I told him. "Her colors."

He bit his lip when he heard that.

Except for Grandma, whose sobbing never stops, the small group of relatives has silently found the seats my father has chosen for us, front and center. If any of my mother's few friends are here, I don't notice them.

Just as the rabbi takes his place at an altar by the coffin, four of my brother's school friends walk up and stand behind the rows of chairs at the back. Years from now, my brother will tell me he hadn't asked them to come and was deeply moved by their show of love for him in the midst of what he called "the great abandonment." Today, we don't say a word to each other; we're just here, like the grass is here, the sky is here.

None of us know the rabbi speaking about my mother. We don't know rabbis. He's a stranger. The funeral home probably recommended him and my father probably gave him details to share. I don't want to hear his words. They come out of his mouth and float away.

The tree beside us is motionless—no birds in it, no breeze in the branches. I hear my heartbeat.

Chapter 13

My mother wanted to be well. But wellness was a steep hill to climb, and she was afraid of heights.

In August, the summer before I turned thirteen, my dad took his kids on a two-week vacation in a rented Winnebago, leaving our mother at home. We drove across three state lines, our ultimate destination Yellowstone National Park. My brother read maps in the passenger seat while Lynne and I played cards, watching a new world pass by the windows. We weathered a rainstorm in Utah, took a guided raft trip on the Snake River in Colorado, gawked at a herd of moose grazing by the roadside in Jackson Hole. It was the best time the four of us had ever had together.

Until we got home. The day we pulled up in front of the house in the motor home, my mother met us at the curb. Grandma Friedman was with her, a surprise.

Right away, I could see that something was off with my mother. Her eyes were too wide. There were dark circles under them.

Grandma was the first to speak. "Hello, Roger, kids. How was the trip?"

My mother nodded hello. Something was definitely wrong.

"Hello, Dorothy. Marilyn." My dad set our three suitcases on the sidewalk.

This wasn't the dad we had just traveled with—the dad who was excited to see moose, the dad who seemed to like us. This was my detached dad. I knew he couldn't wait to get out of there. He gave each of us a perfunctory hug—"Good trip, kids"—and climbed into the driver's seat to start the engine.

I watched as the happiness that had been the last fourteen days with Dad rolled away up the street. I wanted to follow him and go back to the life we'd just had together.

Grandma was gone in the morning. We piled our laundry on top of the washer, and there it sat. My mother spent the days at the dining table, staring at the window to the street, drapes drawn, while we went back to our separate lives. My sister was in her room, door shut. David was in his room, door shut. I was in my room, door shut.

THE PHONE RANG ONE DAY WHEN I WAS IN THE kitchen.

"Don't answer it!" my mother commanded. Warily, she got up from the table and picked up the phone. "Hello?"

She hung up looking shaken.

"Wrong number?" I asked.

"I don't know how they got our number."

"Who?"

"I don't know."

"I'm sure it's nothing to worry about."

"I don't know."

A few days later, another call came with no one speaking when my mother picked up the phone.

I tried to keep my tone light as I asked, "Wrong number?"

She nodded. "It's them."

"Who?"

"I don't know."

I asked how "they" got our number.

"They were in the yard," she whispered.

Our phone number was written on a white sticker attached to the center of the dial on the wall phone. The numbers were written so small I could barely see them from a few feet away.

"Mom. No one was in our yard."

She steadied her gaze on me. I must understand. "They have a telescope." Her tone was so matter-of-fact you could have thought she was saying we were out of milk. This was no-man's-land, dangerous territory. As level-headed as my mother might sound, logic didn't live here.

Recently, she'd told me the Mafia had stolen a pair of her earrings. She didn't know how they'd gotten into the house. "Why would the Mafia want your earrings, Mom?" I'd demanded. She didn't know.

Years later, I would suspect a teenage boy in the neighborhood had come in through the dog door in the hallway and stolen some of her jewelry, maybe even taken some cash from her wallet. (I knew she thought the Mafia had taken money from her purse too.) That same boy could even have phoned the house repeatedly to see if anyone was home and whether it was safe to come in and steal from us. But the Mafia? And the telescope? There was no explanation for that.

In a high school psychology class, I would learn that religious people with paranoid schizophrenia might think the devil is after them or might be excessively concerned about

God's judgments. If they're not religious, their pursuer could be the Mafia.

My mother was decidedly not religious.

LED ZEPPELIN WAS A FAVORITE ROCK BAND OF MINE. One day, I heard one of their songs, "Stairway to Heaven," coming from the living room. My mother liked folk music, not rock. I went in to see what was going on.

There she was, sitting cross-legged on the floor by the stereo cabinet, playing one of my albums.

"What are you doing, Mom? Do you like Led Zeppelin?"

She looked up at me with an eerie smile. "Do you hear what they're saying?"

Robert Plant was singing that words sometimes have two meanings. I knew the song well.

"They know," she whispered. With her eyes, she implored me to understand.

I would never listen to that song again.

The next memory slide drops in without context, but I know it's not long after the "Stairway to Heaven" incident.

It's nighttime and I'm sitting in the green recliner in the living room with a book. My brother's closed door is a few feet away; a neon green sticker reading "David" is taped to its center. All is quiet in my sister's room down the hall. My mother is coming toward me from her bedroom at the back of the house, moving like she's wading through water. Every step is deliberate.

I set my book down. "What is it, Mom?"

She continues toward me and stops strangely close. "I've called your father."

That surprises me. She doesn't even come out of her room to say hi to him when he picks us up on Sunday mornings.

She speaks in a monotone. "He's taking me to the hospital."

That's all I need to hear. I'm up and out, headed to my room. I don't want to deal with this.

She is right behind me. "I know you love me," I hear her say—and as I close my door I hear, "It's okay." Her tone is spooky, right out of a horror movie. "I feel your love for me through the walls. All of you. I feel love from all of you."

That night, my father took my mom to the Westwood Hospital and came back to stay with us, never saying what happened when he took her in or when she'd be home again. I suppose he figured we were old enough to get ourselves to school just fine if she wasn't back when the school year started the following week.

For our part, we were too young or too intimidated by it all to ask questions.

When my mother was discharged from the hospital two weeks later, my father brought her in with her suitcase and a bucket of Kentucky Fried Chicken—a rare treat—and quickly left for home. He'd undoubtedly already heard the news we were about to get from her.

At the dining table, my mother waited for each of us to choose our pieces of fried chicken from the KFC bucket before saying she had something important to tell us.

"Kids, the doctor gave me a diagnosis."

No one moved.

"I have paranoid schizophrenia. With chronic depression and anxiety."

This sounded bad. Paranoid schizophrenia? Depression and anxiety were easier to understand. I had heard of them.

She had started taking a medication for it called Thorazine. The hallucinations and the voices she'd been hearing again would go away. Valium would help with her anxiety.

There was nothing to help with the depression, but that might go away too.

A year or so after this, she would tell me she was also taking a second drug, Stelazine, to lessen the side effects of the Thorazine. Neither one of us knew that Stelazine didn't serve that purpose at all. I know now that it's another antipsychotic drug, duplicative of Thorazine. Most likely her psychiatrist gave her both meds because he didn't know what else to do.

If I had been older than twelve when my mother told me she was starting Thorazine, I might have picked up the phone and called her doctor right away. I might have asked him if he had told her the drug would turn her into a walking zombie. I might have asked if he'd told her she would never read a book or play another Beethoven sonata again. That her concentration would be gone; that she would never be able to hold a job. If I had, of course, chances are her doctor would only have said, "I'm sorry."

Thorazine was exciting to the medical community when it first came on the scene in the early 1950s. The positives of this new fix-it pill, the first antipsychotic medication available, still pushed the negatives right out the window. It wasn't known yet that the drug, which was prescribed in high doses, was like a medicinal lobotomy—that it came with severe side effects and reduced symptoms in only a limited way. Sedation was seen as improvement. Emotional flattening was mistaken for progress.

Today, Thorazine is rarely prescribed because of its severe side effects. There are still no fully reliable drugs for schizophrenia that do more than offer varying degrees of treatment, most of it only masking symptoms. Schizophrenia is an incurable mental illness.

At the time my mother was given the drug, it seemed her only hope.

MONTHS WENT BY, AND THE ONLY THING THAT showed with my mother on Thorazine was that her shoulders slumped, her skin looked pasty, and her eyes were glazed. Sunday visits with Dad continued, although his girlfriend, Jill, and her daughter went with us instead of Lynne, who refused to come anymore.

My father drove a chocolate brown Buick Electra, a big steamboat of a car that easily fit five. When he came to pick us up on a Sunday, David and I went out to wait in the car with Jill and Vicki while Lynne had a screaming tantrum in the house. I cringed while we all acted like it wasn't happening.

Sunday outings usually involved lunch at Marina del Rey or Fisherman's Wharf. Jill looked stylish in a pair of oversized sunglasses and jeans, always with a wide-brimmed sun hat. I could see why my father liked her. She didn't go to therapists, she went to art galleries. She didn't talk about her feelings or ask about his. And she adored her "brilliant Phi Beta Kappa," as she liked to call him.

At home, I lost myself in novels like *The Endless Steppe* and *Manchild in the Promised Land.* Survivor stories. Lately, though, more and more, music, marijuana, and journal writing were my getaways. My journal was a three-ring binder I could fill with as much 8½ × 11 paper as I wanted. And I added paper a lot. I made it through my days with writing as my companion, and romantic fantasies fed story ideas.

Outside my bedroom, the house was a sad place. The only way to know my sister was home was the steady bass beat of hard rock music coming from behind her closed doors, and even David didn't talk much to me anymore. He buried himself in schoolbooks and got straight A's. He skipped a grade. After school, he stopped by the kitchen to grab a snack on the way to his room. He shot baskets in the hoop at the end of the driveway, over the garage door. He might have a friend over to look at his coin collection or trade baseball cards. Maybe they played chess or watched a baseball game. They definitely didn't talk about anything going on in our family.

David was like our father that way. He lived with blinders on, believing things were the way he needed them to be and avoiding the rest. My brother was the Little Engine That Could, cranking his way to the top of the mountain ("I think I can, I think I can . . ."). And he got to the top every time. He was making it in spite of us all. If it weren't for our short dinners with Mom and the sound of the TV in his room after school or the rasp of his clock radio at night, I wouldn't have known he was home. The neon green name sticker on his door was all I knew of my brother anymore.

My brother was on dry land while I sank in quicksand.

RAIN THREATENED THE DAY OF MY THIRTEENTH birthday. I was missing Corinna, who didn't call on Saturdays like she had said she would. We wrote each other letters, but not very often.

My mother tried to talk me out of my funk, assuring me I'd have more friends as I got older. Good try.

Nicki and Debbie came over for lunch. Debbie brought a bouquet of balloons and tied them to a chair in the dining room. Nicki opened the drapes right away. "It's *day*time," she said. "You need some light in here."

She gave me the new Lou Reed album, *Walk on the Wild Side*. Debbie gave me two purple sealing wax sticks and a metal stamp with my astrological sign—Libra, the scales. Balance. Harmony. Whatever those words meant.

After lunch, my mother brought in a chocolate layer cake she'd baked that morning. Thirteen pink candles flickered on top of the cake and two big, unlit candles sat propped at the front of it. Those big candles each had a cartoonish monkey clinging to a yellow number as tall as it was. One monkey held a number "1," the other held a number "3." I thought they were silly, not my style, but my mother seemed excited.

"You're a teenager now!" she exclaimed.

I couldn't see why that was so great.

After cake, my friends left and I helped my mother clean up. Crumpled wrapping paper went into a trash bag, along with paper plates and empty cups. My mother stood at the sink rinsing the goofy monkey candles. "Let's keep these," she said, as she pulled a chair over to a cupboard. "Will you climb up here and put the candles on the top shelf?"

I couldn't imagine why she wanted to keep them, but I did as she asked.

As I stood on the chair and looked at her holding those monkey candles, I saw she had tears in her eyes.

"We can use these again when you turn thirty-one," she said. "We'll just switch the numbers around!" Her eyes sparkled with love for me.

Aha! So that was why she wanted to keep the candles. I took them from her, trying to imagine myself at that age the way she seemed to be doing. The future was a giant blank. Who in the world would I be at thirty-one?

I put the candles into their resting place on the dark shelf.

NOT LONG AFTER THAT, MY MOTHER STARTED A YEAR-long training program to become a courtroom stenographer. This move must have been at her therapist's suggestion. She had to be able to do it, right? She was a fast typist. She had an English degree from Wellesley. Typing was her salable skill.

My mother looked tired when she came in after her first day at stenography school. I asked to see the stenography machine the school had loaned her for the program and she showed it to me, along with a booklet teaching a kind of shorthand alphabet she had to learn so she could document trials word by word.

"I have to memorize the entire book," she said with a sigh, dropping onto the couch to have a cigarette.

I felt sorry for her but didn't know what to do besides leave the room.

I WAS IN EIGHTH GRADE, MY SISTER WAS IN TENTH, and we both were good at cutting school and staying home without our mother knowing it. We wrote our own absence notes; the school never checked.

One morning, my sister tapped at my door to ask if I wanted to try angel dust.

I considered angel dust a drug outside my league, a drug in the danger zone. "I don't know," I said. "It's weird."

"It's fine," Lynne argued. She had smoked it a few times, she said, and nothing bad had happened.

What else did I have to do that day? I gave in.

The angel dust we smoked was in a joint mixed with marijuana and mint, a repulsive flavor combo. I didn't like the strange numbing effect the stuff had on me, either. After two hits I left my sister's room to spend the day alone, listening to music. Once I came down, I swore to myself I'd never smoke the stuff again.

I had no idea what Lynne did outside the house. Lately, she'd been involved in things I didn't want to know about—hanging out with druggie guys she met on a party line and spending time in Vincent's garage. She was also cutting school for days in a row.

When I cut school, this is how I did it: I left the house like it was a normal school day and walked in the opposite direction from the way I knew my mother would drive when she left for stenography school in about ten minutes. I waited behind the bushes in front of a neighbor's house until I saw her car back out of the driveway and head up the street. That was my cue to head back to the house.

It wasn't that home was so great, it was just easier to squander the day there, and that was all I wanted to do. But I only cut school once in a while. Lynne did it all the time, and she didn't even bother to leave the house when she did; she just hid in her closet until our mother left.

That year, it seemed the sun didn't shine in LA. The sky was gray or bright white. At home on those oppressive, gray days, I watched TV and entertained myself touring the cupboards for snacks. Sometimes I walked to the market for a box of corn muffin mix and baked up a dozen to munch throughout the day. The pain from the overload in my stomach didn't stop me.

By four o'clock my mother was home from stenography school, sitting on the couch and smoking with a blank look in her eyes. Stenography school was probably too much for her—or maybe it was the Thorazine.

"How was school today?" I might ask, sitting next to her on a lopsided cushion.

"I'm just typing," was her usual reply.

At that time of day, her plumes of cigarette smoke climbed the dusty ladder of light streaming through the window. Whenever I saw that, I wished I could climb that ladder right out of the room.

My mother may have wished for the same.

AROUND MIDNIGHT ONE NIGHT, I HEARD THE FRONT door open and close. My sister was leaving.

She had told me earlier she would be going to Mark's at

midnight. What concerned me was that Mark wasn't even her friend. Why had she agreed to go?

Feeling protective, I threw on some clothes and walked up to Mark's house to see what was going on.

When I got there, my sister was on the front porch, talking with Mark at his bedroom window. They looked surprised to see me coming. I asked what they were doing. They said she was going inside, and I knew what that meant. I volunteered to go instead of her.

My sister seemed to appreciate that. She stepped aside and let me climb in through the window.

In Mark's room, I drank a big mug of rum he brought me from his parents' liquor cabinet. Then he brought me two more mugs full. He said I should drink fast, without stopping, and I did. After that, I lay back on the bed. The next thing I knew I was waking up vomiting. Mark was frantically pushing me to go out his window to the porch and spraying Lysol air freshener in a useless attempt to hide the evidence of having had a girl there.

I couldn't breathe with all that air freshener swirling around me. I could barely see. Lynne helped me through the window and onto the porch and walked me home, her arm through mine to try to steady me. I climbed into bed and lost consciousness.

Two days passed. I have vague memories of my mother coming to my door to see why I wasn't going to school. I said I didn't feel well. This time it was true.

That Saturday, I met my father for lunch at a restaurant near his office. Without telling anyone the reason, I'd asked for the date because I desperately wanted to talk with him. I wanted him to know that things were really bad at home. I wanted him to save me. I was scared to have gotten so drunk at Mark's that I'd passed out and slept for two days. It sickened me to think my sister was doing anything like that to get the social pass to hang out with those guys.

My father, sitting across the table from me in a suit—no tie, since it was the weekend—seemed miles away. I didn't tell him all of the story, just the part about the alcohol and getting sick.

"Vomiting when you're unconscious can kill you," he said, looking more disapproving than concerned.

"Please help me," I wanted to beg. "This is how bad things are." I wanted him to promise nothing like that would happen to me again. But he didn't. Instead, he glanced at his watch and flagged down the waitress, saying, "I have to get back to the office."

Feeling dirty and disappointed, I watched him pay the bill. We said goodbye out front and he walked back to the office while I got into my mother's waiting car.

"How was lunch?" she asked brightly, like this was something good I had just done, meeting my dad for lunch on a Saturday.

"It was okay," I lied.

That afternoon, Nicki and I got high in my room and listened to Pink Floyd. We were doing exactly what they sang about, ticking away the moments that make up the dull day. It was the soundtrack of our lives.

Nicki lay back on the bed with her eyes closed. Suddenly, she sat up. "I've got it figured out! This is life: Wake up, go to bed, live to eighty-five, then die." She dropped back on the bed.

I was afraid her miserable equation could be right.

When the rabbi who never knew my mother finishes saying whatever he says, everyone gets up to collect their purses and sweaters.

No one reaches out to hug each other or offer comfort. My brother goes to his friends standing at the back, their arms entwined. I see them take him in.

"Marilyn! Marilyn!" Grandma Friedman wails. "My beautiful baby girl!"

Her other two children restrain her to keep her from lunging toward the coffin. "Mom, Mom. Come on," they say.

Her grief is raw and vocal. I know she blames my father for my mother's unhappiness, for her death "so young."

It's time to go.

I start toward the line of cars parked along a street dividing the cemetery into sections. One of those cars has a seat in it for me. All I know to do is go there.

A woman I've never seen before falls into step with me. She looks about my mother's age, mid-forties. Her hair is blonde and loose around her shoulders.

"I'm Jean," she says. "I was in your mother's therapy group."

Do I look approachable or something? I don't want to talk to anyone. I keep walking.

"I am so *sorry," Jean says.*

I mutter, "I am too."

"Your mother could have had anything she wanted! Did you know that? She had the world at her feet."

I like hearing that. But I also know Jean isn't right. My mother couldn't have had anything she wanted. She couldn't live the possibilities of her soul.

I cross the cemetery lawn, avoiding stepping on gravestones as I go. Jean stays by my side, avoiding gravestones too. I realize she may know things about my mother that I don't. I should talk with her. But I can't do it now. And what difference would it make at this point, anyway?

We part ways at the curb.

Chapter 14

I was in the kitchen making a peanut butter sandwich the day my mother answered the phone and gasped. "Three weeks? I had no idea!"

Oh no. My sister's high school must be calling.

I grabbed my sandwich and ducked out the front door. Hell was about to break loose.

After school the next day I came home to find my mother at the dining table with a pack of cigarettes in one hand, a lit cigarette in the other. Her eyelids were puffy and red from crying. I'd never seen her so sad, the corners of her mouth drooping like a painted frown. Her gaze was fixed on the ashtray in front of her. "Did you know your sister wasn't going to school?"

I wasn't sure where to position myself for this line of questioning. I chose neutrality. "I knew she missed school sometimes."

"She missed three weeks."

"Wow."

A stream of cigarette smoke shot to the ceiling. "I took her to my doctor today." My mother's hands were trembling. "He sent her to the Westwood for observation."

I couldn't believe what I was hearing. "Why would he do that?"

My mother took a long drag of her cigarette. "She wouldn't stop screaming. She was completely out of control."

She told me the rest: Medics came from the Westwood Hospital, which was across the parking lot from the psychiatrist's office. They put my sister in a straitjacket and took her to the ICU.

A straitjacket?! The ICU? I ran to my room to get away from this news. I was sure my mother had put Lynne in the hospital because she didn't know what else to do with her.

Later that week, I asked to go with my mother to the hospital to visit Lynne. The only visitors allowed were my parents and the psychiatrist, she told me, but the next week she agreed to take me with her.

I got as far as the grim little waiting room in the ICU.

The receptionist gestured toward a seat. "You need to stay here. Only your mother can go inside."

My mother was allowed though a door, and it closed behind her, while I took a seat on a scratchy couch, still feeling shaken by the sight of the fenced yard I'd seen when we'd pulled up. There was barbed wire at the top of it.

My sister was here. I sat still, without taking a magazine from a corner table, my limbs leaden. I wouldn't have called it love at the time, I wouldn't have known how to recognize that complex feeling when it came to my sister, but the tightness in my chest as I waited for my mother in that airless waiting room was more than fear. That was my sister somewhere inside this prisonlike building, probably drugged and definitely scared.

SHAWN WAS VINCENT'S YOUNGER BROTHER, A CUTE, brown-eyed boy my age with smooth caramel skin and long blond hair he often shook out of his face. He wore motocross T-shirts and faded Levi's and liked to race Sting Rays on the street with me. But mostly we stayed up late in my room, smoking pot and listening to records.

I wanted more with Shawn, but nothing even remotely resembling attraction ever happened for him. He would just sit in a chair, sketching, while I lay on the bed, writing in a journal or doodling up and down margins.

When he found out my sister had been put in a mental hospital, Shawn asked me to go with him to Westwood to see Diana Ross in a new movie called *Lady Sings the Blues*. He thought I would like the singing in it. I suppose it was a thirteen-year-old boy's way of saying, "I care about you."

We took a bus there. Instead of feeling happy to be on something like a date with this boy, sitting by his side in the dark theater, all I could think about was my sister being in a mental hospital. I felt numb.

WHILE LYNNE WAS IN THE ICU, I ASKED MY MOTHER to deliver a letter to her. I wrote a few pages to my sister, telling her I was worried. I said drugs could make her feel worse—that they might even be part of her problem. Somehow I found the words to say, *You need to have hope; life is good.*

When the only response that came back was a request to sneak in some joints for her, I never wrote to her again.

My broken family had completely fallen apart. It was quieter at home without my sister there, but the gloom hanging over the house hadn't left. To escape, I hung out with Nicki and Shawn after school on the front lawn, drinking. I liked that alcohol could soften the edges.

My mother never noticed that her bottles of gin and

vodka were being refilled with inches of tap water. But drinking was pretty short-lived for me. I didn't like "the spins."

Some nights I stayed up watching TV in my sister's room until station sign-offs at 5:00 a.m.

I hated the sign-offs. Another night was ending and I was still on for the ride.

WHEN MY MOTHER WAS AT THE WESTWOOD HOSPITAL, I never saw the place. After my sister moved from the ICU to the west wing, where visitors were allowed, I went with my mother every week.

With its Spanish tile roof and terra-cotta walls, the Westwood Hospital looked more like a sprawling, adobe-style motel than a private mental institution. I was relieved there was no fenced yard topped with barbed wire surrounding the main building, only a grassy yard with blooming flower beds. In the carpeted hallway, a nurses' station sat behind a glass half wall at the junction of the east and west wings of the building. Just past that was the usually crowded rec room with a TV and stereo, both of them on. The doors to patients' rooms were always open, but the rooms were off-limits to visitors. All I knew of my sister's setup was that she had a roommate.

Family therapy met on Thursdays. My father left work to come, meeting us in the waiting room, looking uneasy and out of place. I felt ashamed to have him see us this way. Here he was, trying to have a better life, and we were dragging him down. I couldn't begin to imagine how awful it was for my mother to have to see him there—for that reason; for every reason.

At family therapy we sat on two long couches in an office belonging to my sister's weaselly looking psychiatrist, a man I privately called The Lizard. Skinny and tall, The Lizard sat between the two couches in a high-backed swivel chair, legs crossed, a clipboard balanced on his knobby knees. My father sat next to Lynne, looking like he'd swallowed a handful of pebbles. Across from this unfortunate configuration, I sat on a second couch with my mother and brother.

I wondered if my sister realized that none of us wanted to be there any more than she did. For fifty minutes she glowered, arms folded like a barricade across her chest, while our parents answered The Lizard's questions and asked a few of their own. Any discussion her doctor tried to initiate went south in seconds.

My sister clearly hated us, especially our parents and me. My greatest offense? Being born. The trouble with her mother? She was the reason my sister was there. The trouble with her father? He'd deserted the leaky boat and hadn't thrown her a lifeline.

When the fifty interminable minutes passed with no progress made, we headed to the parking lot, my father hurrying ahead to get the hell out of there and back to work. We didn't even try to catch up to say goodbye.

The hospital disturbed me, but it was also intriguing. Once, on our way out, we passed a woman standing inches from a painting on the wall. She stared at that painting like she was getting some kind of vital message from it.

"Suzy! Come on," my mother scolded. She didn't want me to see the craziness.

It was too late.

THE DAYS WENT BY SOMETHING LIKE WHITEWATER river rafting: You're paddling along peacefully, and then suddenly you hear a watery roar. It gets closer and closer, and soon you're paddling hard, riding the currents and trying to keep from capsizing.

Near the end of summer, after my workout at a gym (my latest effort to be thin), I took a bus with Nicki and my tag-along neighbor, Debbie, to the Santa Monica Mall to try on makeup at Newberry's. Trying on makeup was free fun; it only cost bus fare.

At Newberry's, we sampled lipsticks and explored nail polishes with laughable names like Rain Glow and Once Chiffon a Time. Debbie wanted a red polish but didn't have money. Nicki nudged me, and I knew what she was suggesting. We had been taking small stuff like candy bars and makeup from Thrifty for a while now, and we had it down.

There were three steps to the process. First: Target desired item. Next: Hold your sweater in front of you and lean into the counter, exploring a nearby item. Cover desired item with sweater as you make this move. Last: Pick up sweater with desired item in it and hold casually as you browse for a minute before exiting the store.

It was after this last step, just outside the store, that a firm hand clamped down on my shoulder, followed by the dreaded words—"Hold it right there."

The ordinary-looking man in street clothes flashed his badge at me. I was caught. He frowned at the sight of my two friends hightailing it down the street. *Deserters!*

"Follow me," he ordered, and I did, back into the store.

We passed through the cosmetics area to a flight of stairs leading to a back room outfitted with a desk and three chairs. He flipped a switch to turn on a glaring fluorescent overhead light.

"Wait here," he commanded. "The manager will be in to see you." Then he left and closed the door behind him.

Oh no. Would I be going to juvenile hall? Had I ruined my life over a nail polish for Debbie?

A map of the store hung on a wall near me. I got up to have a closer look. "X" marks written on it seemed to show where the store detectives were staked out. Darn, we hadn't thought of that. On the table below this map sat a stack of papers. Flipping through them I could see they were shoplifter reports; most of the names on them were Hispanic.

Just then, the door opened and I flew to my seat.

A clean-cut man with a name tag on his button-up shirt came in without saying hello and took a seat behind the desk. He rotated his swivel chair from side to side as he looked me over, twirling a pen around a finger. I hoped he thought I looked too young for juvie. He pulled out a pad from a desk drawer. "Name?" I gave him my name and he wrote it down. "Age?"

"I'll be fourteen in October."

He repeated my age, squinting at me. "Fourteen in October? What's your address?" He jotted that down. "Empty your bag." Using his pen, he pointed to his desk as the place to do this.

"It's my gym bag."

He leaned back in his chair. "Empty it."

I wished I hadn't wasted my time studying the detectives map and looking at shoplifter reports instead of stashing the evidence at the bottom of the trash can when I was alone in this room. The contents of my gym bag fell onto his desk: green shorts, a white T-shirt, tennis shoes, socks, the red nail polish, and a pack of Marlboros. He snatched the nail polish and set it beside him, then grabbed the cigarettes and dumped them into the trash. "You're too young to smoke."

"My mother bought them for me."

That got a frown. He looked at his pad. "Is this your parents' number?"

"My parents are divorced."

"Who do you live with?"

"My mother."

"Is this her phone number?"

"Yep."

He started dialing. "I'm sure she'll know what to do about this."

I wanted to say, "Fat chance." But I was worried.

Before long, my mother was knocking at the office door. She glanced at me as she stepped inside and shook hands with the store manager, who suggested she sit next to me.

Stealing was more than my mother could tolerate. One day, in first grade, I picked flowers for her on my way home from school. She wasn't happy when I handed her the little bunch. "You can't take flowers from other people's gardens," she said. "They belong to the people who live there." I tried to understand people owning flowers that grew in a yard. Another time, a few years earlier, when I went to Santa Barbara with my dad, I'd brought home an ashtray from the Miramar Hotel to give to my mother. When she saw the hotel name printed on the bottom of it, she'd handed it back to me. "You took something that didn't belong to you."

And now I might have a police record.

The manager pushed the empty Marlboro pack across the desk toward my mother. "She said you bought these for her."

"I did."

He paused hearing that, but thankfully let the cigarette thing go and repeated the nail polish story I'd told her when I'd called.

"I'm so sorry," my mother said. "She'll never do it again."

The manager stood, and my mother followed his lead. "I'm sure you can take care of this better than we can," he said. They shook hands again.

On the way home I found out what exactly my mother was going to do about this: I was grounded for a month. Eternity.

Two days later, my mother came to my room with good news. No police report had been filed.

Whoopee! I wasn't going to juvie!

But she had bad news, too. I would have to see a therapist.

"Because I stole a nail polish?" I cried. "Are you kidding me?" I had been lying on the bed with an arm thrown across my eyes to shield them from the daylight. Now I turned over to face the wall.

"If you're taking things that don't belong to you, you must feel you're not getting enough of something," she said. "This could help you."

Not getting enough of something? It seemed to me that my mother was the problem. How could seeing a shrink help?

"You're going next Tuesday," she said. And with that, she was gone, her footsteps disappearing up the hall.

On Tuesday, my mother drove me to Dr. Anderson's office. Her shoulders looked stiff and I thought she was squeezing the steering wheel too tightly. Why was she nervous? I was the one who had to see a shrink.

When we got there, I realized I knew the building. My sister was across the parking lot in the Westwood Hospital. Maybe that was why my mother seemed nervous taking me to see Dr. Anderson.

What I didn't know was that I was about to meet a man who would change my life—and possibly even save it.

IN THE WAITING ROOM, I SAT STARING AT MY HANDS while my mother looked at a magazine. Dr. Anderson opened a door and peeked in. "Hello!" he said in a cheery voice. He opened the door wider, stepped in, and warmly shook my mother's hand. "Nice to meet you."

He looked older than my parents, with his gray-flecked

beard and mustache. There were deep dimples in his cheeks, and laugh lines crinkled the skin at the corners of his twinkly blue eyes. "You must be Suzy," he said with a smile.

I nodded and stood up, swallowing my nerves, then followed him inside. *Fifty minutes*, I told myself. My mother would stay in the waiting room.

The office was light and roomy, with windows overlooking neighborhood streets. The air wasn't stale in here like it was in The Lizard's office. It smelled woodsy, like men's cologne. I could see Olympic Boulevard snaking through the west side all the way to the ocean, off in the distant glare. There was an old drive-in theater out there, one with a giant painting of a blond surfer couple carrying surfboards on the street-facing side.

He gestured to an armchair. "Make yourself comfortable."

I noticed he had a big desk with books on it, and framed professional certificates hanging on the wall. He took a seat in a leather swivel chair across from me and rested an ankle on a knee. He wasn't holding a notepad like The Lizard did, and I appreciated that. I always felt like part of a case study when I was with my sister's therapist.

He leaned back in his swivel chair like we were old friends. "Do you have any questions for me?"

The desk clock counted the seconds while I thought about it.

I shook my head. "Nope."

He looked at me with narrowed eyes. "Are you stoned?"

"No! I am not stoned!" How dare he think that! I purposely didn't smoke before coming here. I wanted my wits about me.

"Well, you're either stoned or you have a big scream inside of you."

"I'm not angry!" How embarrassing. I almost shouted that.

For the next forty-five minutes, I answered his questions about school and what I did for fun. Finally, he said the words I'd been waiting for: "Our time is up."

On the drive home, my mother asked how I liked Dr. Anderson. I told her he was okay.

"Good," she said. "You're going to be seeing him on Tuesdays for a while."

I sighed. "Unbelievable."

WITHIN WEEKS, MY RESISTANCE TO DR. ANDERSON, the man I now called Bob, faded. Tuesday was turning out to be the best day in my week. Sunday, Monday, Bob Day. I liked him. He listened. He cared what I had to say, no matter what the subject was.

"What's up?" he asked one Tuesday, leaning forward the way he did when he could see we had a topic to unpack.

"Nothing."

He looked skeptical. "Nothing at all?"

"No. I just hate school."

"What do you hate about school?"

"Everything. The boys in my English class."

"Do you want to tell me about them?"

I liked how he waited for me to say more before he said more himself. I decided to tell him what had happened on Friday in English class.

"We were passing handouts down the row and the guy in front of me stopped when they got to him. The guy sitting next to me said, 'Hey Mike, give the papers to that girl.' Mike said, 'That's not a girl. That's a blimp!' And they both cracked up."

Tears I hadn't known were waiting came pouring out. A blimp, not a girl.

"But it's not true." Bob made it sound like obvious fact. "You're a beautiful girl."

I wiped my tears away, appreciating what he was doing. But I didn't believe a word he said. Not one bit.

"Your eyes are beautiful. What color would you call them? Blue-gray? Green? And your hair is thick and wavy."

I hated my hair. I hated my hands too. I tucked them under my armpits like I had done in English class that morning. Bob didn't miss it.

"Will you show me your hands?"

"I don't like my hands."

"What don't you like about them?"

"They're square. My fingers are chubby."

"Please show me your hands."

Reluctantly, I held my hands out for him to see.

"You have beautiful hands. Capable hands."

That was a laugh. "My fingers are stubby," I insisted.

"Come with me," Bob said. "We're going to look at ourselves."

What was this? I followed him to a door on a far wall. On the other side of that door was a closet with a full-length mirror. A couple of his jackets hung on a coat rack.

"Stand next to me."

Standing next to Bob was new for me. We usually sat in chairs.

"What do you see?" he asked.

"I thought you were taller."

"Impressions aren't always what's true."

"I guess not."

"Do you know you have a lovely smile?"

I didn't.

"Every morning, I want you to look in the mirror and find something you like about the way you look. It could be your eyes, it could be your complexion, it could be your hair—anything. Just notice it."

"I'll try."

"And remember." He faced me, speaking earnestly. "What the boys at school said isn't true. *You* know what's true. And so do I."

That night, before turning off my bedside light, I held out my hands and tried to see them the way Bob did. My fingers looked short and pudgy, not slender and graceful like I wanted them to be. But just for a moment, I thought my hands might be alright.

On a weekday after the funeral, my father is at work when Jill calls me to come downstairs to look through "some of your mother's things," as she calls them. She's at the dining table, sitting in front of a grocery bag full of pill bottles she's taken from my mother's medicine cabinet. A bag next to that holds the pink satin drawer organizer from her dresser.

I sit down with the second bag first, steeling myself for the task ahead.

Jill is quiet, just watching, as I pull the drawer organizer out of the bag. I haven't seen it since the days I entertained myself in her bedroom while she got dressed for the day. I'm sure Jill doesn't think anything in this drawer organizer is valuable. I know everything here is.

I start with the arrowhead in a back compartment. My mother found that sharp triangle of carved obsidian on a hike she took with my dad when they first came to California. I'll keep that and her early 1960s necklace with the purple plastic beads. I'll keep the scarab beetle bracelet her father gave her too, every stone on it a different color. It's hard to believe my mother's treasures are my own now.

"Uck!" Jill screeches. With a grimace she's pointing at a necklace I'm holding up to consider keeping. "Hair!" A strand of my mother's long brown hair hangs from the clasp of the necklace in my hand.

I want to scream at Jill, "That's all I have left of her!" But I don't. I put the necklace back in its compartment in the satin jewelry holder, then turn to the bag of pill bottles and say, "I'm going to throw these out in the alley."

In South Beverly Hills, the garbage cans are humongous lime green plastic containers that line the alleyways along the center of every block. Such unpleasant business as the removal of garbage takes place out of sight in this city.

With burning eyes and a tight throat, I lift the heavy lid of the container in our back alley and empty the contents of one pill bottle after the next, pouring streams of white, blue, and red false promises into the garbage. Next, I toss in the plastic bottles with labels like Thorazine, Stelazine, Valium, and other names I don't recognize. I've wanted to throw away these pills for years.

When it's done I drop the empty bag into the trash can, lower the lid, and bend over it, crying with a kind of sorrow that has no tears. What now?

Chapter 15

My sister didn't do arts and crafts at the Westwood—not her thing. She watched TV, went to therapy appointments, and slept the days away. She made friends with a few boys who brought her cigarettes after their days out on a pass. I didn't ask if any brought pot back for her, but they may have.

Her roommate committed suicide one night; she overdosed while Lynne slept in the bed across the room. Lynne's doctor got her a room change, moving her closer to the rec room, where the commotion of the TV and records clashed and the cloud of cigarette smoke was constant.

Now and then I still went along with my mother when she went to the hospital to see Lynne and her doctor. I usually didn't talk with anyone; I was interested in seeing their world, but I didn't want to be part of it.

Daniel, with his big paunch and greasy red hair, was a regular. He always stood close enough to a small group of people to hear what they were saying, but far enough from them to whisper furtively into a microphone attached to a tape recorder without being overheard. The guy seemed to be documenting everything happening around him. Which wasn't a lot. I wondered what he did with all those tapes.

A tall, skinny girl with a mane of blonde curls showed up in the courtyard one day. She stood smoking a cigarette, then pulled a chair up next to mine and sat down, dropping one long leg over the other. "You new?" She nervously wagged a sandaled foot.

"No, my sister's here. I'm waiting for my mom."

She didn't ask my sister's name and I didn't offer it. "I'm manic-depressive," she said flatly.

I didn't know what that meant, but I wasn't about to ask.

"I tried to commit suicide. That's why my parents sent me here again. Ugh. I hate this place." She twisted two long, bony fingers together and groaned.

I noticed a bandage peeking out from the sleeve at her left wrist. "How long have you been here?" I asked.

"Three weeks."

I didn't tell her my mother only stayed here for two weeks when she tried to kill herself.

The girl went on. "My parents think I'm anorexic."

Another new word for me. But I appreciated that she thought I was someone she could talk to. I nodded like I understood.

"Why is your sister here?"

"She got caught cutting school. For a month." That second part seemed important.

"That's stupid. So they put her in a mental hospital?"

"There are other reasons too. She has problems."

The girl let that go by. "God, I hate this place! One girl's parents put her in here because they found her stash in her bedroom. And your sister's here for cutting school."

"Something like that," I said.

"Hey, do you want to have dinner with me tonight?"

"I can't. My mom's coming for me soon." I hoped I didn't sound too happy about that.

"See ya, then!" And with that the girl was up and gone, disappearing through the door to the cafeteria building.

In the car on the way home, I asked my mother what manic-depressive meant. She explained it. Then I asked what anorexic meant.

"Bring a book next time," she said.

TICK, TICK, TICK, TICK. THE TICKING WALL CLOCK IN MY classroom moved like a spoon stirring a bowl of molasses. Another dull day at school. Walking to school that morning, I had caught a glimpse of my reflection in a store window on National Boulevard. I looked like a shadow passing by. Everyone driving past me was hurrying to get somewhere. I didn't know why they cared.

Nicki was going to an alternative school in Venice, where ninth grade was the first year of high school. I was still at Webster, a junior high that went through ninth grade. I was stuck in the same old place with the same old teachers, the same old everything. I had tested into Honors English, but in math I sat with the other end of the academic spectrum, kids who didn't know what to do with numbers. I couldn't understand why the term "math problems" was used. All math was a problem, if you asked me. Making it worse, my math teacher this year smelled of alcohol in this first class after lunch period. He always looked like he was in over his head.

It was about five weeks into the fall semester. When the bell rang after lunch period that day, instead of heading to math class, I went to my locker and pulled out all of my books and Pee-Chee folders. "I can't do this anymore," I muttered. It was impulsive, and I didn't care. I walked out of the school gate with the heavy armload and no one stopped me. It was that easy.

My mother wasn't there when I got home. I sat on the floor in my room, leaning against the bed and listening to *Tales from Topographic Oceans* with my headphones on.

When my mother came home and saw my bedroom door open, she came in looking worried. "Suzy! Why are you home? Are you sick?"

"I'm fine," I said. "I hate school. I'm not going back."

"You can't leave school because you're having a bad day."

"It's more than a bad day, Mom, trust me. I'm never going back to that school."

She called my father at work, and by the next week we were looking at private schools a friend of his at work had recommended.

I chose an alternative creative arts high school in Santa Monica called Horizons.

Horizons started with ninth grade. The school had only seventy students, which meant classes were small, six to ten students in each one. After lunch everyone had three hours of classes in their arts specialty. This was called "studio," and the options available for studio were music, dance, drama, or art. You had to choose one for the school year. I chose music.

Alan, a neighbor on our street, was in drama studio at Horizons. I would drive in with him in the mornings and take the bus home.

Something good was finally happening.

IN LA YOU CAN TELL IT'S WINTER MOSTLY BECAUSE IT gets dark early. Bad weather is rain, and it doesn't rain too often, which was perfect now that I commuted to school in Alan's noisy little MG convertible. I loved that car. I also liked that between the constant roar of the engine and the whipping wind in my ears at fifty miles an hour, we didn't have to talk.

At Horizons, my teachers went by their first names. A few were in grad school at UCLA. Some were musicians; a couple of them were artists. Most classrooms had conference tables with seats around them. A lounge had a bank of windows overlooking the parking lot out back and floor ashtrays three feet high. We could smoke at school. Huge canvasses hung on the walls in a big art studio at the end of a long hall. The intoxicating smell of oil paint drifted through the building morning and afternoon. "PE" was yoga or modern dance in a big room with a mirrored wall. I chose dance.

For the first time, school interested me. I took notes in class instead of doodling. In Western Civ we read Homer and novels about classical Greece by Mary Renault. In English we read Herman Hesse and Thomas Hardy. I saw a new side of the world in an anthropology class, reading about Pygmies in a rainforest in the Congo. And Barry, my wiry biology teacher with scruffy dark hair that flew out from both sides of his balding head, made science interesting. He poured an endless stream of information, sometimes so excited by what he was teaching us that he went up on tiptoe.

But socially, school was hard. There were cliques—the cool kids, the artists, the musicians, the actors, the stoners, and the misfits. I was the new kid, starting school two months late. Even the misfits ignored me.

It quickly became clear to me that school and home were different countries. Home might be dismal, but at least I knew the language there. At school I wasn't sure what to say to people, so I didn't say anything. Everyone already had friends or was too self-absorbed to care.

The wealth gap was a wedge too. One boy was a TV star. A few kids had parents or grandparents who were famous directors or actors. Horizons was in a part of Santa Monica far from the gated mansions north of Sunset and nowhere near Malibu, Benedict Canyon, and Topanga Canyon, which meant these kids either had drivers or had their own cars. I was one of only a handful who rode a bus home.

And so it was that I encountered a whole new host of ways to feel left out. Every week my rut dug deeper, making it harder to speak up or meet anyone.

Through Nancy (a stoner), the one girl who would share a cigarette in the lounge with me, I learned I had a reputation for being spaced out. I was sure that was thanks to Alan complaining to his fellow thespians about the neighbor he had to drive to school every morning. And the truth was, I *was* spaced out after staying up until two o'clock every night, getting high and listening to music in my bedroom with my friend Shawn.

Thanksgiving came, and we were only three at home. David watched a football game on the TV in his room while my mother stuffed and roasted a turkey. She called me in for my annual job of opening the can of cranberry jelly and slicing the slippery cylinder into one-inch rounds. I cut those gelatinous maroon discs with a flower-shaped cookie cutter and set the flowers on a white serving plate on the table. Then I put on the Crosby, Stills, Nash & Young album *Déjà Vu* and sat in the living room listening to it in front of the fire my mother had agreed to make for me in the fireplace. The oil painting of the clay pot tipped on its side that she'd bought in Ojai hung above the mantel. A picture of desolation.

IN DECEMBER, ONE WEEK BEFORE GRADUATING, MY mother quit stenography school. We didn't talk about it. I only noticed her stenography machine was gone and she wasn't leaving the house in the morning anymore. I imagine she realized she wouldn't be able to perform in a courtroom under pressure, typing every spoken word into a transcription machine using the special code she'd been taught.

What did my mother do at home all day? She sat on the couch smoking in front of the empty fireplace, looking like her last hope had been flushed down the toilet.

Her face was puffy. Her clothes were drab. She put on lipstick and sometimes a little eyeliner before leaving the house for therapy or to drive to the Westwood Hospital to see my sister and her doctor. Was her brain blanked out by a medicinally tranquilized nervous system? The days of doing anything like inviting an African man she met at the market to talk to my class at school seemed so long ago.

The only thing that stayed usual was dinnertime. Every night at six o'clock she put a simple dinner on the table for the three of us. As soon as we finished eating, she disappeared into her bedroom.

One Saturday I was in my mother's bedroom, in front of her mirror, practicing blowing smoke rings like Diana Ross in *Lady Sings the Blues*. My mother sat on her bed, idly watching.

The phone on her bedside table rang. "Oh, hello Roger," she said coolly.

Wavering circles of cigarette smoke rose to the ceiling, evaporating on the way. I was getting good at this!

After listening to my father for a minute, my mother said, "Goodbye, Roger," and hung up.

I knew it must be bad news. She looked sucker punched.

"What did he want?" I blew another set of smoke rings, all of them perfect circles rising to disappear above my head.

"Your father's moving in with Jill."

CHRISTMAS CAME AND WENT WITH A SMALL, FLOCKED tabletop tree my mother agreed to buy when we were grocery shopping at Hughes one day. There wasn't much to the holiday at my house, but I liked putting a few wrapped presents under the tree even if no one else did. We hadn't lit the Hanukkah candles since my dad lived with us.

In the spring, a little more than a year after going into the hospital, my sister was home again. Her diagnosis? Chronic depression. It would be thirty years before other identifiable issues would lengthen the list of the challenges that made life hard for my sister—borderline personality disorder, OCD/hoarding disorder, dyslexia, and ADD among them.

Rage still ran her. She yelled at our mother for anything and everything. She stayed holed up in her room, refusing to join us at the dinner table. My mother enrolled her in a remedial high school, hoping she would graduate on time next June. I squirmed thinking about the drives my mother made with her resentful daughter across the city to school and back five days a week.

My sister. The Great Unknown. Once, when she wasn't home, I peeked into her room to get some idea of what she did in there. Her unmade bed was covered with rumpled clothes, possibly clothes she hadn't worn since before she left for the hospital. Maybe she had tried them on; maybe she just wanted to see them again. Her unpacked, open suitcase lay on the floor by her bed. I cautiously took a step inside to have a look at the record albums stacked by her stereo.

Before I touched the stack, something creepy caught my eye. Across the front of a Cat Stevens album, in black marker, someone had scrawled, "God is June. June is God."

I ran from the room.

BRYAN WAS A CLASSMATE OF MY SISTER'S AT HER REmedial high school. Late in the day, he'd come over to drink beer with her in her room and play records. Loud.

I was the one who answered the door when he knocked. His broad shoulders looked good in a tight white T-shirt and I liked the way his hair hung in a ponytail past his shoulders. Bryan was a big cinnamon bun, sweet and soft-looking. A recipe for disaster for this teenage girl. Before long, when I let him in I invited him to my room after he visited my sister, to smoke a joint.

After that, he came to see me instead of her. Too young to be ethical, I shrugged off stealing my sister's only friend.

Nicki wasn't around much now that we went to different schools, but she came over to meet Bryan and she liked his ragtag buddy Prett—an edgy, angry, hard-drinking guy who looked straight out of *Oliver Twist*, with his shaggy mop of blond hair, freckles, and pale blue eyes. She thought Bryan was a "dolt" but Prett was defiant, an outcast, a bad boy—exactly her type.

It was summer, and the days were long, with temperatures in the 90s. I shied away from the heat, preferring my room, with my stereo and a book. If Nicki came over and Bryan and Prett showed up, we walked to Hughes to get a bottle of tequila to drink on my front lawn. Prett sang when we walked, usually Bowie songs from his album *Hunky Dory*. I started listening to Bowie all the time. Songs like "Rock 'n' Roll Suicide," where time puts a cigarette in your mouth, spoke to me, carried me.

Getting tequila was easy. The boys knew how to tuck a bottle in the front of their baggy jeans and walk out of the market like it was nothing. Shoplifting was how Prett ate too. But mostly he drank. He showed us how to swipe a cut lemon across the top of our hands and sprinkle it with salt to lick before throwing back a swig of tequila. I never drank enough to get the spins, but those few shots I took each time we hung out put a numbing wedge between me and everything around me.

Bryan was a drinker too. I knew his parents were alcoholics, and so was his sister. If his parents cared that he drank, they were too drunk all the time to do anything about it. Prett basically had no parents. "You should appreciate your mother," he said once, when I complained about mine. "You're lucky you've got a mother at home." He didn't know his mother at all. He didn't know his father well, either, though his father showed up occasionally to crash at the shack Prett called home—a run-down, one-room building behind some abandoned railroad tracks in an industrial part of Culver City.

Bryan and I wanted to see where our friend lived. Eventually, begrudgingly, Prett agreed to take us there.

We rode a bus to Culver City and got out in a desolate area Prett said was his stop. Broken glass littered the railroad tracks where we walked, following our fearless leader like dedicated rats behind a cheerful pied piper. He led us to a small building in back of an abandoned warehouse, and opened its single door with a key he wore on a chain around his neck.

There wasn't a speck of furniture in the place besides a warped mattress on the floor, under a pile of questionably clean blankets. "Dad's on a drunk," Prett said.

I walked over to the rusty old refrigerator, the only thing that made that part of the room look like a kitchen, and opened it. There was an unopened can of grapefruit juice on the top shelf inside.

I could see why Prett didn't like staying here. All that connected him to this place and his father was the key the man had given him.

Bryan's situation wasn't as outwardly gruesome as Prett's, but after a few months, the bottomless alcohol tank that was my boyfriend's body was beginning to wear on me. He even nodded off once during a drunken kiss. But I kept up the charade, wandering lost in the desert as I was.

Until the time his mother found us in his bed.

I had left home at nine o'clock to go to Bryan's that night. My mother knew I was going and she didn't want me to. Perhaps because it was late. Or maybe she knew that everything about it was a bad idea. She followed me out to the sidewalk begging me not to go—"Please, not so late."

I didn't want to hear it. My teenage hormones were fueled by anger with her for making my life so unhappy. So off I went to Bryan's, walking the mile or so up National Boulevard to drink together at his house and then lie down on his bed to sleep. Alcohol was his lover, not me.

At two o'clock, soon after we turned out the light, his parents came home. His mother opened his bedroom door and saw us sprawled out across the mattress, sleeping in our clothes.

"Get out!" she shouted. "Get out now!"

National Boulevard was an eerie walk at that hour. Houses were dark, parking lots were vacant. Before I was halfway home, the only car on the road slowed to almost a stop beside me. A quick glance at the driver told me he was too interested. I had to get out of there fast. I couldn't knock on doors this late to ask for help, and I knew better than to run. Prey shouldn't show weakness.

Without looking at him again, I picked up my pace. The car continued down the street.

At home, I heard my mother's voice inside before I touched the doorknob to go in. She was saying, "I'm so worried about her," and crying as she spoke.

Who could she be talking to at this hour? Her sister in New York? It was three o'clock. She wouldn't call my father at that hour.

I had no interest in seeing her right then. Her station

wagon was parked in the driveway. I thought about going in there and lying down in the back to sleep; the third seat faced out the rear window. But it seemed too cramped and too visible.

I went to the other side of the car and curled up on the neighbor's lawn. The grass felt cold and scratchy, but at least no one could see me.

I felt wretched knowing my mother was inside crying about me. I lay there, feeling miserable as night fell harder and the darkness deepened. Eventually, I drifted into something like sleep, until the haunting cries of the mourning doves—*who-who*, *who-who*—woke me at dawn.

I lay in the blue half-light, chilled by the cold, chilled by my misery.

A week after the funeral, my father takes me to Santa Barbara to pack my dorm room and leave that school for good. Tomorrow, two weeks to the day after she died, we'll clear out my mother's house so he can put it on the market. He's paid for that house since buying it in 1962, when the family was young, my mother was well, and hope for everyone's future shone bright with possibility.

David will leave soon for summer school in Massachusetts, at Andover. I start classes at UC Santa Cruz next week. Lynne is back to her job working as a receptionist at a boarding hotel for cats, a job our mother helped her get.

Outside the passenger window of my father's new white Jaguar—a car Jill encouraged him to buy—dizzying rows of green crops flash past for miles. The last time we drove this road north together, my father was taking me to college. It was September, and I was about to start what he would call the best years of my life.

"Your grandmother was part of your mom's problem," he says now, interrupting the memory of my life eleven months ago. I've never heard him talk about my grandmother. "She talked out of both sides of her mouth. Your mother never knew what to believe." He says this like it's a certain reason for my mother's demise.

Really? I think of the time when Grandma set a second piece of date nut bread on my plate, only to tell me I shouldn't have it, that I needed to lose weight. But that wasn't the reason for my mother's problems. She had a serious mental illness. You don't get schizophrenia because your mother says one thing and means another.

He still doesn't get it. He can't take it in. Even though he read her suicide note too. She said she couldn't live with the fears and hallucinations any longer. She couldn't live with the medications, or without them. How could that be plainer?

We pass Ventura without another word, each of us lost in thought after the emotional avalanche the last two weeks have been. Buildings and billboards mean the Pacific will peek out soon from around a corner up ahead. After that we'll be in Santa Barbara, packing up my freshman dorm room, and this part of the nightmare will be over.

Chapter 16

A good teacher can be a ray of light. That light in my life was Lara, my psychology teacher at Horizons. A Swedish grad student with hair so blonde it was nearly white, in my first year at that school Lara opened my eyes to humanistic psychology and radical thinkers like Carl Rogers and Carl Jung, with his theories about the collective unconscious. I learned in her class that R.D. Laing believed insanity was a perfectly rational response to an insane world. Could he be right? Maybe the craziness of this world had affected my mother, and that was what was wrong with her. I read *The Art of Loving*, by Erich Fromm, learning that if you love yourself you can feel loved all the time. Unfortunately, I finished that book and the school year still wondering how to do that.

But Lara stayed in my thoughts. She taught us about art therapy. I could see myself someday being an art therapist myself, helping people into breakthroughs talk therapy couldn't seem to touch.

I could see myself in the future. That was new.

Corinna and I were completely out of touch by now, which was fine with me. There was so much I didn't want to tell her about. My biggest secrets were about who I was spending time with. She would have called Bryan and Prett "scuzzes," and she would have been right. But I also worried about what she'd say if she knew what I was doing lately with her ex-boyfriend, Vincent.

Vincent's nighttime visits to me started with a question, after an evening I'd spent with Shawn at their house. Vincent was watching TV when we walked by on my way out—nothing unusual, except that tonight he smiled at me when he waved goodnight. "Like to smoke a joint sometime?"

I hoped he wouldn't notice my joyous teenage soul lifting from the earth as I somehow returned his smile. "Sure," I said.

Shawn rolled his eyes and held the front door open for me to go. But I had no loyalties to keep. Shawn was a friend, nothing more. "Knock at my window at eleven thirty," I told his brother.

I was weightless walking home, dancing on air. Gone were Sherman Tank and Fatso. I wasn't a "blimp, not a girl" anymore. Dream Boy wanted me.

Later that night I put on a pink satin 1940s nightgown with spaghetti straps, something I'd picked up at a thrift shop in Venice. Should I stay barefoot? Brush my hair again?

A tap came at my bedroom window right on time. Jittery and not a little afraid, I opened the window wider.

"Hey there." Vincent flashed his charming smile and, with an effortless jump, he was through the window and inside my room.

What now? I had never been alone with Dream Boy before, not even for a minute. From my seat on the bed I watched as he suavely eased the tension by pulling a cigarette case from a back pocket and taking out a fat joint.

He held it up for me to admire. "Thai stick."

I nodded like I knew what that meant.

Streams of white-gold moonlight poured through my window as he lit the joint with a lighter and we took a few hits off it. My big night was off to a good start. He tugged his T-shirt over his head and tossed it on the bed, showing off a smooth, melted-caramel chest. That expensive pot sure was strong! I hoped I would know what to do. He leaned in close for a kiss and our lips met. When I opened my eyes again the white glow of moonlight on his bare shoulders left me breathless.

I had stashed my bag of birth control in a bathroom cupboard before he came over that night. Now seemed the perfect time to excuse myself to go get something from it. I prayed my sister wouldn't hear me and come out to see what was going on. I felt incredibly stoned, higher than I'd ever been. That must be what he'd meant by Thai stick. This stuff was strong—out of my league.

In the bathroom, I opened the bag I'd stashed, took out the bottle of foam, and used it. I went back to my room to find Vincent lying naked on the bed. He leaned back against the wall with both hands folded behind his head.

The dance he led us in was something like what I'd imagined, except without a single word of affection between us or another kiss until he was dressed again and ready to hop out the window. After he left, I closed the window and lay back on the pillows, drawing the covers to my neck to muse about what had just happened. Of all people. Vincent. My first time.

I didn't feel happy or unhappy. I felt empty. More amazed than anything else. My pleasure that night was having Vincent want me that way.

Three or four more late-night knocks came on the window that summer, and I paid a few late-night visits to his house too. But eventually I lost interest in our clandestine capers. They didn't make my heart sing.

One night I answered his knock with practiced words and no move to open the window wider. "I think it would be better if you don't come over anymore."

He flashed his charming smile and whispered, "See ya."

And that was it. He was gone. No biggie.

Exactly the problem.

THE SUMMER OF 1974 WORE ON. PINK HEARTS AND White Crosses were amphetamines, and Prett knew how to get them.

"Don't take them all at once," he warned, pouring a few feel-good pills into my hand one day. "This is all I've got."

I liked those pills. They gave me energy. And they took away my appetite. I was already thinner, probably because I was still growing—I was almost five foot nine now—but I didn't mind the idea of losing more weight. I loved the swing in my skirts, the loose waistlines in my pants. I felt pretty.

One Sunday I was sitting on the front lawn with Bryan, Nicki, and Prett when my father pulled up to the curb in his Buick Electra. Our Sunday outings were long over by this point. He felt like a stranger.

"Oh, no," I murmured.

"Who is that?" Prett asked.

"It's her dad." That was Nicki.

Bryan stared as my dad got out of the car. Prett stood up and gave his too-big jeans a yank. "Hullo!" he called out gaily.

My father hurried past us to the front door without a word. He was carrying his briefcase, his mouth set tight.

"Okay, then," Prett said, and he shrugged. At the sound of the front door closing, he picked up the tequila bottle we'd been sharing and tucked it under an arm. "Later." He was off, heading up the street.

Nicki and Bryan got up and followed him.

I went into the house and found my parents in the living room, my dad seated on the carved wooden chair from Ojai, his briefcase spread open on his lap. My mom sat on the couch, across from him.

"Hi, Suzy," she said, and her voice sounded light, like she might even be happy about this visit.

My father didn't look up. He scribbled on a yellow legal pad with a Cross pen.

His wedding was in a couple months; I figured my parents were finalizing their divorce papers. But I didn't ask what they were doing. And I didn't stay.

BOB USUALLY STARTED. HE COULD GET ME GOING BEfore I even knew I was headed somewhere. I might be telling him about something that happened with my parents or sister and he'd grab the foam bat he kept beside him, the Bataka, and slam it hard on the couch arm. He said what I didn't have the guts to say: "Dad, I'm pissed you never call me!" *Slam*. "You act like it's a chore to see us!" *Slam*. Then he'd look at me and point to the Bataka propped next to my chair. "Your turn."

Bob had been right the day we met. I did have a big scream inside me. At the time, all I knew was that my mother had problems, I hated my sister's temper, and my father hurt my feelings all the time.

I might start a Bataka session by reaching out from the chair to hit the couch arm closest to me. In seconds I'd be standing and using both hands to really whop that couch arm. I hit it over and over, slamming out my frustrations with all my might.

"Whew!" I'd finally sigh, dropping into my chair to catch my breath. "That was good."

I didn't tell Bob what I was doing at home—hanging out with Bryan and Prett, drinking tequila out of the bottle and finishing quarts of beer with them—and I didn't tell him about my forays with Vincent, either. I didn't want him to know. He was my only support and confidant, and I was ashamed of myself.

WATERGATE WAS IN THE NEWS THAT SUMMER, WITH President Nixon possibly resigning over it. But I didn't care about politics. I only cared that I was going away to the Trinity Alps for the entire month of August. David was coming to camp this time too—he was finally old enough.

We could never have guessed how profoundly those four weeks would impact the rest of our lives.

That year at camp I'd applied to live at an outpost in the woods a few miles away, near a tiny town called Hyampom. I was thrilled when I was chosen; only a handful of us were selected to go. Seven city kids would share the magic of living in the woods with two outpost leaders, Cathy and Jim. Meanwhile, David got settled into his boys' cabin on the side of a hill overlooking a gorgeous, mountainous landscape.

At the outpost, my idyllic outdoor playhouse in the woods, there were no walls or doors. At night we slept in sleeping bags on canvas cots stretched over stripped pine logs. I counted seven falling stars every night in the astonishing umbrella overhead before drifting off.

The kitchen was an area where large sheets of burlap had been draped over ropes tied to trees. Jim hauled in blocks of ice every few days for the wooden ice box that held our perishables. Every morning, Cathy poured water over the burlap covering those ice blocks, to keep the eggs and produce in there cool. A retired US Army blood bank held foods that could have attracted unwanted visitors (think bears).

In the forest, I bathed under a stream of water from a water tank that was heated by a wood-burning fire. Birds chattered in the redwoods around me. Burlap curtains strung on ropes were my privacy curtain.

Work projects were optional, which meant that every morning I could spend time on my own in the barn while the others sawed and hammered, building new troughs for the horses.

I loved the cool dimness of the barn, where hay bales were stacked to the rooftop. I was Fern in *Charlotte's Web*, climbing bales to the eaves to gaze into the treetops through an open window near the peak of the roof. I lay back on a hay bale and sang Joni Mitchell songs into the endless blue.

A younger boy named Everett hung out with me sometimes. We chewed the tips of hay stalks like we were two country kids who knew what we were doing. We hiked a trail circling a lake on the property where water skeeters skimmed the surface, dragonflies danced at the edges, and toads jumped from rocks to land with lusty splashes. Wispy white thistle seeds wheeled by like friendly ambassadors, welcoming me into their high mountain home. I resisted falling to my knees when I caught an intoxicating whiff of August pine and sun-warmed redwood. I hadn't known life could be this good.

One day I sat with Tony, the oldest boy in the outpost, on a rocky outcrop overlooking a sea of mountaintops as sunset softened the light on their jagged peaks. Tony was a wholesome redhead who looked like he could star in a skiing commercial. Listening to his stories about backpacking in Alaska while we smoked a joint I'd snuck into camp in a Tampon box, I felt happier than I ever remembered being.

I belonged with people who felt good about life and knew how to live it.

THE END OF AUGUST BROUGHT THE DREADED LAST morning in Trinity. It was time to roll up our sleeping bags, pack our duffels, and leave the kitchen and sleeping area looking like it had when we got there. I didn't like thinking of others living here after us, counting falling stars from their sleeping bags at night, talking and laughing until they couldn't stay awake any longer.

Everett was up and packing when I peeked out of my sleeping bag. Tony's belongings were already gone. The others lay cocooned in their down bags, looking reluctant to start the day. No one had talked about their lives at home all month. It was perfect. But those days were done. Reality had descended.

At breakfast, my little camp family met for the last time at the table in our kitchen. Disheveled was our usual look. Without mirrors, we didn't comb the night out of our hair and we didn't care. I sat watching a block of ice melt in the dirt by the emptied ice box. Cathy served us plates of scrambled eggs and toast while some of the kids talked about the horses they were going to miss. Cathy read us a poem she said she'd written the night before, with lines about each one of us and what we'd meant to her. About me she wrote, "Sue is joy and sorrow. She reminds me that light comes even to dark corners." No one had ever written about me before.

When the pickup truck was packed, Jim suggested we take a last walk in the woods. Everyone wanted to go. With Jim and Cathy in the lead, we followed a trail into the woods, people chattering as though leaving wasn't the worst thing they could be doing. I looked to the trees around us. *Can I stay with you?*

Hoping no one would notice how far behind I was getting, I slowed my pace. No one noticed. Then, without a plan or destination, I ducked off the trail.

After walking for a few minutes, I saw a circle of trees off to one side. Cathy had told us circles like this were families of trees. They were connected by roots under the earth's surface. I headed to that family, avoiding tangles of brush and stepping over fallen branches. When I reached the circle, I lay down in the center of it, my arms and legs stretched out like a windmill.

Years ago, in Sequoia National Park, my mother had said, "Listen." She knew the woods were sacred. And here I was, listening again, hoping this time the forest could save me.

Under and all around me, brittle pine needles vibrated with life. I knew their history. With time, green branches had turned brown and fallen, joining thousands more on the ground to disintegrate into soil that fed the trees that grew new branches that eventually dropped to become soil again.

Tomorrow would bring more dreary days at home in Los Angeles. I wanted to die here. It was scary to have that thought—and exciting, too. I wondered if I could stop breathing if I tried hard enough, and become a part of the earth I lay on. I decided to try.

After my next exhale, I lay as still as I could and tried to keep from inhaling again. It was impossible. On their own, my lungs filled with air. I tried again and lost, tried again and lost.

Cathy's voice rang out from somewhere too close by. She sounded worried. "Suzy! Where are you? Suzy!" She was coming closer. "Suzy! Come back!"

I looked into the treetops high over me, creating their own sky. Such magnificent presence. Such complete indifference. They couldn't help me. The forest would go on through this year and the next and for decades and centuries, whether I was here or not. It couldn't take me in or erase me.

"I'm here," I said finally, rolling to my side. "I'm right here."

THE LAST EVENING IN TRINITY ENDED BACK AT MAIN camp with Vespers, a nonreligious, spiritual evening on a grassy cliffside meadow. Campers and counselors came silently to sit together on the grass. There was no stage or moderator, but people took turns playing music on guitar or flute, reading poetry, and performing the occasional skit for a laugh. Presenters knew their order; it was planned ahead. When their turn came, they simply stood up, in the same spot where they had been sitting, to perform. Between presenters, minutes of stillness would pass before the next person would stand in the seated crowd to speak, sing, or play music.

At Vespers on my last Sunday, I sat alone in the meadow, watching broad-winged birds dive and soar across the canyon of sky with their wild wings spread wide before looping back for another graceful sweep. Golden sunlight kissed the mountain peaks and the coming night wrapped its darkness around their bases while lyrical melodies drifted in from the forested trail and campers came in to find their seats on the grass.

Just then, I heard someone crying. The sound seemed so out of place. Quickly scanning the seated crowd, I saw where it was coming from. My brother! David, whom I hadn't seen in four weeks, was walking through the seated crowd with his arms outstretched. He appeared to be looking for someone, or maybe he was just in despair.

I got up on my knees and called out, "David! I'm over here!"

He changed direction and headed my way. When he reached me, he fell into my open arms.

I drew him close. "What is it?" I stroked his thick hair as he sobbed into my neck. We had never hugged before. "What's wrong?"

"We have to go home tomorrow."

I squeezed him harder. "I know."

Another wave of sobs shook his body. "What are we going to do?"

Oh, my dear brother—my sweet boy. I hated that I was part of the problem he must feel he faced going home. I was also sure he knew I was the only one who might understand. A new feeling filled my heart. I wanted to protect him. This wasn't supposed to be how our lives went.

"It'll be okay, Dave," I promised, rocking him gently. "I'll make it okay." I knew I had to. I hoped I could.

At home again, no one said a word about camp. The house was stuffy, with windows closed and drapes drawn day and night. The living room reeked of cigarettes. I sat in my bedroom, gazing out the window at the static, unchanging street. Directly across from me was Ann's yellow and brick house, her barking dog behind the fence, the white sedan in the driveway.

I didn't know how much longer I could take it here.

After the trip with my dad to UC Santa Barbara to collect my things, I sit with him in the den. Jill painted this room a deep chocolate brown with a cream-colored ceiling to make it look bigger. I call it the cocoon room. A colorful Hundertwasser print my father likes, Bleeding Town, *hangs on the wall near his high-back chair. The print seems out of place, like a laugh track in a sad movie.*

My father's hands lie limp and empty in his lap. It's a wonder that even hands can look sad. "The coroner said most suicides happen on Sundays around four o'clock," he tells me.

I know that Beth, a next-door neighbor, said she heard two gunshots at four. I have nothing to say.

I feel sorry for him. He tried to help my mother in the only ways he knew how. He paid for mental hospitals and psychiatrists. He paid alimony and child support. He identified her body on the bathroom floor for the police. He helped his son pack a suitcase. He called Mom's family. And through it all, how much compassion did he get from Jill?

Mental illness? Horrible. His ex-wife? Worse.

When my father dies, twenty years in the future, and my uncle Leonard is gone too, I'll see a file my father kept in his office at home. The coroner's business card is in the file, stapled to a sheet of paper, along with a policeman's business card. That sheet of paper is a page of notes dated June 11. My dad has written, "She talked to Leonard today on the phone." Beside that is one word: "hopelessness." When I see that note, I'll be curious to know why she talked with her brother earlier on the day she died. Did he call her or did she call him? Did he know she was suicidal? And what difference would it make?

"It's been hard for your mother," my father says.

His next words spill out like a confession: "It was your mother who wanted the divorce, you know, not me."

My mother wanted the divorce, not him? Why is he telling me this now? We've never talked about their divorce, not once. Alimony and child support were about to end. Is he blaming himself for her death? Does he think she would still be alive if they had stayed married?

I can't tell him what she said long ago, that she couldn't stay with him if he didn't believe she was hearing voices and hallucinating. His refusal to believe her was a deal-breaker. When they first split a decade ago, the illness seemed to have gone away. She thought she could make it without him, or with someone else. But the illness came back and ruined her.

And there's more I can't say. Their styles were too different. He was more conventional. I will always remember the time we went hiking, when they were separated. My mother beat us back and sat cross-legged on his car hood, waiting for us. Before he could scold her for sitting there, she hopped off, singing out, "Hello, slow pokes!" I felt embarrassed by her because he was. But my mother was just being herself. Jonathan Livingston Seagull flying high. Doing it differently, doing it her way.

"It's not your fault, Dad," I say.

He looks devastated. I can see he really loved my mother, and not just once upon a time. I want to console him and I don't know how.

Jill is rattling pans in the kitchen, making dinner. The little time I have alone with my father is short and precious, saying and not saying things about what's happened. There's nowhere else I want to be. If only we could console each other. I'm wondering how to initiate this when Jill calls out from the kitchen, "Roger! Your dinner's ready!"

Our time is up. Like I'm not even here. This is what he's left with.

Chapter 17

My father married Jill the first weekend in September, on her father's birthday. The dress my mother bought me for it was floor-length and black, with a deep V-neck. I had a choice of black or maroon, and we both liked the black one better.

Grandpa Sherman was there from New York. My grandmother had died of a heart attack two years before, and he quickly remarried someone very different, someone splashy. That marriage ended in less than a year, leaving him a handsome, divorced widower at seventy-one.

The morning of the wedding, Grandpa drove to our house from his Marina del Rey hotel in a white rental car. He had what looked like an awkward conversation with my mother at the front door, then we headed out to the valley for the wedding. Grandpa Sherman smelled of cigars and Paco Rabanne aftershave, and the car did too. I rolled down my window.

The sun was already hot when we pulled into the temple parking lot at eleven o'clock. I stayed behind to have a cigarette and try to accept this was really happening, while the others went in. My father was getting married and my mother was at home alone. I felt like a traitor to her by coming.

Inside, seats surrounded an area at the center bordered by bouquets in tall ceramic planter boxes that looked like Roman columns. More than half of the seats in the place were empty. They wanted family only, my father had said, and there weren't a lot of us. Jill was an only child, and her daughter was too. Vicki sat by herself in a front row, looking as uncomfortable and uncertain as I felt.

"Where's Grandpa?" I asked my brother, taking a seat beside him. My sister sat on his other side.

David nodded toward the ceremony area. There was Grandpa, talking with Jill's parents for what may have been the first time.

Jill's parents were a sharp-looking British couple happy to have their daughter marrying well again. Her new husband was a Beverly Hills lawyer, for God's sake.

The ceremony went quickly—with music but no procession down an aisle, I was relieved to see. They recited their wedding vows, followed by the ceremonial crushing of a wrapped glass under the groom's foot. Mazel tov! Hallelujah and good luck. My father was married again.

THE WEDDING RECEPTION AT JILL'S PARENTS' HOME in Bel Air was mostly a party for them and their friends—I didn't see anyone my father's or Jill's age. Dressed in his cheery red vest, her father greeted each person at the door with a quick kiss on the cheek or a firm handshake and a backslap and pointed them in the direction of a bar set up in the living room.

Meanwhile, I wandered the house, wondering where to go. I'd never been in a home like this before, with paintings lit by a mounted wall light above them. Waiters with a linen cloth draped over an arm strolled the crowd, offering hors d'oeuvres from trays. This had to have been Jill's idea; it certainly wasn't my dad's style.

I looked for my brother and sister and couldn't find them. Maybe they were out taking a walk. My grandfather, the consummate New York gentleman, held court with a few attractive older ladies, a boutonniere on his collar and a glass of wine in his hand.

Eventually I gave up trying to make small talk and retreated to the guest bathroom. The room, however, was no retreat. It turned out to be just another room in this foreign country. Paper-wrapped soaps tumbled over each other in a crystal bowl on a black marble sink. A stone statue of a bird rested on a pedestal in the corner. Where in the world was I?

I jumped when a knock came at the door.

"Hullo in there!" It was a British voice; it had to be Jill's father.

I had met Jill's father a few times before. The man intimidated me. With a background in the Hollywood costume industry, he was all about good looks and biting wit, and I was a fourteen-year-old girl without a lot of either. I opened the door and sure enough, there he was—Mr. Jovial, holding a highball. He extended an arm for me to slip mine through.

"Let's have a little walk, what do you say?" he said. "I've got some photographs in my office that should interest you."

Not sure what else to do, I took his arm and let him lead me downstairs to his office for a tour of the mostly black-and-white photos decorating the walls. I appreciated that he was trying to put me at ease in what he rightly guessed had to be an uncomfortable situation. I hoped I could act right, whatever that meant.

He nodded toward a photo that showed him much

younger, posing for the camera beside a gorgeous actress. I recognized her immediately.

"Any idea who that great lady is?" he asked.

"Audrey Hepburn."

"Jolly right, that's who it is! And that's me right there. Can you see that?" He raised his glass like we were having a toast.

I had to admit he looked good in the photo, with a full head of dark hair and a sunny smile—and yes, the costumes in *My Fair Lady* were sensational. We oohed and aahed over other photos on his office walls with movie stars on movie sets.

Eventually I headed upstairs again, where I stopped by the bar table for a glass of wine before going outside to the deck. The house was in the hills, backing up to some scrubby terrain.

I leaned on the railing and sipped my wine, breathing in the scent of wild sage lifting on the breeze. So this was my father's new life. How very far from home he had gone.

AT BOB'S ON TUESDAY, I SKIPPED OVER THE WEDDING details and didn't tell him about camp or Vespers and what had happened with David. Instead, I told him I hated being home. I was suffocating there.

"I'm not sure how much longer I can take it," I said. I told him about trying to stop breathing when I was in the woods in Trinity.

Looking concerned, Bob leaned forward in his chair. "Can you move in with your father?"

That was a definite no. "He wouldn't want me to. Plus, he just got married to Jill."

"Right. I may have another idea for you."

He had a client, a twenty-five-year-old woman named Andrea, who had just moved out of her parents' house in Cheviot Hills. She lived in a small house near my school.

"She might like a roommate for a few months, while we look for something more permanent for you," he suggested.

Something more permanent? Leave home? What about David? What should I do? I was afraid to leave and sure I didn't want to stay. My gut said, *You better jump off this train before it derails.*

I took a deep breath and said the one word that would put this monumental change in motion: "Okay."

I hoped with all my heart it would be.

WHAT FOLLOWED HAPPENED QUICKLY. I DON'T KNOW what they said. I only know Bob convinced my mother I would be better off living somewhere else.

The next morning, she knocked at my bedroom door. She didn't look upset, she didn't ask questions—she just said, "You can go if you need to."

I'd like to think we reached for each other then and held on tight: *I love you, I need you, don't go.* But that's not what happened. I just nodded and looked away.

I wanted to believe Bob had tossed me a life preserver, but he hadn't. I was the Little Match Girl walking barefoot in the snow.

That Saturday morning, I packed a suitcase while my mother sat on the bed watching. She looked defeated. At noon she would take me to Andrea's house in Santa Monica.

What do you pack when you have no idea how long you're going away for? Or if you're leaving home forever? I chose a few pairs of pants, some favorite shirts, and two nightgowns. I added a second pair of shoes and counted out a week's worth of underwear and socks. My record albums would have to stay for now.

My top dresser drawer held half a baggie of pot and a chamber pipe. I covered them with a scarf and left them there. My bedside alarm clock would come, and so would three earrings. I had two holes in one ear and one hole in the other—unusual at the time, but that's what I wanted.

Lynne was out that morning, probably to avoid a goodbye to me. I was glad not to have that conversation.

I zipped my suitcase closed. "I guess that's it."

I knew we were both acting strong and I didn't want to break that spell, so I didn't reach out to hug my mother.

"Now I have to say goodbye to David." This was the next big hard part.

My mother said she'd take my suitcase to the car for me. "I'll wait for you there." She picked up my suitcase and left the house.

David's door was closed, as usual, when I went to say goodbye. I knocked on it, just below his neon name sign. "It's Suzy."

"Come in."

My brother sat on the bed, watching a ball game with two bowls on his lap. One bowl was filled with sunflower seeds, the other held empty shells. His horn-rimmed glasses and thick hair obscured his eyes, but he wasn't looking at me anyway. The TV screen had all of his attention.

"I'll be staying somewhere else for a while," I managed to say in a voice as weak as I felt. This was the great betrayal. I had made a promise I couldn't keep.

He spit a seed shell into a bowl and popped a fresh one in his mouth.

"I'll visit soon."

No reaction to that. Nothing. Just the sound of the basketball game, the crunch of seeds splitting between his teeth.

"I'm so sorry, David."

My apology sounded lame hanging in the air. I wished he would say something, anything, and make this easier. But he didn't.

Finally, I left. Walking out of the house, I felt like a colossal failure.

IN MY NEXT MEMORY SNAPSHOT, MY MOTHER SITS IN a chair in the living room of the house where I'll be staying. We're in a quiet neighborhood in Santa Monica. Andrea looks like she's in high school, with wavy brown hair in a ponytail and a pink cardigan sweater pushed up to her elbows. She's on the couch, pouting like a spoiled child, answering my mother's small-talk questions like all of this is a big bother for her.

My whole life is turning upside down and this woman seems to think these critical minutes are just a drag. She doesn't even try to help my poor mother make conversation.

We've probably been there fifteen minutes when my mother gets up, saying she'd better go now. Memory gives me that and little more. I get a vaguer glimpse of a goodbye hug before she walks out the door.

I know I stood at the window for as long as I could, watching her drive away. I hated having her leave me there, but I had asked for this.

What now?

"I need to tell you the house rules." Andrea motioned for me to follow her, and I did, moving in slow motion through outer space.

She led me down a hall to a bathroom we would share. "You can put your cosmetics bag here," she said, pointing to an area she'd cleared on a shelf next to a set of matching glass containers filled with Q-tips, bobby pins, and cotton balls.

"I don't have a cosmetics bag," I said.

Either ignoring that or just not hearing me, she continued, "Use the washcloth and towel I put out for you. And *never* leave your hairbrush out. I don't want hair in the sink."

I promised to never leave it out. We went to the kitchen.

"I don't have a dishwasher. You'll have to wash your dishes." She said this like it was an inconceivable truth, not having a dishwasher. "I don't want dishes in the dish drainer. Dry your dishes and put them away."

I promised to do that, too.

An oversized gumball machine filled with colorful gumballs stood in a corner of the kitchen. I was impressed to see it had a coin slot and a metal chute where the balls rolled out. For a moment I thought Andrea might actually be a little fun. "You have a gumball machine!"

She wagged a finger at me and narrowed her eyes as she warned me never to use it. "My father gave me that as a housewarming present."

In the living room, she showed me the couch where I would sleep. She wanted me to keep my suitcase behind it. She'd loan me sheets and a blanket.

"I leave for work early in the morning, which means I go to bed at nine thirty," she said. "You can watch TV, but not after nine o'clock. Do you understand?"

I did.

"Good. I'll make dinner."

With that, Andrea was off to the kitchen, rattling dishes a few feet from where I stood wondering what in the world I'd gotten myself into. It was only four days earlier that I'd told Bob how depressed I was at home.

I felt like I was running down a steep hill and the only way to stop was to fall.

ON MONDAY MORNING I WALKED THE FIVE BLOCKS TO school from this new location, feeling like a foreigner in my body. But I felt a little special too. I was only in tenth grade and I had a roommate in a little house in Santa Monica. I didn't live at home anymore. McCabe's Guitar Shop was within walking distance. I could look at guitar books and try out an Ovation guitar. My future might be uncertain, but maybe it was going to be better.

Every night I made the couch into a bed with borrowed sheets and pillow and blanket, and in the morning I folded up that borrowed bedding and set it on top of my suitcase behind the couch.

One night I dreamt of a giant butterfly flying in close to me. It spread its wings over my left eye and rested there. With that eye covered completely by the butterfly's feather-light wings I could see out of only one eye—my right eye, my stronger eye. Below my waist, above the front pocket of my pants, a safety pin the size of a hair comb clung to my jeans. I wanted it off, but the metal safety clasp was so big it wouldn't budge.

My pounding heart woke me up.

Before my dad puts the house on the market there will be a garage sale. First we have to sort through our belongings and decide what to toss, sell, or keep. We have one day to get this done.

Coming in through the front door, I shake off the ghost of a memory—saying goodbye to my mother in the entry hall three weeks ago, on Memorial Day. I imagine the others are seeing ghosts too.

"Take a few of these." My dad is doling out grocery bags Jill has labeled with a black marking pen: "giveaway," "garbage," "keep."

David heads to his bedroom carrying a stack of bags. He's the only one of us who still lived here; he has a lot to pack.

My sister goes to the hall bathroom. I don't see where my dad goes. I'm on my way to my mother's bedroom, the worst room I could go to and the only one I want to see. I don't want to sort through her clothes, I don't want to empty her dresser, I just want to be where she lived and died.

Her bedroom door is open. I turn on the light and look for bloodstains. They're here. Bloodstains on the wall where her pillows were. Bloodstains on part of the mattress. Bloodstains on the carpet between the bed and dresser. I take a step inside.

I know my dad and Jill cleaned up in here, but there's so much that can't be erased. There's a bullet hole staring down from the ceiling over the dresser. I shudder. She must have tried to die in bed, but things didn't go that way.

The coroner's report showed there were two bullets. The first bullet went through her forehead. It must have landed right there in the ceiling. I'm sure she was determined not to be found half-dead like last time, when I found her after she OD'd. She fired the second shot in the bathroom. I'm not going in there.

Turning, I see a loose piece of paper on the second dresser, the one by her closet. Can this really be what I think it is?

I pick it up and see a Hollywood address printed at the top and, next to that, the date. May 30. Below that, in handwriting:

.38—11-day hold

An eleven-day hold means she had this planned when I saw her last. That was Monday, May 29—Memorial Day. She went out and bought the gun the next day. On Sunday, June 11, my father took his son to The Gap to buy some new jeans for the summer. When they got back, David went for a two-hour run. He was captain of the cross-country team at Beverly High and he trained on weekends. At four thirty he was home again, and he lay down to rest in his room before going to Mom's room to ask about dinner.

A note taped to her door stopped him cold: "David, don't open the door. Call your father."

He opened the door.

I drop my forehead to the dresser and hold on with both hands. "Mom," I whisper. How am I going to get through this?

I lift my head and find I'm looking at her black-and-white print of a seagull. Jonathan Livingston Seagull.

I have to go.

Chapter 18

A third weekend at Andrea's was coming. With no stereo, I had no music. And I had no friends at school or from the old neighborhood. I was lonely.

Not knowing what else to do, I called Bryan. It wasn't that I missed him. I didn't miss him at all. He was just the one person I knew who might be willing to take a bus this far to see me. I told him where I was and invited him over for Friday night.

On Friday, Bryan took three buses to get from his house to Andrea's in Santa Monica. I introduced them at the door and was relieved when Andrea promptly disappeared into her bedroom after that.

It felt so familiar yet so wrong, being with Bryan in my new, temporary home. It was like spilling red wine on a beautiful white dress.

"Let's get some beer and watch TV," I suggested.

He liked that idea. We walked a few blocks to the convenience store on Pico. Beer was easy for me to buy at fourteen. Maybe it was my height, I didn't know, but people always thought I was older. Bryan waited outside for me and was impressed when I came out carrying a bag with two six-packs.

Back at Andrea's, we sat together on the couch watching TV while he downed one beer after the next, tossing empty cans into the paper bag at our feet. As I could have expected, having him over wasn't helping my mood. We had nothing to talk about. Around midnight, we lay down wrapped in each other's arms to be able to fit on the couch.

Which is how Andrea found us in the morning.

She went ballistic. "Get *out* of my house! Get out right now!" she shouted.

Bryan was up and out in a flash. She kicked the bag of empty beer cans across the floor, scattering them. "Bob said you were a sweet girl! He was wrong! You're not! You're terrible! Drinking beer in my living room! Having a boy stay the night!"

I hugged my knees to my chest and buried my face in them.

"I'm calling Bob. You have *got* to go!"

She stormed into the kitchen to make the call while I sat wondering what would happen. I couldn't go home again.

In no time Bob was pulling into the driveway in his orange 240Z. Andrea flung the front door open and pointed at me sitting on the couch with my knees drawn to my chest. I had thrown the bag of beer cans into the trash can outside, then collected my things from the bathroom and zipped my suitcase closed while Andrea watched, fuming. If smoke could have come out of her ears, it would have.

Bob came in looking concerned and curious, wearing jeans on a Saturday morning. Andrea launched into her tirade, shouting about the mess that was me. She looked desperate, like a little bird trapped in a room with a cat. "She had a boy spend the night! They drank beer! She used my gumball machine after I told her not to!"

"Be quiet," Bob told her, but he kept his gaze fixed on me. "Are you alright?"

Andrea went on with her list of complaints. He wasn't listening.

"Get your things," he told me. He turned to Andrea. "Stop it." And she did.

Bob ushered me out the door.

AT HIS OFFICE, I SAT IN MY USUAL CHAIR AND HE SAT in his. I couldn't look at him. I covered my face with my hands.

"I'm so sorry, Sue. I thought she was ready."

I felt a little dizzy, not fully attached to the floor by the chair I sat in. I couldn't breathe in all the way. I had failed Bob. Shameful. And I couldn't imagine what my mother would say when she heard about this. Kicked out of Andrea's after three weeks?

He apologized again. "You didn't deserve that."

All of me felt weary. I needed help but didn't know what to ask for. "How do you do it?" I asked finally, hoping for a hint about how to keep going.

"Do it?"

"Every day."

He sat back to consider my question. "I'll tell you. Every morning I start with a hot shower. I think about the day with the water pouring down the back of my neck. The water feels good. I think about what I want to get done and the order I'm going to do things in. When I get out of the shower and dry off, I'm ready to start the day. Awake, refreshed, interested in what's ahead."

His shower idea wasn't working for me. I never had days like that. I didn't have a list of things to get done and I wasn't that interested in having one.

"Can you stay with your father?"

"No. And he's still on his honeymoon."

Bob said he knew a boarding school near San Francisco that could be a good option. It was an alternative school like Horizons, with small classes.

I couldn't go to boarding school. That was for other people, not me.

"Is there a friend you can stay with until your father gets back and we can talk about what to do next?"

A friend? I thought of Nicki. She was my best bet. Bob said I could use the phone on his desk to call her.

Nicki answered, and when I told her what was happening and asked if I could stay with her for a week, she said, "Hang on, I have to ask my parents."

There was a loud bang, like she'd dropped the phone. I waited.

When she came back on the line she said I could stay the weekend but I had to leave Monday. Her parents would pick me up at Bob's office in an hour.

I felt like a lost dog.

Lying in bed next to Nicki that night, I took a free fall. I banged my forehead on the wall over and over—feel something, feel nothing, feel something, feel nothing. The pain felt good.

"Stop it," Nicki growled. "Let me sleep." I lay crying quiet, useless tears.

After that weekend, I moved on to stay with Nancy, a stoner friend from school. She was an odd one, with a lantern chin and deep-set eyes, though I did like some things about her. She called butterflies "flutterbys." It made sense. I also liked that she was willing to help me out, no problem.

A week later, my dad phoned me at Nancy's. He was back from his honeymoon and he was mad. "Where *are* you? I'm coming to get you."

I figured my mother or Bob had told him the story of these last few weeks. "I can't go home, Dad. I really can't."

"I know," he said wearily. "I talked with Bob. You can stay with us until we figure something out. Put Nancy's mother back on the line. I need directions."

I handed the phone to Nancy's mother and went to my friend's room to pack my suitcase. Things were definitely spiraling down.

IT WAS LATE OCTOBER WHEN I WENT TO STAY WITH my dad at Jill's house near Century City. She had a spare room upstairs, right across from their bedroom and connected to Vicki's bedroom by a bathroom with a door on each side. It was a relief to have a room with a door that closed, for the first time in a month.

The single bed in that room doubled as a couch with an ugly ochre cover and bolsters in orange corduroy. A metal file cabinet and still-sealed cardboard boxes belonging to my father shared a wall beside it. Besides those boxes, there was no sign of him in the house. A cushioned window seat overlooked a grassy backyard where Jill's little cockapoo, Lolo, liked to sniff around and frolic. I sat watching her, thinking of my mother at home. I had never meant to hurt her—not by doing this, not by anything I'd done.

There were rules at Jill's house, lots of them, and Jill was chief rule-maker and rule-keeper. I had gone to school barefoot the entire time I'd been at Horizons; we were allowed to. I liked being barefoot. If shoes weren't required, why should I wear them? My mother hadn't minded. Even my dad didn't say anything about it when he drove me to school on his way to work. But Jill wasn't having it. For her, I was an unwelcome guest, and my going barefoot to school was an offense she couldn't tolerate.

One morning, as I waited in the living room for my father to be ready to take me to school, Jill came out of the kitchen, where she was making an open-face grilled cheese on sourdough for herself and Vicki.

She pointed at my bare feet. "Where are you going like that?"

"School."

"And where are your shoes?"

"We don't have to wear shoes at school. I never wear shoes there."

"Well! You have to wear shoes here! Shoes are required in this house. Now go put your shoes on. And never leave the house without them again!"

Everything at Jill's was different than what I was used to. The phone was my only connection to the few friends I still had, and now, the only phone I could use was a shared phone in the living room. But lack of privacy wasn't the worst part. Jill enforced a six-minute rule for calls. If I didn't hang up after six minutes she'd walk over with a smirk, press the peg, and hold it down, rudely ending my call.

I had chores at Jill's. I had to change my bed on Saturdays. I had to wash and dry my sheets and make the bed again with them as soon as they were dry. And at six thirty I had to help Vicki set the dinner table, putting small side plates to the left of every place setting, whether we would use them or not. Forks went on a folded white or apricot two-ply paper napkin, knives were put with the serrated edge facing in, the spoon went to the right of that. Filled water glasses were set at the tip of the knife point. The salt and pepper shakers and the covered butter dish went in the center of the table.

I actually liked all of this housekeeping. I wanted to learn about it. But I never would have let on about that; I just did what I was told to do.

Like clockwork, at six forty-five every weeknight, my father came home from the office, went upstairs and changed out of his suit, came down and poured himself a glass of Scotch in the kitchen, and sorted through the mail Jill had left for him on an entry table in the hall. At seven, standing at her prized Wedgewood stove, Jill plated four servings of a dish she'd prepared, serving my father first and herself last.

WEEKS WENT BY AND NO ONE SAID A WORD ABOUT why I was there or for how long I would stay. I didn't see Bob anymore; there was no way to get to his office and then out to this house after school. And my dad seemed to think my problems were over now that I didn't live with my mother anymore.

How wrong he was.

Barry was a gay artist friend of Jill's from Venice. I'd met him at her art studio once or twice and I liked him. He wore a small hoop earring on the left and paint-spattered jeans and always had paint flecks in his dark curls. A decade later, when the AIDS epidemic hit, I would ask after him and Jill would snap, "Well, of course he got AIDS. What do you think?"

One night, when my dad stayed late at the office for a meeting, Barry came over for dinner. Instead of plating dinners at the stove, Jill brought three steaming plates of spaghetti smothered in tomato sauce to the table. She served her friend first, her daughter next, and then me. When she set the plate of spaghetti in front of me, she delivered it with searing words that would stay etched in my memory: "I didn't expect to get two Shermans when I married one."

I flew out of the room like my chair was on fire, glimpsing Barry's worried look as I passed. Upstairs, I dove face-first into my pillow and smothered my sobs in it. Didn't she understand? I wasn't trying to crash her marriage. If I could have been anywhere else, I would have been in a second. I hadn't expected this either. I knew the timing was bad.

When I heard my father come home sometime later, I was still lying on my bed in the dark with my clothes on. He would never know what had happened. I reminded myself I just had to get through this until a better arrangement could be made.

In the ghost town that is the hallway leading to my mother's room, I start with the bookshelf, filling paper bags with books. I drop Manchild in the Promised Land *and* The Autobiography of Malcolm X *into a "giveaway" bag. I remember when* Between Parent and Teenager *showed up on her shelf. I was too young to be the reason she bought it. Giveaway.*

Her yellowed collection of Louisa May Alcott books, dating back to her childhood, go into a "keep" bag. I read every one of those books when I was in elementary school. I open a book of poetry by John Keats, wondering which bag it belongs in. It was one of her favorites from college. Tucked inside, I find a folded piece of paper with a typed sonnet she wrote as a freshman when she was eighteen. It's called "On the Death of Janey Snow." The first part reads:

> How carelessly did Death invade my brain
> And bury all thoughts of Hope and Love
> It made its presence known with naught to prove
> except that separation brings wild pain.
> I see Death when I look at Life—in rain

That plummets to its grave from high above
And disappears

I keep the poem and put the book in giveaways. The Angry Book *is here too. I leave that book on the shelf for someone else to decide about. Years ahead, when my father dies, I'll find out he kept that $2.95 paperback in a file drawer in his desk at home. The book is a treasure chest, filled with reasons for the demise of their marriage detailed in my mother's penciled margin notes. I'll never know why he kept that book. When I look at it I'll see they were reading it when they were seeing a marriage counselor in the late 1960s. I recognize their therapist's name in one of her margin notes. In one note she's written, "Roger stifles his anger to avoid ruffling feathers and risking rejection." And in another, "He's a workaholic."*

On the last page, she wrote, "I love you, Roger."

My dad's script appears only once in the book, on the last page. It's an observation, nothing personal.

Below the bookshelves are two deep cupboards. Old purses fill most of one of them. I feel around inside their zippered pockets or pouches for any clues to her life. All that's here is the musty smell of leather and a psychologist's business card with an appointment time written on the back.

Her quilted sewing box is next. I know there is a pair of pinking shears inside it, a tomato pincushion, spools of thread, a measuring tape, a thimble. "Giveaway" bag.

Revealed on the shelf under the sewing box is something curious. It's an envelope addressed to Fannie Sherman, my dad's mother. The date at the top of the letter inside reads July 8, 1961.

"David! Lynne!" I shout. "Come here!"

In minutes, we're huddling around the desk lamp to read our mother's unsent letter.

"Dear Fannie, I am so unhappy with Roger. I love him, and I don't know what to do."

Just then my dad appears, peering over our shoulders. "What is this?"

He snatches the letter and takes off, ignoring our protests.

"I don't see why that letter belongs more to him than to us," I say to my brother and sister.

David looks weary. He walks away, headed back to his room to finish packing. Lynne sticks around to see what else might show up in the hall closet.

While she digs around in the back of the shelf where I found the letter, I notice a sketchpad I may have seen before—perhaps the sketchbook she brought home from day care at the hospital years ago and didn't want to show me? I take it before my sister can and go with it into the privacy of Mom's bedroom.

The first pencil drawing is a profile of an eagle's head. The single menacing eye looks terrified and terrifying. The hooked beak is a sharp dagger. Fear incarnate. A few blank pages follow. The next drawing is a brick well in an empty yard, with a bucket hung over the opening, a rope dropping into the depths. Isolation. The rest of the pages are blank.

I hand the book to my sister on my way out. "Don't let him see this."

Chapter 19

Some months before I moved out of my mother's house, I gave her one of my favorite Joni Mitchell albums to listen to, hoping the lyrics might speak to her like they did to me. I wanted her to be able to travel with Joni to other places and feel better, like I did listening to her sing. Music was my only currency for connection with my mom.

She gave me the album back, saying Joni's voice was untrained—it roamed all over the octaves.

"That's her style, Mom," I protested. "Try her again."

She didn't want to.

At my dad's, I listened to *Blue* and *For the Roses* on the old turntable in the room where I stayed, singing along to every song. "Michael from Mountains" had me dreaming of the magical mountain man Joni sang about. I wanted him to hold me through the rain until the sidewalks were dry, too.

And then, one day, I met him.

I was in a neighborhood park one summer evening, walking Jill's cockapoo. A bearded man with a ponytail left his volleyball game to fall into step with me. We exchanged names. We talked about music. He listened to the blues, he said, and named musicians I didn't know—Muddy Waters and Lightnin' Hopkins. I said I played guitar.

I had no idea this man would take me down a dark path that would end up turning my life around. I left the park with his phone number in my pocket, skiing on air.

Kurt was twenty-four, but our almost ten-year age difference didn't bother me. What bothered me was finding out his mother was in a mental institution. He'd been born there. He lived with his adoptive parents. He didn't drive. But what did I know about red flags?

I wanted to believe this was the man Joni had sung me into meeting. These details didn't fit with that vision, so I looked the other way.

We went to a guitar concert at McCabe's. We made out in the park. I agreed to go to his house one Friday night and stay over, sure I could get away with it. I would take a bus there, and his parents would drive me home in the morning. I would tell my dad and stepmother I was staying at a friend's house in my old neighborhood.

Kurt's parents were in their room when I arrived that evening. He took me to the kitchen for a cold drink. He had a new carbonated water machine he was excited about, and he poured tap water into it and pressed a button to make me a glass.

I didn't ask why he didn't make himself a glass of this "best stuff ever" too. Another missed red flag.

In Kurt's bedroom, the flag was waving, and it was big, but I didn't see a way out. He pulled his bedcover down, revealing bedsheets covered in nonsensical babble written with black marking pen. The man was insane. I'd missed the clues.

I had no bus money. I didn't even have a purse. Where could I go?

And then came the blackout. Memory has me taking a

seat on that mattress—the canvas for his craziness—and seeing glimpses of skin and nothing more. He had put a drug in that glass of bubbly water he was so excited to have me drink.

AFTERNOON SUNLIGHT STREAMED THROUGH THE bedroom blinds when I finally woke up. Kurt sat in a chair across the room from me, dressed and smiling like the Cheshire Cat.

I panicked. "What time is it?"

"Four."

"Four o'clock! Oh no! I'm so late!" I jumped up and frantically dressed while he sat watching, looking amused. "I need a ride from your parents!"

He shook his head. "They're out."

"Shit."

I ran out the door and up the street, afraid and with no idea how I was going to find my father's house from here. I saw a man across the street getting into his car, and I ran over to beg a ride to Santa Monica Boulevard. I knew that street was nearby and knew it passed through my dad's neighborhood, miles away.

The man dropped me at a bus stop in front of Vons Market on Santa Monica Boulevard.

Looking around, I could see I was in Hollywood, nowhere near where I needed to be. In the fading daylight I walked around the market parking lot asking strangers for a quarter for the bus. I knew my outfit was ridiculous (my mother's slinky maroon midi dress, no purse or shoes). No one looked convinced I needed that quarter for a bus ride home.

After a few minutes of getting nowhere, I went to the curb and stuck out my thumb. I had never hitchhiked before, but it was my only option. In minutes, a sedan pulled over, a balding, middle-aged man behind the wheel.

I sucked in my breath and got in.

"I'm going to Century City," I said as the man merged with the westbound traffic. "I'll recognize my corner when I see it." I knew that sounded lame, but I didn't know the name of the street that met Santa Monica Boulevard and led to my street, and I wasn't about to give him my address. I held onto the armrest, prepared to grab the door latch and jump out if he tried anything.

A pack of cigarettes sat on the console and I asked for one. A lit cigarette could be a weapon if needed. He handed me a cigarette and lit it with the car lighter. Then he made a sudden turn off Santa Monica Boulevard and started up a residential street.

"Stop the car!" I said.

His beady eyes looked lecherous. "It's fine. I'm just stopping by a friend's house for a minute to pick something up."

I pulled the door latch.

"Wait!" The man slowed the car to almost a stop and I jumped out and ran the half block back to the busy boulevard.

Heart pounding, I put out my thumb again.

My next ride was in a big white van with six rowdy Canadians who were in LA to play soccer and "have a good time!" They were fine about dropping me off at any corner I wanted. Again, I rode with one hand on the door handle. The second I saw my corner approaching, I called it out, and the driver pulled over.

"Have a great day!" he shouted, and the van joined the stream of traffic heading west.

I stood on the corner for a moment, reveling in my good luck. Then I started running. I ran five blocks through the neighborhood, powering through a painful side ache. When I reached the house I climbed the steep staircase and knocked, ready with my alibi. I had been at the beach with Marla, we'd lost track of time, the bus had come late.

Jill flung the door open, her eyes fiery with rage. "Wait here until your father gets home!" *Slam.*

Uh-oh. I sat on the top step, rubbing my side ache, suspecting I'd blown it.

Before long, my father pulled into the driveway and parked, then climbed the staircase carrying his briefcase. Jill must have called him at work.

"Hi, Dad," I ventured.

He sounded sad. "You shouldn't have lied to us about where you were last night."

My stomach turned over. "I don't know what you mean."

"We bumped into Marla. She had no idea where you were."

Bumped into Marla? I knew that couldn't have happened. Marla lived near my mom's house, too far away for them to bump into her. But I wasn't about to argue. My alibi was blown.

I followed my dad through the front door, passing Jill, who looked horrified to see that my father hadn't even raised his voice. I went straight to my room and closed the door. The maroon dress came off first—goodbye, horrible night. I didn't count the hours between Kurt handing me that drink and my waking up at four o'clock the next day, but I knew some very wrong things had happened.

I put on a pair of Levi's and a T-shirt and sat down on my bed with my journal. My journal that year was a spiral-bound notebook with a full-sized photo of a wish weed on the cover. I lay down with my journal and started to write.

I will never ever take a chance like that again . . .

I kept writing, begging a God I didn't believe in to *please please please don't let me be pregnant.* I couldn't imagine things getting worse, though I knew they could.

The door flew open. It was Jill, one hand on the doorknob.

"Whore!" she shouted. *Slam.*

Had she really just called me a whore? I had just had one of the worst nights of my entire life. This new punch she threw only added to the pain.

The door opened again.

"Liar!" she shouted this time. *Slam.*

That did it. My armor cracked. I cried as quietly as I could, my tears blurring the ink on the pages of my open notebook. What a mistake. I had lost my chance at a better life. How could I have been so stupid? The wet tissues were piling at my side.

Then the solution came to me. If I wanted a better life, I had to change.

In my journal I listed what I needed to do.

1. Give up my friends from the old neighborhood.

2. Do whatever they want from me at Dad's.

3. Break up with Kurt.

I prayed on the page again: *Please please please don't let me be pregnant.*

From Vicki's room on the other side of the bathroom I could hear late-Saturday-afternoon sounds from a normal girl in a normal house doing normal things.

The door flew open. It was Jill again, but this time I turned to face her, my journal open in front of me, my pen in hand. I braced myself for the next stone she would throw.

This time her anger was more controlled. It was clear she wasn't done with me, but she had calmed down. She put a hand on her hip and glared. "You have to remember one thing. I make a much better friend than an enemy. And you have a long way to go to change that." She closed the door hard, but didn't slam it.

THAT EVENING, JILL AND VICKI WENT OUT AFTER dinner, not usual for them. My father sat in an armchair in the living room, reading a contract balanced in his lap. I lay on the sofa across the room from him with my feet on the armrest and an arm over my eyes.

What a muddle I was in. I wondered if he was thinking about his daughter being with a guy all night. I had confessed to being with a guy I knew, not saying who it was or what had happened. There was no way to explain it. I knew, too, he might not be thinking about any of that at all. He might simply be worrying about his new problem. He had brought someone from Family #1 into the mix, and in doing so he'd messed things up with Family #2.

I started to cry.

In seconds, he was at my side, on his knees just inches away. I didn't look up when he put a hand on my shoulder. "I don't know what to do," he whispered.

"I don't know either," I whispered back.

What happened next? Did my father wrap his arms around me? Did he say *I'm sorry it's so hard* or *I wish I could help*?

I have no idea. The scene evaporates.

ON MONDAY AT LUNCH, I SAT ON A CURB ON THE RESidential street across from school and lit a cigarette. Nancy wandered over and sat down next to me. She lit a cigarette off mine and lay on her back on the lawn, blowing smoke streams into the air.

I noticed an empty soda can in the street. Wondering if I had the guts to use a blade on my skin, I picked up the can and twisted off the pull-cap. To test it, I lightly dragged the sharp edge of the metal cap across the skin between my thumb and forefinger.

Droplets of blood appeared to mark the line I drew. There was no pain.

I scraped a second line, coming at it from another angle. Still no pain. I turned the cap for a third angle, swiping across my skin. I watched this happen like I was seeing it from high above. I felt careless, detached.

Nancy shocked me back onto the lawn. "What are you doing?!"

"Nothing."

She sat up to get a better look and gasped. She snatched the metal cap from me and threw it into the street. "Come on. We have to get back to school."

I walked back to school with her, keeping my scratched hand out of sight.

I continued to hide it through the rest of the day. It wasn't hard to do. In music studio, my checked-out teacher with the big hair and handlebar mustache didn't care what I did as long as I tinkered with the piano keys in front of an open music book for the hour I sat there.

After school, upstairs in the spare room, I put on a Joni Mitchell album. Minutes later, Jill was calling me from downstairs. "Sue! Get down here right away!"

Oh no. I was in trouble again.

I found Jill in the laundry room with the washing machine lid raised up. "Look!" She pointed into the washer bin.

At first all I saw was the clump of wet clothes clinging to the center post. Then I saw the problem. Every hole lining the washer bin was packed with tufts of tobacco. White and brown flecks speckled the wet clothes. My cigarettes had gone through the wash cycle.

"*Clean this up!*" she shouted. "I don't want to see a single sign of this mess when you're done!" Then she noticed my hand. "What is this?" She grabbed my forearm to get a closer look.

I yanked my arm away from her. "I was playing with a cat at school."

I could see she didn't believe me, but she didn't press the issue. "Clean this up," she snapped.

And with that, she was gone, leaving me to figure out how to do what she'd asked.

Bob called that night. Nancy must have told the owner of our school what I had done at lunch, and the owner knew Bob.

"Your father said you cut your hand?" He said the last few words quietly.

"It's nothing," I assured him. "I wasn't trying to do anything serious."

"Can you come see me tomorrow at four?"

"No, I don't have a ride." I knew Jill wasn't about to take me there, and my father would be at work.

And that was the end of that. The incident was never mentioned again.

But conversations between my father and Jill apparently continued behind closed doors: What were they going to do with me?

ONE NIGHT, NOT LONG AFTER THE HAND INCIDENT, I was on the living room couch reading Hesse's *Narcissus and Goldmund* for English class. Vicki was in bed; Jill was in her room with the TV on. My father sat in the armchair on the other side of the room, looking at papers in his lap. The room was quiet. He wore a brown paisley robe over his pajamas. The homey time together felt good.

At nine o'clock I closed my book and waved goodnight as I got up to leave for bed. "'Night, Dad."

He set his reading glasses on a table by his side. "Can you stay a minute, Sue? I'd like to talk with you."

Was this going to be "The Talk"? He motioned for me to follow him into the kitchen and I did, wondering why he hadn't initiated this conversation sooner. We had been sitting together for an hour and all he had said that whole time was, "What are you reading?"

I knew plans had to be made for next year. I had two more years of high school. Jill didn't like having me live with them. Vicki never said what she thought about anything.

He closed the kitchen door behind us and faced me. He was six feet tall; we stood nearly eye to eye. "You said you wanted to go to boarding school."

Yep. Here it was. The Talk.

"If you still want to, I'll send you. If you want to stay here with us, I want you to know you have a home."

Had I heard him right? *I want you to know you have a home.* The earth turned a complete circle. In one moment. I had never dreamed of hearing those words, not even for a second.

To my father, what happened next may have looked seamless, but I had to reach across a gaping cavern when I held out my arms to fall into his. He held me close and rocked me, humming a sweet and tuneless melody—something that sounded like consolation for a lifetime of sorrow.

The last frontier in the house clear-out is the kitchen. I know the monkey candles from my thirteenth birthday, the "1" and the "3," are in the cupboard in there. I know I'm the one who has to decide what to do with them. But I'm not ready.

I start with something easier. The refrigerator.

I open the refrigerator and a sleeper wave hits me. There are a few items in there: a carton of eggs, two unopened blocks of cheese, a milk carton with an expiration date of June 21. She must have bought groceries recently so no one would guess she had plans to go and bring this house down.

I feel a little sick to my stomach as I close the fridge and turn to the bread drawer. I always hated this deep drawer when it was filled with creepy, moldy loaves. I open it with apprehension, knowing they may be here again.

There are loaves inside, but none, I'm relieved to see, are moldy. I discard them and dig deeper to pull out a couple of old cookbooks and an old metal index card box with the typed words "Yale Law Wives" taped to the front. Into the "keep" bag.

Among some scattered recipe clippings floating around at the bottom of the drawer is a yellowing baby formula recipe. Why is this still here? Sentiment? Disregard? "Garbage" bag.

I pull a chair over to the cupboard with the monkey candles and climb up on it. Fancy silver-plated platters are on the top shelf alongside other never-used serving items, probably old wedding gifts.

Next to those are the monkey candles. The future my mother will never see. Everything that's been shot away.

Holding the candles to my heart, I think of her standing right there next to me, smiling at me with so much love in her eyes. "We can use these again when you turn thirty-one. We'll just switch the order around!"

I keep her with me as long as I can—seconds only—then climb down from the chair and walk out of the room, leaving the candles on the counter for someone else to decide about.

Things have developed in the living room. My father has moved the vase with the sprays of pussy willows from the piano to the coffee table for the divide-and-keep when we're ready. He's moved the carved wooden chair from Ojai to the center of the room for one of us to claim.

Over the fireplace, a few birthday cards stand on the mantel. I see the one I sent, with a flower garden and butterflies on the front. I go to it and read my note to her inside (loving wishes for her future) and lay the card face down on the mantel.

The afternoon is late when we're done doing what we can to put our childhoods into bags to donate, throw away, or keep. My father drives us to Goodwill with the bags of giveaways. It feels good to be out, even doing this. It's been a long day. Thankfully, the hard part is almost done.

We return to the house to finish the job. Dad has it all figured out.

My brother, sister, and I sit cross-legged in a circle on the living room floor with the curtains to the backyard open wide. It's lighter in here than I ever remember seeing it before.

"I've emptied the 'keep' bags you kids made here on the floor," Dad says. "Go around the circle and take turns choosing what you want. I'll be right here." He takes a seat nearby.

Most of the choices about her belongings are hard to make because we're too young to know yet what we'll need. Lynne has her own apartment, but when will she need silver platters and linen tablecloths? Those unused wedding gifts from the 1950s aren't her style. David is in high school. I live in the dorms.

Our dad says he'll get a storage unit to hold everything for later.

For the first time ever, I feel like we're comrades as we go around the circle, taking turns, choosing from a collection we've all contributed to making. There's not a single argument. If one of us says we want something before it's our turn, the others immediately agree it will be theirs the next time their turn comes around. If anyone has memories of something, it's theirs to keep.

I keep most of the things my mother bought on her trips to Ojai. The piano will collect dust at my sister's apartment until I can send for it someday. The Martin guitar is saved for last. No one but me remembers her telling us she wanted David to inherit it when she died.

She had told us the day she called us into her bedroom to say that she had changed her will. It was right before Dad and Jill got married. I was fourteen. She told us she'd decided to be buried, not cremated, when she died. She didn't say why. I imagine she wanted to be remembered and was afraid she wouldn't be. David and Lynne left the room almost immediately—Oh no, Mom's talking about dying, gotta go—but I stayed to hear what she had to say. She was giving me and my sister each a bracelet she'd been given by her mother and mother-in-law, she told me. Her Martin guitar should go to David, because it was the only heirloom she had for a boy. That upset me. I was the only one who played guitar.

Now that the time is here, everyone is glad I remember what our mother wanted us to have. My brother says, "Let's share the guitar." And we do.

Chapter 20

In a storm, rivers widen narrow channels, draw new curves along the shore. Tree branches toss for turbulent miles before finally landing on dry sand. My life was like a river in a storm.

After my father invited me to live with him and Jill long-term, not much looked different: I still slept in the spare room, on a bed made to look like a couch. My dresser was a suitcase; a few shirts hung in Jill's mothball closet. Yet so much was changed. The new curve? I wasn't just "staying at my dad's" anymore. I had an address.

Rain fell for days, finally taking a break one weekend to lay a gray blanket over the city. I put a jacket on and took a walk up the street to breathe in the day.

Birds twittered in the jacarandas, whose spring blooms were long gone. Neatly tended lawns glowed a vibrant green. Near the corner, a garden bloomed with poppies. Their fragile, shivering, red-and-yellow petals floated on wiry stems. Puddles left from the sky's onslaught filled their centers. A few stems gave way under the weight of that water, bending down deeply, yet not a single petal touched the ground. The flowers were broken, but beautiful anyway.

NICKI WAS TAKING LSD WITH FRIENDS FROM SCHOOL, and she loved it. One day, she called to ask me over to see a painting she had stayed up all night making.

"I have a whole universe in my room!" she told me.

I had to go see.

Barefoot and glassy-eyed from either drugs or lack of sleep, she greeted me at the front door and led the way upstairs. She stepped aside at the doorway so I could look into the world she'd created.

A rainbow arced across a wall from one bottom corner to the other, touching the ceiling at the center. Within the frame of that arc, a galaxy of stars and planets glittered in bright reds and golds, some of the planets small, others as big as basketballs.

"What do you think?"

"Wow," was all I could say. Nicki was clearly traveling in a different orbit.

I was curious about LSD. When Nicki had started taking it a few years earlier, I hadn't wanted to try it. I was afraid of it because it was hallucinogenic. My mother hadn't liked marijuana because it made her feel like she did when she'd been sick. What if this drug triggered something in my brain that gave me what she had? I didn't want to take the chance of opening Pandora's box and never being able to come back. What if that echo in my head as a kid was a sign of things to come?

But Nicki had said you could really *see* on that drug, and there were some things I wanted to see. I wanted to see my mother beyond her illness. I wanted to know who she was as a person. And I wanted to leave my childhood home more consciously than I had when I'd left three months earlier, feeling like a deserter.

After school the next day, I walked up to the library to see if I could find out about this drug Nicki liked so much. I found *Me, Myself, and I: Psychiatry's Newest, Most Potent Drug, LSD* on the shelf. It had been published in 1965, when the drug was legal.

I took the book home and read it in a night.

LSD was clearly more than an amusement park ride for the mind. The author wrote about having twenty-three sessions with her psychiatrist using LSD, and making progress she had never been able to make with talk therapy. She hadn't slept well in years because of a tic in her neck that started the moment she got into bed at night. With her subconscious made more accessible on LSD, she was able to uncover the reason for the tic with the help of her therapist and ultimately overcome the problem.

Reading that book, I also learned that you could change habits on LSD because your subconscious was more accessible. I had smoked a pack a day for three years by now. I felt short of breath running for the bus in the morning, which worried me. For a science class experiment, I blew a stream of cigarette smoke into a petri dish to see what would grow on it. Within days, long wisps of freakish black mold appeared in a stripe across the container of clear gel. If cigarette smoke could do that in a petri dish, what could it be doing to my lungs?

I decided New Year's Eve would be a perfect time to try acid. New year, new start. I would take a hit of acid at my mother's house, quit smoking, and move out, consciously this time—and for good.

CHRISTMAS WAS COMING. JILL LOVED CHRISTMAS. Presents! Color! Cinnamon sticks simmered in a pot on the stove, filling the house with a warm and spicy fragrance. We brought a Christmas tree home from a parking lot sale one Friday, roped to the roof of her car. I'd seen people driving home with Christmas trees tied to the roofs of their cars all my life; now I was finally getting to be one of them.

My father didn't seem to mind the Christmas tree or that Hanukkah was completely ignored in this house. He hauled the tree upstairs and let Jill guide him in arranging it in a metal stand by the fireplace to "rest" overnight. But he did have his limits. After Jill's traditional breakfast of kippers dipped in bowls of vinegar on tree-decorating day, he left for the office well before the boxes of decorations came out.

Happy with their holiday task, Jill and Vicki oohed and aahed over the Christmas ornaments they brought up from the garage. Vicki's job was to hand her mother wire hooks and help her choose where to hang them. Mine was to sit on the couch and watch.

Jill clapped her hands like a schoolgirl every time another box was opened. "Fabulous! Vicki made this one in second grade!" She held up another painted clay ornament for me to see.

I did my best to act interested from my seat on the sidelines.

A week before, at a lunch out, my mother had given me a gift to take to my dad and Jill. "Be sure to give it to them before Christmas," she had said. "It's for their tree." I'd promised I would.

When the tinsel came out, I went upstairs for my mother's box. "This is from my mom," I said, handing Jill the gift.

She frowned and took the box. I watched her pull out the satiny red bow, lift the lid, and peek inside. "I don't want it." She gave the box back to me and resumed hanging strips of tinsel.

I felt punched. How could she do that? Turning away from her, I opened the box. Four adorable gingerbread men lay on a bed of green tissue paper, three small red candies lining their fronts like buttons. Christmas tree hooks were attached to black top hats.

"Throw it in the can outside," Jill said, not looking up. "I don't want ants in my kitchen."

I would never tell my father about this or ever mention it to my mom. I tucked that punch into the place where all my pain stayed, deep in my aching heart.

ONE AFTERNOON, I WAS IN THE KITCHEN, HELPING Jill get dinner ready. We'd had roasted turkey for dinner on Christmas, and now she was making a soup with the left-overs. The carcass simmered on the stove in a big pot with carrots and celery and a bouquet of fresh herbs tied in cheesecloth.

"Shoot!" she cried, turning the front burner knob on and off a few times. "It won't stay lit." She found a box of wooden matches in a kitchen drawer and the burner finally caught light. "Ha! Got it. Throw this out for me will you please?"

She handed me the smoking match. I took it from her and ran the tip under the faucet, then tossed it in the trash can under the sink.

Jill watched all of this from the stove, standing with a hand on her hip. "That was very careful," she said, with a tinge of sarcasm in her tone. "Wetting the match before you threw it away."

I went back to setting the dinner table. "Just makes sense."

A few days later we were in the kitchen again, making dinner. She wore her usual cooking attire: a button-up turquoise-and-white-checkered apron over jeans and a crisp button-up shirt. She always accessorized with an interesting beaded or silver necklace and bracelet, and her lipstick was freshly applied in anticipation of my father's return home at ten to seven. But something was different tonight. There were tears in her eyes.

"I want to give you something." She came closer and pulled a small jewelry box out of an apron pocket. Inside, perched on a bed of black velvet, were two gold and pearl earrings shaped like grape clusters.

For me? "Jill! They're beautiful!"

Sniffling, she wrapped her arms around me and gave me our first-ever hug. "You've changed so much. I love you."

I accepted her hug, feeling bewildered, and we laughed a little, brushing our sentimentality away.

"I want to put these in my room," I said. "I'll be right back."

Upstairs with the door closed, I stood holding the jewelry box to my chest. Jill had said she loved me. She had cried. I looked at the earrings again. They were way too fancy for me—gold with pearls. I would never wear them. I guessed they had been a gift to her and she didn't like them enough to wear. But giving them to me was huge. With this development, I knew I would do whatever it took to keep things this way. I would keep going with her to do the grocery shopping on Fridays after school. I would help in the kitchen with the cooking and setting the table. I would keep my room clean and do my Saturday chores. I didn't use the phone anymore; I had no one to call anyway. I could do this.

I tucked the jewelry box in the zippered pocket of my suitcase for safekeeping. Maybe her love was conditional, but I needed this life.

The garage sale is advertised in the newspaper for 8:00 a.m. Saturday, which means we have to get to the house by 7:00 to set up. My dad drives me and David. Lynne has a car and will meet us there.

As soon as we arrive, my father asks me to make a sign advertising the garage sale and post it in front of Hughes Market. He hands me a roll of duct tape Jill sent with him. "Tape it to a lamppost by the street," he says, then heads to the garage with David to set up a card table and put price tags on things while I make the sign.

I walk to the market holding the garage sale sign I've made and the roll of tape to put it up with, wishing, not for the first time, that I wasn't me. I pass Shawn and Vincent's house at the corner of the street, wondering if they even live there anymore and not feeling curious to find out. I know Mark and Alise's family moved away a while ago.

It's overcast but not cold on this summer morning, as I struggle to secure the cardboard sign to the curved lamppost so it faces approaching cars. "Garage Sale—Everything Must Go." I put the address below that.

Surreal. People driving by have no idea how awful this is. "My Childhood Home—Everything Must Go."

When I get back to the house, a few early garage sale shoppers are already in the house. I hurry inside to make sure my mother's bedroom door is closed. That room is off-limits.

Strangers wander the living room and kitchen, eyeing our belongings, hoping to find a deal. Some may live in the neighborhood. Tragedy rubberneckers. The back door is wide open so they can go out to the garage to see more stuff and pay.

Debbie comes by. She looks sad, and curious, like she has a hundred questions and doesn't know where to start. I don't want to tell her anything anyway. The last five years feel like an eternity. We catch up a little, tell each other we're in college, say where. After that, she hovers, watching the house she knew through her own childhood taken apart piece by piece.

Chapter 21

On New Year's Eve, my father dropped me off at my mother's at seven o'clock. David was at a friend's for the night. Lynne would be home. It would be the three of us.

No one answered when I knocked, but the door wasn't locked. I opened it. "Mom?"

The first thing I noticed was a bong on the coffee table. I'd never seen *that* before. The house reeked of cigarette smoke, as always.

I set down my overnight bag and the extra suitcase Jill had loaned me to pack more clothes while I was here, and called to my mother again. In minutes, she came out of her bedroom looking puffy and disheveled. She may have just woken up.

"Hi, Mom."

She gave me a listless hug. "Hi, honey."

Things seemed worse here since I'd left. I didn't remember the gloom being quite this bad. Holding suitcases in front of my mother didn't feel good either. I told her I needed to put them in my room and hurried down the hall with them.

I looked forward to being in my room again. I'd spent

so much time in there; in ways I missed it. But the sight turned out to be disturbing. No one had gotten it ready for me. The room was a mess. The bed was covered with a tangle of yellow sheets I didn't recognize and a couple of scratchy-looking blankets.

My mother had told me a guy my sister knew from the mental hospital was staying in my room and would be away on New Year's Eve so I could stay there. That must have been his bong in the living room. But leaving my room like this? It wasn't going to be hard to say goodbye in the morning. I was already gone.

Depression hangs heavy when it's trapped between four walls, and I could feel it in every room of this house. At my dad's, windows were open in the daytime. Jill put fresh flowers in vases around the house. Rooms were dusted, couch cushions were smooth and plump. This was how I lived now and how I always wanted to live.

At eight o'clock, I left my room to go to the garage. It was time to take the tab I had gotten from Nicki. The small square of paper with the hit of acid on it was tasteless on my tongue—in my mouth and absorbed in minutes.

I sat down on a dusty cardboard box to wait for whatever would happen next. More boxes were stacked against the walls and it was hard to see anything in there. The only light came from a single lightbulb hanging by the wall. I could make out my old red wagon in the shadowy dark, the one I'd tied my neighbor Phil to when we played Bonnie and Clyde. Deciding I was Bonnie *and* Clyde, I'd tied him up and left him in the garage in that game. That was the last time we'd played together. By then, his mother, Ann, had stopped coming over to visit with my mom over coffee.

I'd written down Nicki's advice about how to avoid a bad trip on acid, and I pulled the paper out and read it now: *If you feel a bad trip coming on, change your focus right away.*

I sat in the dim, dusty light until I felt my heart beating faster. When I closed my eyes, images swirled behind my eyelids. *Uh-oh, time to go.* I didn't want to come on in the garage.

In the house, I walked past whoever was sitting in the living room without saying anything and went straight to my bedroom. I took a wary seat on the edge of the bed. Taped unevenly on the wall beside me were two colorful illustrations that looked pulled from a desk calendar. I didn't like them at first. I hadn't put them there; it felt strange to see them.

Then I noticed the illustrations were moving. Fantastical colors flowed like water in intricate, intertwining patterns. I realized the guy staying in my old room must take acid. I wondered if my sister did too.

After some time, I knew I had to be brave and go find my mother. I wandered into the wasteland that was the living room to find her sitting in an armchair, looking like a sad queen on her throne. A full ashtray was balanced on the arm of the chair. Smoke rose from a burning cigarette in her hand. Across from her, the velour couch looked like a saggy, oversized basset hound. I tried not to laugh at the thought.

The best way to connect with my mother seemed to be by getting in front of her. I sat down cross-legged at her feet and from the floor looked up at her, full of love and apprehension.

How sad she looked on her smoky throne! Creases framed the sides of her mouth, melting into longer lines that dissolved into tears streaming down her chin and dripping off. Her whole face was crying.

I reached out with both hands, wanting to console her. "You're crying!"

My mother's sad melting face morphed into a scary mad face. "Are you on hash?"

Hash must have been the strongest drug she thought I could possibly take, and she could see I was on something strong. If I answered her question I knew I might laugh, and laughing would be a terrible idea right now. I looked away and the wall glided backwards and then rose up at a skewed angle. I had read that proportions could seem off when you were on LSD, but knowing that didn't help. I didn't like where things seemed headed. A bad trip couldn't happen, not here.

I reached for Nicki's tip in my back pocket once again. *Change your focus if you feel a bad trip coming on*, I reminded myself. I got up and took off for my room without looking back. Sam, our dog, followed me. I closed the door behind us.

The quiet of my bedroom was a relief. I already felt better. "Sam, come here." I patted the mattress and he jumped up, his tail wagging. "How are you, Sam?" I kissed his bony head and stroked his silky ears.

Sam's brown eyes looked soulful. I knew his thoughts! He wanted to run free.

"Do you want to go out?" He loved that idea.

Out! Out! I opened the window next to the head of my bed and watched him leap through it to disappear into the night.

Time to pack my suitcase. I opened the closet. Oh no! What chaos! Fallen shirts lay on top of a riot of shoes. Toppled planter pots had spilled loose potting soil onto the closet floor. Why were there planter pots in my clothes closet? Had I put them there?

I was ashamed to see I hadn't cared how messy it was in here. Ashamed that I hadn't even noticed. I pulled wire hangers out of the tangled mess and shook soil from the scattered clothes. With a hand, I swept the potting soil into a mound. And what delicious distraction that turned out to be. The soil was alive with rainbow particles.

Then I remembered I had something important to do.

Brushing off my hands, I abandoned the closet to face a bigger situation that needed cleaning up. One of the reasons I'd come here was to quit smoking.

I positioned myself in front of the full-length mirror on the back of my bedroom door, opened my mouth wide to see the tender flesh of my throat. *I breathe with this throat*, I thought. *I swallow with this throat. I sing and speak with this throat.* "My body is precious," I said out loud. I looked at the blue veins below my pale skin on the underside of my forearm. Currents of lifeblood coursed through this body. "I need to take care of you," I said.

Looking into my own eyes, I made a pact. Aloud, I said, "I am not going to hurt you anymore. I am not going to smoke."

What next? Going back to the living room to be with my mother didn't seem a good idea right now. I straightened the itchy blankets and sat next to them on the bed. Light trails followed my hands as they passed over the fabric. I was captivated, playing with streams of colored dust specks to see what they could do.

Just then, I heard a knock at my bedroom door. It was my sister. "Did you let Sam out?" she snarled.

I stood up to face her and kept my cool. "He wanted to go out."

"We don't let him out at night! You think you can come here and do anything you want!"

I knew I had to change things, and fast. "I'll get him! I'll get him right now!" I pushed past her, hurried through the empty living room, and left the house to search for our dog.

On any night, I didn't especially like the dark—but on that night, I didn't have time to waste worrying about possible phantoms lurking. I had to undo the damage I had done. I had to find Sam. But how far did I dare walk looking for him?

"Sam? Sam?" I started up the street, walking in the center of it so he could see me better if he was nearby. The houses I passed looked like lifeless boxes. I thought it must be past midnight.

I heard an airplane and looked up at the sky. Two ribbons of red light dragged across it. The hum of freeway traffic on I-405, a few blocks away, sounded unnatural. Motors were humming up above in the starless sky and down on the ground. What if I got lost out here?

I pulled Nicki's tip out of my pocket again. *Change your focus.* I turned and walked back to the white house with the black shutters in the middle of the block. My house.

Inside, the living room was dark. A ribbon of light glowed at the bottom of my sister's door. I tiptoed past it, went to my room, and quietly closed the door. Then I lay down on the scratchy blankets. Nothing bad dared happen.

WHEN THE SUN ROSE OVER A SLEEPING CITY ON NEW Year's Day, I put on my shoes. Both suitcases were packed. It was only six thirty, but I knew buses ran at this hour. I would take the #13 on National and transfer to the bus at Santa Monica Boulevard, traveling to where I needed to go: my new home with my father and Jill. At the bus stop, I would toss my pack of cigarettes into a trash can. I wouldn't smoke again for years.

In the hall bathroom, I splashed cold water on my face and went to my mother's room to say goodbye. On the way there I saw Sam curled up in the corner of the couch. Good. My sister, the night owl, must have let him in.

Quietly, I opened the door to my mother's room. She lay sleeping on the covers, her head at the foot of the bed, her feet up by the pillows. I couldn't begin to imagine why she was in this backwards position. A thick, black-and-white mohair bedspread cradled her like a hoary cocoon. I had hardly seen her last night.

"Goodbye, Mom," I whispered.

At the sound of my voice, one sad brown eye opened. Unfocused, it stared past me into somewhere so distant and so desolate I shuddered. If only I could protect her from her horrid life. I wanted to scoop her into my arms and hold her tight. I wanted her illness to disappear so her intelligence, her talent, her beauty, and her loving heart could be free to thrive. I wanted to say, "Mom, you're the one I want to live with. There's no one I want more."

Her gaze caught mine and held it for a moment, and then that one woeful eye closed.

"Is the whole set for sale?" a woman shopping the garage sale asks me. She's excited about the Encyclopedia Britannica *collection my dad gave me for my thirteenth birthday, happy or relieved I had asked for something so adult.*

"It is," I tell the woman. "The whole set's for sale."

She opens her wallet.

"My father's in the garage." I gesture toward the door that leads to it.

Another woman likes the oil painting of the tipped-over clay pot hanging over the mantel. "What a nice painting," she says with a nervous smile. "If you're ready to sell it, of course."

I've never liked that painting. I've always thought it looks like desolation. But I don't say that. I say, "My dad's in the garage."

At the end of a long day, my father finally says we can leave. He'll come back next week and take what's left to storage and Goodwill.

Three months from now, the house will sell to neighbors who *will spackle the bullet hole in the bedroom ceiling, repaint the walls inside and out, replace the carpeting, and rent it out. One day, the modest three-bedroom my father bought in 1962 for less than $15,000 will sell for $2 million. But at a time like this, who has eyes to the future?*

Chapter 22

After two bus rides across a still-sleeping city on New Year's Day, I was home in time to find my father, Jill, and Vicki at the breakfast table in bathrobes and slippers at 9:00 a.m. I waved from the doorway.

"Morning, Sue." My dad set his newspaper down. "Did you have a good time last night?"

"I did. Happy New Year."

"Happy New Year," said Jill.

Vicki murmured hello.

No one asked me to join them, which was fine. Saying hello was all I wanted to do. My dad got up to help me with the suitcases.

"No thanks, Dad. I can do it." I waved for him to stay seated and took the suitcases upstairs.

In my room, I stripped off the night and gratefully stepped into the shower. The warm water streaming over my skin felt delicious. I stood with my head under the spray, watching what felt like thousands of days of despair disappear down the drain.

When I was finishing dressing for the day, a knock came at my door. "Can I come in?" It was Jill.

I found her standing with the huge phone directory in her hands. "You need to make a dentist appointment."

"It's New Year's Day, Jill." I couldn't believe she was doing this right now.

"You need to get your dentist's phone number so you can call for an appointment first thing in the morning. Before school." Message delivered, she handed me the heavy book and left, closing the door behind her.

They must have had a talk last night about her new role as stepmother now that I was staying. I knelt on the floor and spread the phone book open to reveal a dizzying number of pages full of names and numbers. I had never made my own medical appointment before and she wanted me to do this today? She sure was big on sink or swim.

I turned page after page until I finally found my dentist's number. I wrote the number on a slip of paper and put the paper where I could find it in the morning. I was going to do this.

A FEW MONTHS LATER, AT THE DINNER TABLE, MY father had some big news. "Girls, we bought a house."

The floor dropped out from under me. They were moving?! I had been coasting downhill and hadn't seen this pothole coming.

"You two will have bedrooms upstairs and share a bathroom like you do now." Jill's voice was bright with excitement. "I want to take you to see the house after school tomorrow."

Wait, I was moving with them? This was not what I expected.

Vicki started to cry.

"What's wrong?" Jill tapped the table with a painted fingernail.

"I don't want to move!" Vicki sobbed. She was about to start sixth grade. She didn't want to have to change schools and leave her friends.

My father offered her a box of tissues from the phone stand by his side. Vicki cried harder.

"We need a bigger house," her mother said. "You'll like it, you'll see. We'll make your room pretty. And there's a swimming pool out back."

Vicki was a swimmer. She wanted to be on a swim team someday. But the news of the pool didn't sway her.

"I don't want to move!" she cried.

I watched the mother-daughter drama like I wasn't part of the same story. But I was. We were moving as a family. I would have a bedroom upstairs. I was really going to live with them. I felt like Cinderella with a ticket to the ball, and the night was young.

THE NEW HOUSE WAS A SPANISH-STYLE TWO-STORY in South Beverly Hills—a fixer-upper, Jill called it. "We're going to roll up our sleeves and get dirty this summer," she said when we drove there with Vicki after school the next day. She had been an interior decorator; she knew how to improve the look of the house upstairs and down.

In June, working together, the three of us yanked dusty drapes in the living room and carried them to the alley behind the house. We pulled musty carpets and got rid of them. Using crowbars like hammers, we knocked dingy brown tile out of the living room hearth and Jill replaced it with decorative blue and white Spanish tiles. We wore rubber gloves and spread a stinky chemical solution on the baseboards with paintbrushes. The caustic liquid blistered the paint so we could take it off with a metal scraper to show the natural wood underneath.

A housepainter painted the bedrooms. The master bedroom was a beautiful teal blue. "You should always paint your bedroom a color you look good in," Jill told me. My room was powder blue with white trim. Vicki's was a light spring green with yellow daisies on green shades. I sewed white lace curtains for the two French windows in my room and helped Jill paint flowers on a wrought iron headboard a friend of hers gave her for me. She hung an antique bookcase on my wall and bought a wall mirror and dresser at a secondhand store.

But it wasn't all perfection in paradise. The week we moved in, Jill and I came back from the paint store one afternoon to see a small potted tree waiting on the doorstep. It was a lemon tree.

"Oooh!" My stepmother clapped her hands. "A housewarming present!" She read the card tucked into the branches and dropped it like a thing on fire. "This is from your mother!" She called to the gardener planting zinnias in the front garden. "Diego!"

"Sí, señora?"

"Diego, take this tree away for me today. I don't want to see it again."

The lemon tree was gone before my father even knew about it.

I DIDN'T LIKE BEVERLY HILLS. WEST LA PEOPLE DROVE Fords and Chevrolets, not Porches and BMWs. The opulence in this city revolted me. I cringed seeing Rolls-Royces parked near the yellow cabs in front of the Beverly Wilshire Hotel, three blocks from our house. The rich leisure look turned me off—men with styled haircuts and white loafers, women dripping diamonds and walking in three-inch heels. Jill, in contrast, seemed excited by them and everything else around her. Beverly Hills was the end-all, everything she'd hoped for.

When we ran errands—to the stationery store for cards or to Gelson's, an overpriced, upscale market—I waited in the car while she and Vicki went in. I understood something about elitism, and I didn't like it.

To his credit, my father didn't seem impressed by the riches around us either. Wealth didn't woo him; work did.

How my father looked away from Jill's racism was something I couldn't understand. The first time I saw it we were riding an escalator up to the second floor in Robinson's. Two beautifully dressed Black women passed us riding down the escalator beside us.

"Ooh, they sure can look good, can't they?" said Jill.

I didn't like her comment or her tone. I had to speak up. "I can't believe you said that."

She didn't say a word back, but I knew she'd heard me. Her mouth looked tight.

Another time, before she and my dad were married, I made the mistake of telling her I was dating someone, as I rode in the car with her one day. I thought she would be impressed because he had a car.

"How old is he?" she asked.

"He's nineteen," I said. "And he's cute. He's about six foot two and he's Black—"

"You're dating a Black man?" She gasped. "What are you doing? You're saying your own race isn't good enough for you!"

I wanted to jump out of the car but we were on the freeway. Did my father know she thought this way? How could he miss it?

IT WAS MY SECOND YEAR AT HORIZONS, AND ELEVENTH grade started with a five-day retreat at De Benneville Pines in the San Bernardino mountains, ninety minutes southeast of Los Angeles. At the retreat, teachers presented on subjects we wouldn't have time for at school. I took yoga and got to walk in the woods with my roommate Liza.

At a swimming hole, Liza swam out to a dock to tan in the sun while I stayed in the cold water, dipping down until it came up to my chin. The chill almost hurt, but it felt good. I dropped my head back to let the glittering waterfall spilling over the rocks behind me rush through my hair.

That week, Celia, an art teacher, and Lara, my beloved psychology teacher, offered a self-awareness workshop inspired by the new book *Our Bodies, Ourselves: A Book by and for Women*. I arrived early for the workshop and sat looking through a copy of the book they had left on a table for us. Chapters were about reproductive health, the menstrual cycle, and the birth process, as well as sexuality, body pride, and self-empowerment. I'd never even heard of those last two.

A black-and-white photo on one page captivated me. There was a group of girls a little older than me sitting with their arms around each other. They looked so happy leaning against each other and smiling. One girl wore a beret. I wondered if they were lesbians. I tried to imagine how it would feel to be part of a group of friends like that.

In the workshop that day, along with about ten or twelve other girls, I sat on a yoga mat I'd spread out on the carpeted floor and listened as Celia and Lara gave a short talk about learning to love our changing bodies. Then they passed around speculums and handheld mirrors so everyone could have a look at their cervix—which, they said, was an important part of our body we never got to see. Uneasy laughter went around the room, and I was right there with it. Look at my cervix?

I left before anyone could try to talk me into using the speculum. Way too personal.

FIVE DAYS PASSED QUICKLY. ON THE LAST NIGHT OF the retreat, a dance was held in the dining hall. Liza didn't want to go, so I went by myself to see what was happening. I was curious about these kids at school who were so hard to get to know.

The dance floor was empty when I got there. A cluster of boys stood next to a DJ station near the back. I found a seat. Near me, Mo, Liz, and a new girl I hadn't met sat in a group looking bored. I thought of them as the Cool Clique.

Liz got up, holding an album she'd brought, and walked up to the DJ to have a chat. The other girls watched her go. She came back smiling. "He's going to play it!"

Mo punched the air. "Yes!"

Seconds later, a singer's raspy voice filled the room and all three jumped up to dance. I had never heard the music before, and I liked it. I sat grooving to it in my chair.

Mo waved me over.

Really? Those girls never even looked up when I walked by in the lounge at lunch.

"Come dance with us!" She waved me over again.

I took a deep breath and got up to join their circle, dancing and shouting out the lyrics with them when the singer belted, "G-L-O-R-I-A, Gloria!"

When the song ended, we went back to our seats to collapse.

Mo waved me over again. "Come sit with us." She tapped an empty chair beside her.

I had a good feeling about Mo. She looked cool pulling into the parking lot in her red convertible sports car, wearing mirrored sunglasses. Her blonde hair was short; her eyes were ice blue. Liz had long, jet-black hair and dark, judgy eyes. She had a way of looking put out, like she couldn't believe she had to be at school. Her father was a famous Italian actor; he ran with the big stars. She was too good for this shit. Up close, though, I thought she might actually be nice.

"So," she said, turning her chair to face me. "You like Patti Smith."

"I like that song."

Everyone nodded.

"Do you like Cris Williamson?"

That was Mo.

"I don't know her."

Liz frowned. "We brought her album too. But that asshole over there won't play it. You know."

I didn't know, but I commiserated with them.

The new girl introduced herself as Elise. She was pretty, with green eyes and auburn hair that cascaded in waves over her shoulders. Her skin looked silky. "Were you at that speculum workshop today?" she asked. "We thought we saw you there."

"We were going to go," Mo added. "Until we saw all those mats on the floor. We took off running."

They laughed.

I admitted I had gone. "But I didn't stay for the speculum thing," I added quickly.

More laughter.

Mo said I could borrow her Cris Williamson album if I wanted. I said I would like that.

And that's how I suddenly had friends at school.

On Monday I sat with Mo's clique in the lounge at lunch. She brought her Cris Williamson album, *The Changer and the Changed*, for me to borrow. I played it in my room every day, twirling in front of my big wall mirror. Just like "Song of the Soul" said: I wasn't dying, I was dancing.

I bought my own copy a couple weeks later and gave Mo her album back.

"So you liked it?" she asked, with a curious smile.

"I play it all the time! I bought my own copy."

And then, like it was nothing, Mo said, "Would you like to go out Saturday night?"

I didn't ask where to or what time and I didn't care. I finally had a friend at school. And she had a car.

ON SATURDAY NIGHT I RAN DOWNSTAIRS TO ANSWER the doorbell the second it rang, but Jill beat me to it. She opened the door, took one look at Mo, and shut the door in my friend's face.

"What are you doing?" I whispered. "That's who I'm going out with tonight!"

Jill looked disgusted. "Is she a lesbian?"

"I don't know."

"Where are you going?"

"I have no idea!"

It was obvious Jill didn't believe me. "Whatever you do, don't go to one of those women's bars downtown."

I had never heard of a women's bar, but I didn't say that. "We're not," I whispered, and I reached past her to open the door.

Mo wore denim overalls over a T-shirt, and she wasn't smiling. She was looking at her feet. "Hi, Sue." She started walking to her car.

I walked out without saying goodbye and hurried to catch up with her. "That was my stepmother," I said apologetically.

Mo didn't respond. I hoped Jill hadn't blown my evening with my new friend.

"So where are we going?" I asked.

"There's a great women's bar downtown I want to take you to. I think you'll like it."

I had to laugh. Quietly.

Mo parked in a dark alley deep in the heart of downtown LA. She walked with the confidence of someone who knew this place, heading for a brightly lit doorway where a woman in a jeans jacket and black motorcycle boots sat on a barstool checking IDs. I wasn't nervous; I was sure Mo would know what to do.

"Hey, Sandy." She casually gestured at me without mentioning our ages or showing her driver's license. "This is my friend Sue."

Sandy nodded, and we passed by without missing a beat. Mo must be a regular.

The door we entered led into a nearly empty room, where two girls danced at the center, entwined so tight their bodies seemed to breathe together. I recognized the song they were dancing to; it was "Sweet Woman," one of my favorites on the Cris Williamson album.

"I love this song!" I slowed to look at the girls. I had never seen two girls slow-dance together.

Mo kept walking. "Come on. There's another room."

The next room we entered was bigger, and it was packed with women. Girls sat or stood clustered around high cocktail tables; some sat on another girl's lap. Arms were wrapped around waists. Some couples were making out. Mo urged me on. She steered us to a table with a few empty chairs. And someone I recognized.

Elise stood up to give Mo a hug, smiling over her shoulder at me. "Hi, Sue!"

I couldn't believe what I was seeing. "Like a beer?" Mo asked. She excused herself to go to the bar while I sat with Elise, looking around and wondering what to say to her.

I thought about the album I had been listening to. Was Cris Williamson a lesbian? How could I have missed it? I had gotten here without even planning to come.

Mo appeared, emerging from the crowd at the bar with two frothy glasses of beer in her hands. She set them on the table and sat down.

"Thanks, Mo." I reached for a glass. Oh no! Instead of grasping it, in my nervousness, I hit the glass I had meant to pick up, dumping sixteen ounces of beer across the table.

Mo jumped up. Elise backed out of the way as beer spread across the table. The glass lay on its side.

"I am *so* sorry!" I cried. "I'll get a towel from the bartender!"

What could be worse? Humiliated, I fled to the bar.

The girls crowding the bar counter stood three layers deep. Bodies pressed in from all sides. If I tried hard enough, I could catch a glimpse of the bartender over the tops of everyone's heads. I waved a hand to catch her attention. She seemed to be flirting with a few girls at the counter. Her long ponytail almost touched the bar towel tucked in a back pocket of her jeans.

"Can I use your towel?" I called out to her. "I spilled my beer!" Ugh. Now everyone knew.

The bartender flashed me a smile and reached out with a towel. I took it from her, promising to bring it right back. I had to get to my seat as fast as I could to undo the damage.

Turning with the towel in hand, I found myself face to face with a girl I recognized from grammar school.

"Susie Gottlieb!"

Susie had been in my sister's grade at Mar Vista. I was sure she didn't recognize me. Back then, I'd been chubby, with thick short hair that stuck out. Now I was tall, with long, wavy hair, and I wore dark plum lipstick. Susie didn't look too different except that she was taller and had a crewcut now. I remembered her as a skinny tomboy who always sat alone at lunch. I hadn't seen her in years.

She cocked her head to one side and said, "M'name's Frank."

I could have fainted.

The mood was strained back at the table, with Mo standing up waiting and Elise looking a little out of sorts. I mopped up the spilled beer and was starting to tell the story of running into a girl from grammar school when who came sauntering up but none other than Frank herself. She headed right to Elise and swooped in for a kiss on the lips, then slipped into the seat beside her and pulled her chair up close.

"Hello, ladies," she purred. "How ya doin' tonight?"

"Just great," Mo murmured, keeping her eyes fixed on the dance floor. It looked like she was scanning for a possible dance partner.

On the drive home, I wanted to hear about Frank.

"I dated Frank last summer," she said. "Until she met Elise. But they won't last long. Frank goes through girls fast."

I stared at passing cars to keep from staring at Mo. There was so much I hadn't known about. As we drove on, she filled me in about the lesbian scene at school. I hadn't known there was one. That explained how Elise had gotten into Mo's clique so fast when she started school in the fall.

I got home just after midnight. There were no awkward moments in the car when we pulled up. Mo seemed ready to get the hell out of there. I'm sure I had been a disappointment, but I had far too much on my mind to feel bad about that.

The house was dark. I went inside and tiptoed upstairs, hoping no one would poke a head out to ask about my evening. Once I was safely behind my bedroom door, I leaned against it with a sigh. What a night.

Mo's clique were my friends at school for the rest of the year, but when Mo and Liz graduated in June they disappeared from my life. My friendship with Elise soon fizzled away too. But meeting those girls gave me a lot to think about.

In my journal that year, I pasted a photo clipped from a magazine of two men and two women dancing in a circle, their hands clasped and raised high in the air. Below it I wrote, "We're conditioned to be one way or the other, straight or gay. But I think everyone is really bisexual. And I am."

I didn't know where this new understanding would take me, but I was ready to find out.

I'm in the back seat of a cab, riding from the San Jose Airport to UC Santa Cruz on a winding mountain road. I feel like I'm in a picture in my Sierra Club calendar, with all these pines surrounding me, the blue sky overhead. We turn on Bay Street and climb a road through a meadow that leads into campus. From here I can see the small town and the Pacific.

In front of Crown College, the driver comes to a stop. "This is it," he says.

I open the car door. The second my feet touch ground, I know this is the place for me.

I'm enrolled in two classes for the next six weeks. In one of them I'll read short story collections by Fitzgerald, Hemingway, and Hawthorne. In the other, a writing class taught by a Jungian psychology grad student that I'll appreciate for the rest of my life, I'll get to write freely on soul journeys after guided visualizations. That three-hour class five days a week will turn out to be the best medicine I could take.

My room is at the back of a half-empty dorm building. I

have my few books, a metal-framed single bed, a desk, a closet, and a window that opens to scraggly trees on a hillside of dirt. Rain would be nice, but it's still June. I long for the sense of protection this bare room could give me in a falling rain. But it's just a bare room.

In the weeks to come, I'll read short stories and write papers about them in my room. Images of my mother lying in a coffin in the cold ground will haunt me. I can't help her! *Then I'll remember I don't need to. It's over. Done.*

Countless times, I'll cry, sitting on the floor with a book, and end up on my knees, face down and crying into my flimsy mattress. My heart is breaking. The person I loved most in this terrible, beautiful world is gone.

Chapter 23

Cigarettes were over, and so was smoking pot. But the weight of emptiness was still inside me. Food had been my ally and my enemy for as long as I could remember. Food entertained me. Food anesthetized me. I loved it and I hated it. And living with Jill, food was a new problem.

Temptations loomed around the house. In the kitchen, it was the cookie jar. Jill would put a cookie on a plate for dessert after lunch, or sit down with a cookie on a plate and a cup of tea at four o'clock.

I wasn't about to use a plate for a cookie. I didn't avoid the cookie jar completely, but I did avoid eating cookies around Jill. And the jar of roasted peanuts mixed with peanut M&M's that she kept in the living room for my dad plagued me. The container was clear glass, so I refilled it whenever it got visibly low and finished off the bags of nuts and M&M's in my room.

Jill's concern about my weight didn't help. Once she castigated me for eating "an entire" three-ounce can of tuna after school. Vicki was there for the interrogation.

"Who did this?" Jill held up the empty can for us to see. "You never eat a whole can, never!" She shook the can at me. "One can of tuna fish makes three servings."

I had to admit guilt. If I finished a three-ounce can of tuna after that, I always carried the evidence to the garbage can in the alley.

Sneak-eating had an edginess to it. After school, if Jill wasn't home yet, I went straight to the refrigerator. A Sara Lee pound cake was a constant presence at the back of the second shelf, its cardboard lid clamped tight with foil edging. I didn't even like pound cake, but I couldn't resist it.

I might start by opening the box and cutting a paper-thin slice from the tasteless loaf. After eating it, I'd wash and dry the knife and put it back in the silverware drawer and then replace the cake lid, returning the box to the exact place it came from. Next was a spoonful or two from a plastic container holding last night's leftovers, maybe a pasta or a stew. The cheese drawer was another safe bet. I could unwrap a wedge of Jarlsberg and shave off a few wafer-thin slices with the cheese slicer, then replace the wrapping and wash and dry the cheese slicer before returning it to the utensils drawer.

Bread was risky because she kept it in the freezer. Eating a piece involved the toaster oven. Defrosting took time, and crumbs were hard to sponge up quickly if I heard her car pull into the driveway.

Nerve-racking. Addictive. If I ate too many of my father's Fig Newtons in the freezer, I walked to Safeway and bought a new pack to replace the right amount so he'd never suspect.

Mistakes were unavoidable. Once, a peanut butter and jelly sandwich brought me to the kitchen for an interrogation. I had rinsed the knife and put it in the dishwasher. I had cleaned the counter of every crumb. I couldn't imagine how Jill could know.

"Did you have peanut butter and jelly?" She waved a sponge so I could see the purple stripe of jam across it. "That's a lot to eat after school, peanut butter and jelly. Too much. Don't do that anymore."

But her notes to me in the refrigerator were the worst. She'd leave them propped against containers of left-overs—"Sue, don't touch." I hated all of it.

After a refrigerator tour I'd go upstairs to my room, in pain from the overload. Lying on my side on the bed didn't help. I tried vomiting once, but only succeeded in pulling a tongue muscle.

And I couldn't stop. As soon as the pain in my stomach began to subside, like a zombie I was up and heading down-stairs to have a little more. I was amazed I was doing it, but I kept going anyway.

I came close to telling Jill about it once, mistakenly thinking she could understand. A friend of hers was married to an alcoholic. The woman left their toddler with him one afternoon and came home to find the child drowned in the swimming pool. Her husband was drunk.

"How can anyone be so out of control?!" Jill shrieked when she hung up after hearing the news. "He has no discipline!"

I took the moment to try to explain what I knew about addiction. I told her about the trancelike feeling I knew from my after-school eating binges.

Her eyes went wide and all she said was, "You need to have more discipline!" It was clear she didn't understand, not in the slightest.

Jill bought my clothes. At Ohrbach's, the dressing room was sadly the same ordeal it had been at Lane Bryant with my mother years before. I felt like a giant next to her, with mirrors in front of me and to the sides, showing all angles. I would fight back tears as she handed me yet another offensive shapeless blouse or pair of plain navy blue or black pants to try on. ("Dark colors are slimming!") She would tug the clothes into place and pronounce them a fit while I tried not to cry.

After that we'd go home with another shopping bag full of solid navy blue or vertically striped blouses ("never go horizontal"), grabbing some navy blue socks on the way to the register ("color lines should be continuous").

Even shoe shopping was a disaster. I wore a size 10—not unusual for a girl my height, but Jill didn't seem to care about that. In a shoe store one day, she grabbed a shoe I had just tried on and held it up, cackling like a mean schoolgirl. "It's so *big*!"

One day, after returning home from one of these godawful shopping trips, I sat in the den, too worn out to climb the stairs to my room. Shopping with my stepmother took everything out of me. Uncharacteristically, she came into the room, sat beside me, and, in as kind a tone as she could probably muster, said, "You really need to stick to your diet. You're wasting the best years of your life."

The best years of my life? I ran upstairs to my room.

THE SUMMER BEFORE I TURNED SIXTEEN, JILL ENrolled me in a driver's ed class at Beverly High to get my learner's permit. I made a new friend there, a wiry little guy with a goatee named Josh. Josh was short and clever, with a father who wrote the music for a popular miniseries. We dissolved in laughter over the teacher's name: Mr. Dodge. How had a driver's ed teacher gotten that name?

I liked Josh's sense of humor. He was a DJ at the school radio station, with a show called *Radio in the Nude*. He promised me a spot on his show as a guest DJ if I went to school at Beverly in the fall.

Wholesomeness had arrived on my doorstep. Josh asked me to see a play with him in Westwood Village and took me to Equus in Hollywood. We saw a movie one Saturday night in Beverly Hills and afterwards we kissed, leaning against his father's car. It was a disaster of mismatched heights. My attempt to lose ten inches standing with my feet set far apart didn't work too well.

We never tried again.

But romance was ready for me.

Nicki and I were out of touch by now, but she called one day to tell me there was a guy from school she wanted me to meet (read: unload). William had a crush on her, but she liked his friend Paul. Both boys had just graduated.

"William's a reader," she said. "He's just your type."

Curious to see my old friend and meet this guy she thought I'd like, that weekend I took a bus to her family's new apartment in Brentwood.

The apartment was modern, with a cottage cheese ceiling. I found the three of them waiting for me in her bedroom listening to music.

Paul was cool and cocky—just Nicki's type. Mr. Slick. His black hair was tied back in a ponytail that hung to his waist. Faded Levi's fit his slim hips and the flask in his back pocket held whiskey. He smoked hand-rolls.

William, in contrast, was tall, a softie, with fair hair, smooth round cheeks, and wide-set eyes as turquoise as tide pools. His hands looked like they had never done more than hold a joint, a hamburger, or a book. He seemed shy. And smart.

Nicki was right. I was interested. Anything I might do with a girl would have to wait.

We played the Velvet Underground while Paul rolled cigarettes using the Stones' *Sticky Fingers* album cover for a surface. When he was done he set six perfect cigarettes in a silver case and held it up for us to admire. "I'm getting to like having summer for the rest of my life," he said in a gravelly voice I was sure Nicki found sexy. "Let's take it outside."

Later, when the boys were getting ready to leave, I realized I had better make a move if I ever wanted to see William again. I found a scrap of paper and jotted my number on it. "Call me sometime?"

William looked surprised. "Why, thank you, Suzanne."

Suzanne. No one had ever called me that. On William's lips, the name my parents had given me at birth suddenly fit. I had been Suzy. I had been Sue. I was ready to be Suzanne.

MY NEW BOYFRIEND LIVED IN A LOW-RENT DISTRICT across the city, in a small, three-bedroom house with an overgrown, weedy backyard. The oldest of five, he had his own room while his three brothers—the youngest of them eleven-year-old twins—shared a room and his sister slept in a windowless cubby off the kitchen.

The third bedroom in that house theoretically belonged to his mother. Mostly, she was at her boyfriend's house or at the bar where he worked, BETTY'S Drink All Night PISTOL DAWN.

William's parents had divorced when he was six and the twins were babies. He barely knew the man. What he knew were collection agencies. When the electric company came a-knockin', the five kids hid in the closet until the doorbell stopped ringing. He laughed telling me about it, hiding and all that. The phone was turned off sometimes. He took it in stride. "Don't worry," he'd say when we finally spoke. "She'll pay the bill eventually."

William's mother left food money when she came to the house every few days, but the cupboards were bare. It looked like the kids lived on bread with bologna and mayo, potato chips, and chocolate chip cookies. Sometimes I saw Taco Bell takeout bags or a half-empty box of doughnuts on the counter. Once I took a peek at a soup their mother had left simmering on the stove. It was a watery brew of cabbage and carrots—maybe a chicken neck was in there too. Grayish bubbles collected at the surface. "Is anyone going to eat this?" I asked, replacing the pot lid in a hurry. William assured me they would eat it; they always did. I could see they lapped up their mother's meager attention like kittens in front of a bowl of cream.

Had I fallen for another broken boy? I had wanted to leave my seat on that trouble train.

William's room was big enough to hold a double bed and a dresser. A ceramic jug on top of the dresser held loose change and dollar bills—his savings account. He was also proud of his '64 Chevy Impala, though it needed water poured in the radiator every few hours when he took it out. Mostly, he rode the bus. They were cheap and someone else was at the wheel, which meant he could read.

In William's bedroom, "lost" library books, used books, and borrowed books were stacked high along one wall. The world went by while he read, his mind busy beyond the mundanities the rest of us lived with. Sometimes he laughed out loud when he read, even when he was walking. Somehow, he always managed to look up when the stoplight turned green or the bus was half a block from the stop. I never saw him without a newspaper or a novel to read in any spare minute, and that would stay true for the ten years we would spend together.

Besides books, movies were William's passion. He tried to talk about films with my father the few times they met, but my dad didn't read Pauline Kael like William did; he was on the business end, too busy to be a movie fan or critic. And no matter how warm and friendly my dad was, William felt shy around him because of my dad's stature as an attorney in the film business.

Jill did her best to be pleasant to William, but she was not impressed in the slightest. Sure, I had a boyfriend, but he looked like a hippie from the other side of the tracks, with his long hair and run-down Chevy. The day they met, she sniffed deeply and frowned. "I smell cigars."

Amazed, William admitted to having a half-smoked cigarillo in a back pocket.

As soon as Jill was gone, I whispered, "I told you, she can smell water boiling."

He assured me nothing like that would ever happen again.

THREE YEARS HAD PASSED SINCE I'D MADE THE PROMise to my brother in Trinity that I would make everything okay at home—only to move out soon after we got there. When I saw a flyer for a backpacking trip at the local rec center one day in April, I grabbed the chance to get him out of the house and into the mountains again.

That three-day trip over Memorial Day weekend changed David's life. He clicked with the other backpackers, all of them down-to-earth, athletic Beverly High students on an A-track to Ivy Leagues. He was starting high school in September, and they wanted him to come to Beverly High with them.

He signed up as soon as he got home, using our father's address for admission. He would remain lifelong friends with those kids. One would become a rabbi who would officiate at his wedding. Another would become a doctor who would say kaddish for our grandfather when he died at ninety-seven.

David would later call that weekend in the mountains pivotal; I would call it a promise kept.

With my last year of high school coming, I had to make a decision myself about high school. Beverly High was only a few blocks from home. I'd been sure I didn't belong at that school with all those snobby rich kids, but now my brother was going to be there.

I decided to change schools.

I HAD BEEN SEEING WILLIAM FOR THREE MONTHS, which to me at sixteen meant we were serious. I wanted him to come to the birthday dinner my mother was making for me in October. I wanted them to meet—but more than that, I wanted him to know this was where I was from, not Beverly Hills.

William said a bashful hello to my mother when she greeted us at the door that night and welcomed us into the house. I could tell by the smile she gave me that she liked him already.

Lynne lived in an apartment and had brought her boyfriend that night too. After saying a quick hello, they disappeared into her old bedroom and shut the door. My mother led me by the hand into the living room and the three of us took a seat.

David was in his bedroom, watching a game on TV.

"Dave?" my mother called to him. "Come say hello."

When he peeked out from his doorway, she tapped the couch cushion beside her. "Come sit with us. This is William, your sister's boyfriend."

He waved a hand to say hi. "Game's almost over. I'll be at dinner."

Conversation flowed between Mom and us three kids at the table that night while the two boyfriends sat quietly. Those boys could have thought we had dinner together and talked so easily all the time.

After dinner, my sister got up without being asked and helped our mother clear the table. She knew about the cake our mother had made and was excited about it. I wasn't used to seeing her like this. I waited at the table with the others while she helped light the candles in the kitchen and they carried the cake out, singing to me.

The cake my mother had made was her most spectacular one ever—and she hadn't made one in years. She'd baked the cake in a rectangular pan and cut it in the shape of a guitar. A round block of chocolate was the sound hole, long strings of licorice lining the neck were the strings, and six chocolate Tootsie Pops were tuning pegs at the squared-off top. Everyone applauded.

After cake, Manojit, the UCLA grad student renting my old bedroom, came home. He stopped in to the living room to say hello and gaily offered to take a photo of everyone. I didn't tell him we didn't take family photos, we never had. And yet no one protested. David ran to get his Instamatic 110 from his room.

"I'll watch from here," William said, and he took a seat cross-legged on the floor off to the side.

"Perfect!" Manojit pointed to my mother, David, and me. "You, you, and you, sit on the couch. You two, stand behind them."

Lynne and her boyfriend took their places behind the three of us on the couch.

In that one existing family photo—or something like a family photo—my mother sits between me and David, holding my hand and beaming like she's just won first prize. Dressed in a floor-length maroon dress with an embroidered bodice she bought me at an African dress shop after lunch one day, I'm wearing a smile like the Madonna. David looks very fourteen: He's just gotten his braces off and he has a soft brown mustache coming in. Lynne and her boyfriend wear red and blue silk-screened T-shirts. My sister's has a sleeping black cat on the chest. His has a picture of a heavy metal band, Iron Maiden.

This was my odd and fractured family that October night I turned seventeen, the last time we were all together.

I MET MY MOTHER FOR LUNCHES OUT, AND FOR DINners sometimes too. We liked a restaurant in Westwood Village called the Bratskellar. It was roomy, with two floors and hanging plants, and the dim light gave us a feeling of privacy.

I had a lot to tell her about my new school. In my poetry class we got to listen to Simon & Garfunkel songs and analyze the lyrics. In ceramics, I threw pots in a studio with twelve potter's wheels and shelves stocked with glazes. I was taking a psychology class, and a French class with a teacher who wore a beret. Business typing was picking up my typing speed.

Things were going well with William. He was funny, smart, gentle. She smiled hearing that he read authors I said I'd never heard of—Raymond Chandler, W. Somerset Maugham, Vladimir Nabokov. (She knew them all.) He read historical fiction, literary fiction, and crime novels. He wrote me love poems. Once, we lay beside each other on a grassy knoll above Highway 1 with the ocean in view to feel the energy radiate between us without touching. It was deliciously hard to do. Our song, "Miracles" by Jefferson Starship, said it all.

Music was a currency for my connection with my mother again, and it felt good. David Bowie and the trippy music of my younger years—Pink Floyd and Yes—was over for now. When Joan Baez played LA, we got tickets to see her at the Universal Amphitheater. During her encore, we sat enraptured listening to her a cappella rendition of "Amazing

Grace," her gorgeous voice soaring into the glittering night sky as we stood with thousands of fans holding lit matches high: "I once was lost, but now am found, was blind and now I see . . ."

Sam was sick and had to be put down that year. We'd had him since I was six. David had known him for most of his life. I went to the house to be with my mother and David the afternoon he died. Lynne wasn't there; she had a job as an ambulance dispatcher and had to be at work into the evening.

It wasn't only because of Sam that I felt sad that day—haunted, really. It was the look on my mother's face when she told us about their goodbye at the vet's.

"He knew he was going to die. I could see it in his eyes." She said this like it was something special she shared with our dog.

I was shaken. She had been at death's door before too. She'd recognized the look in his eyes. I wondered if I would ever see that look in *her* eyes. Would I know it if I saw it? What would I do if I did?

I'm in an office at UC Santa Cruz, making copies of a piece of writing to share with my class, when an old love song called "More" comes on the radio at someone's desk on the other side of the counter.

I stop what I'm doing. "More"? My mother used to sing that song at the piano years ago, after I went to bed. I've never heard it on the radio before, and yet here it is playing in the few minutes I'm here.

I look around to see if anyone notices. Of course they don't. I know something everyone around me doesn't. It's the great divide—me and them.

I quickly gather my papers and duck outside to sit on the grass and drop my forehead to my knees. Is this how it's going to be? Am I going to have to run from certain songs for the rest of my life?

At mealtimes in the cafeteria I sit alone, eating whatever I want. I don't care about calories or carbs anymore. I say to myself, My mother just died. *And take another bite.*

At an art store in town I buy a pad of watercolor paper, a palette of paints, a mason jar for water, and three brushes. Maybe I need something different—colors, not words.

I take my art supplies to Natural Bridges, at the end of West Cliff Drive. I want to capture the beauty of the glittering blue water meeting the sandstone cliffs, the contrast of moving water meeting static stone. But the scene I wanted to capture blurs into a wash of color on the paper. I don't know how to create that beauty.

I pull my brushes out of the jar and pour the blue water over the rocks. I don't even know what I'm looking for.

Chapter 24

Predictability can be a comfort when so much feels unhinged, and for my mother, routine gave her some of that. She shopped at the same market every week. She bought Crest no matter how great the sale might be on another brand of toothpaste. She served a simple dinner at six on the dot, no deviation. She fed the cats morning and night. When street construction in the neighborhood blocked her usual route, she didn't want to take the detour; she made a U-turn, went back home, and missed our lunch date. When I called her to ask if she was okay, she told me about the detour and said she was afraid she might get lost if she took it.

I didn't remind her she had lived in the neighborhood for over ten years, that she knew her way around. No point.

At school, I was making friends. Through Josh, I met Susan, a spunky, unaffected girl with straw-colored hair and a button nose. Halfway into lunch the day we met, she surprised me with the news that she was deaf.

"I read lips!" she insisted when I said I couldn't believe it.

Susan was an inspiration. Nothing held her back. Her laugh was contagious, her smile was sunny. She danced when we played records in her living room, feeling the beat through the floor. In a store, when a saleslady replied to me instead of to her, she told the woman, "I'm the one asking the question," and tapped her chest to make her point. Her older sister helped her make calls to me. "Suzanne! Do you want to go out with me Friday night? I can take the car!" She'd hand the phone to her sister to take my reply, then grab the phone again to answer or ask her next question.

I didn't dream of telling Susan about my life before I lived at my dad's. There was no reason. Everything seemed exactly as it needed to be. I didn't tell her about my mother's struggles, or the hard stuff I heard when I saw her for lunch one Saturday.

That day, my mother had looked worried.

"Dave wants to go to summer school next year at Andover."

"Andover?" I had never heard of it. "Where's that?"

"It's in Massachusetts. I'm sure he'll go to college on the East Coast, too—maybe to Yale, like your father."

The surprising part came next. Child support would end when David left for college. My mother's too-wide eyes said, *What am I going to do?* The only paid work experience she had was teaching third grade when they'd lived for two years near the Air Force base in Delaware. She'd loved it, and the children had loved her. Once, up in the attic, I'd seen a drawing one of her students had made her with a note in crayon on it reading, "Yer the best teacher." But I knew she couldn't be a schoolteacher again. Not now.

My mother always looked good on our dates together—her hair brushed, her lipstick freshly applied. Today, I noticed she hadn't taken a bite of her salad.

"Eat your lunch, Mom."

She poked at her salad with a fork. "I'm not very hungry."

"How about getting a job at May Company?" We had shopped at that store for as long as I could remember.

She shook her head no, she couldn't do that. "I check the classifieds every morning. Next week I have an interview at a law firm in Century City." She hoped her degree from Wellesley and her typing speed would make up for her lack of work experience. Century City was near Beverly Hills. She could take David to school in the mornings.

Conversation continued at tables around us—silverware clattering, glasses clinking.

My mother got the job. She had a paycheck. David had a ride. Things were looking up.

IN NOVEMBER I GOT A JOB TOO, MY FIRST, SELLING tickets at a movie theater a few blocks from home. The theater had been built in 1929, when stars arrived in Rolls-Royces for movie openings. Almost fifty years later, ornate chandeliers still hung on a high, ornate ceiling, and carpets upstairs and down were a plush burgundy. But the player piano was gone, popcorn was stored in giant plastic bags in a closet until it was needed for concessions, and there were bargain matinees on weekends.

Three nights a week I worked a four-hour shift in the stuffy sidewalk box office, wearing a terrible orange polyester minidress. I sold movie tickets, answered calls about movie times, gave directions to passersby on Wilshire when they asked, and stared interminably at the bright neon sign across the street advertising Nathan's Hot Dogs, waiting for my shift to be over.

For the first three months I worked there, *Tommy*, a rock opera starring The Who, played almost twice every shift.

When I finally escaped my two-by-three cage I was singing like Roger Daltrey—"*I'm free!*"

William got a job at the theater too, working the concessions counter. On breaks we made out downstairs in the dressing room and upstairs in the empty balcony seats. After our shifts he walked me home, leaving me to float upstairs, get into bed, and wait for his goodnight call.

I was writing poetry lately, inspired by E. E. Cummings especially. One Sunday at the Bratskellar with my mother, I shared a poem I'd written. In it, I described early mornings in my powder-blue bedroom with doves cooing in the trees outside the French windows. The first words of each stanza formed their own poem, read vertically. I was afraid she would feel uncomfortable hearing about my good life and knowing she hadn't been able to give it to me. Still, poetry was a language I knew we both understood.

As I handed the poem to her, I told her I was feeling a little nervous to share it.

"Thank you," she said. "I would love to read your poem."

I watched her read thoughtfully, then took the paper when she held it out to me.

"It's very beautiful," she said with a sad smile. "Show me your poetry anytime."

I promised I would.

But our blossoming friendship wasn't fated to last.

On my seventeenth birthday, my mother gave me tickets to a guitar series at UCLA. Every few weeks we were going together to see top classical guitarists—big names like Andrés Segovia, Christopher Parkening, Julian Bream, and John Williams. I had suggested we have dinner before every concert, at a different ethnic restaurant every time. We could try Indian, Japanese, Moroccan, Ethiopian, a restaurant with Spanish foods. She thought it was a great idea.

On one of our concert nights, we were crossing the lobby of the auditorium at UCLA when my mother stopped suddenly. She stood staring at the floor while concertgoers streamed past, headed for the auditorium, like we had just been.

"What is it, Mom?"

She opened her purse and pulled out a concert ticket. Without looking up, she held out the ticket and said, "I don't feel well. You go ahead. I'll wait here."

My stomach turned over. What could have triggered this? "I'm not going in without you, Mom," I declared.

She shook the ticket toward me. "Please go. I'll find a place to sit out here and wait." And then she said the dreaded words: "I feel anxious."

I hadn't noticed anything was off. Should I stay with her? Go in alone? She was the reason I'd come in the first place.

I took her hand. "We can leave."

"Please go," she repeated.

I looked around us. The room was enormous, with a polished wood floor. I saw two chairs by a wall near the bathrooms and pointed to them. "You can sit there, Mom," I said. "I'll find you after the show."

She kept her eyes to the floor. "Just go."

Unable to do anything to help, I took my ticket and left her standing stiffly in that spot.

In the crowded auditorium, I found our seats in the middle of a row and sat down, my heart pounding hard. Why was she anxious? Weren't her medications working? It scared me to think what this could mean.

Thunderous applause brought the star onto the stage. I watched him stride confidently across the stage to take a seat by his instrument. When the audience quieted, he began to play. I sat feeling gutted, unable to enjoy the music.

It felt so wrong to be sitting there without my mother at my side.

But before long, to my surprise, she was on her way to her seat, navigating our row while the audience applauded between songs. She slipped silently into the empty seat beside me and hugged her purse tight to her chest. She was here!

I leaned in and whispered, "Are you alright?"

She nodded, her gazed fixed on the stage like she didn't dare move.

Intermission came, and instead of talking about what we'd just heard and how amazing the guitarist was, we looked at our programs without a word. After the show we said goodbye at her car without mentioning what had happened, but now I knew a time bomb was ticking.

The next time we went out it was to Westwood Village to see a new movie called *I Never Promised You a Rose Garden*. I regretted having suggested that movie the second it started. What could I have been thinking? The movie was about a teenage girl with schizophrenia who was admitted to a mental hospital after a suicide attempt. Had I thought my mother would like the movie because she could relate to it? Bad idea.

In one especially disturbing scene, a loud, chaotic mechanical sound something like a racing train played. The girl was the only one who could hear it. She was hallucinating. I didn't want my mother to know things like that could happen, though of course I knew she already did.

Mom was riveted to the screen, her expression lit up like she was almost enjoying this. I, meanwhile, squirmed all the way to the closing credits.

When the movie ended, she whispered in my ear, "It's just like that."

I grabbed my purse. "Let's go."

FOR YEARS GROWING UP I WAS AFRAID OF PROWLERS. Recurring nightmares always involved my frantic rush to shut a window just as a man's hand reached out to force it open. Unsafe. Pursued. I had never been attacked, but a few times I had been followed.

In ninth grade, when I was attending Horizons, a man in a pickup followed me from the bus stop on my way to school. I was barefoot and wearing a long, Indian print wraparound skirt with a black button-up shirt tied at the waist, and I was carrying my guitar for music studio. The pickup truck was the only moving vehicle on the residential street.

When I told my mother about it after school that day, she was quiet.

Worse than being scared for my safety was having my fear of prowlers follow me to my father's house. With some of the perspective I had by then, I tried reasoning with myself. I had seen my mother frightened by invisible threats long before I was old enough to tie my shoes. But she had a serious mental illness; I did not. Still, I tortured myself wondering if my fears were learned or if the threats to me were real.

One night at my father's house, after midnight, I was startled awake by red lights spinning circles around my bedroom. A man's voice called out from the neighbor's driveway, below my open French window, "Come out with your hands up!"

I sat up and pulled the sheet to my chest. Sounds of a ruckus below came at the same time my father and Jill flew from their bedroom to run downstairs.

Minutes later, they were talking to an officer at the front door. I listened from the landing. There had been a robbery in the neighborhood. Police had chased the suspect down our street and up our neighbor's driveway. The suspect had been climbing the tree outside my window, trying to escape, when the police caught him.

"We have him in the squad car now," the officer said. "Everything's fine." Really? I wasn't fine. Whatever dividing line there had been between imaginary and real was gone.

The McHenry Library at UC Santa Cruz is a modern building in a forest where redwood trees climb to the sky outside three-story-high concrete and windowed walls. You reach that library by a shady trail through the forest, and I take that trail on my first week at summer school. I want answers. I want to learn about schizophrenia and the drugs they gave her for it. And whether I can inherit it. Suicide may have ended her life, but schizophrenia is what really killed her.

I start at the reference desk. The girl working there brings me a fat binder of psychiatric journals. "You have to read these here," she whispers in her library voice. I whisper back, "I will," and head off to the stacks to find books about schizophrenia.

It's crowded in here on a weekday morning. Students with daypacks slung over their shoulders wander the stuffy book aisles. I find a few books about mental illness, none of them with the word "schizophrenia" in the title or even the table of contents. I head upstairs, past a boy napping in a chair, hoping I'll get some privacy on the third floor.

Perfect. I come out of the staircase and into an empty, spacious room with floor-to-ceiling windows. I'm in the treetops. Removed. Private. I take a seat at one of the long tables and open the binder of psychiatric journals. It's obvious the articles and ads in here are aimed at psychiatry professionals. Just what I'm looking for.

My heart is thumping hard as I read names of medications I don't recognize. Then I find exactly what I'm looking for. An ad for Thorazine. It's a full page.

"At Last!" the oversized text at the top of the page boasts. "A drug to treat patients with schizophrenia. Most patients can function with regular treatment." Thorazine's great virtues are listed. Below them are the warnings: "(1) Patients should avoid consumption of alcohol. (2) Patients should never stop Thorazine suddenly or without medical supervision or catatonia can occur." My mother made both of those mistakes.

Possible side effects fill an entire third of the page: "mask-like face, loss of short-term memory, drowsiness, dizziness, inability to concentrate, blurred vision, confusion, psychotic reactions . . ."

Wait a minute. The drug was supposed to stop *psychotic reactions. I fling the binder across the table and watch it slide to the floor.*

High in this modern treehouse, I'm suspended in time. And sick to my stomach. My mother's doctor had her on a medication that could cause the problem it sought to cure? No wonder she took herself off of it when he wouldn't.

Steeling myself, I turn to my short stack of books about mental illness. The first one I open is so choked with convoluted language and jargon it's hard to skim. I'm stumbling over nails scattered on a floor.

Finally, I land on the word I want: schizophrenia. A few sentences describe it. That's all I get.

Ever since my mother was given her diagnosis five years ago, I've never been convinced her diagnosis was right. The illness seemed to come and go, or else she did an amazing job of hiding it from us for months and maybe even years at a time. If you can even hide schizophrenia. Her depression and anxiety, however, were year-round. Nothing I find today in the library helps me understand.

I dig deeper, eager to find information about heredity with this illness. And there's nothing here. Scientists don't know yet that schizophrenia tends to run in families. When they do finally know that, they will also determine there is no single gene considered responsible for the illness. That complicates things.

On my own, in my twenties, I'll make some important discoveries about heredity. In the summer of 1986 I'll stay with my brother for a month in Ithaca, where he's in graduate school at Cornell. Our aunt Barbara, who doesn't live far from Ithaca, will drive up to spend a weekend at David's house with us.

I like being with my aunt. I'll be surprised to hear my mother's laugh in hers. I'll also see my mother in the way Barbara sits, with one knee bent, bare foot on the chair, and the other bare foot tucked under her. We'll talk about her dogs and drink coffee, the way I'm sure my mother and I would have done.

On the second night my aunt is there, the two of us will go to see a new movie about Mozart called Amadeus. *Moments before it starts, when Barbara comes back from the restroom and takes her seat, she'll whisper in my ear, "I feel a little funny. I'm getting used to a new antidepressant."*

Did she say antidepressant?

As the theater goes black and Mozart's dramatic "Symphony No. 25 in G minor" fills the room, I'll lean in to ask, "How long have you been on antidepressants?"

"Fifteen years."

My stomach will be in knots through to the closing credits.

On the way back to my brother's house, I'll ask her about the antidepressants. She'll say she can't function without them, though she'll also be quick to add, "But I don't have what your mother had."

Can't function without them?

"Uncle Leonard has taken antidepressants for years, too. Did you know that?"

I did not.

In time I'll find out the genetic strings may have been even longer. Her grandmother, my great-grandmother, was known to stay in bed for most of the day when her daughters—one of them my grandma Friedman—were little. This was in a Lower East Side tenement in the days before electricity and indoor plumbing, and she had five daughters. Was she in bed all day because she was overwhelmed with so many kids in this foreign country? Was she depressed? Or was it something else? I'll never know. I'll only know for certain that her three grandchildren—my mother, my aunt, and my uncle—didn't slip by like David and I did when the genetic roulette wheel was spun.

Sitting at a table on the third floor of the McHenry Library, combing the pages of the last book I've found on mental illness, I see something worrisome that I also want to know about: age of onset. If a person is going to get schizophrenia, the book says, they can expect to see symptoms by age twenty-five. I wonder if my mom did. Then I think of the echo I heard when I was eight. Was that an early symptom?

I'll spend the next seven years on the watchtower, looking for signs.

Chapter 25

Six weeks after she was hired by the law firm in Century City, my mother was fired for not performing well (the words they used). She went back to the classifieds and right away found another job as a legal secretary, this one at a small law office on Westwood Boulevard. She asked me to stop in sometime to say hi.

The day I dropped by after school, the single-story office building was quiet as a library. I opened the door and took a cautious step inside. Vague scents of perfume and coffee hung in the air. There were no windows, open or closed, in the large room. Three secretaries sat at desks in front of typewriters. The office doors of the attorneys they worked for were closed behind them.

"Sue!" My mother jumped up, excited to greet me at the door. We had a warm hug.

"I'm just stopping by for a few minutes, Mom." This came out like an apology to the other secretaries, who kept their eyes on their work.

With an arm around my waist, my mother proudly steered me over to their desks. "Janice, this is my daughter, Sue."

So embarrassing.

Janice looked half my mother's age, early twenties. She nodded a quick hello and rolled a clean sheet of paper into her typewriter carriage. In a second, her fingers were flying over the keys, the rapid *rat-a-tat-tat* of the IBM Selectric ball sounding like a volley of bullets. The other secretary, Pamela, ignored us completely. I wanted to say to them both, *Give my mother a break. She needs this job.*

She lasted four weeks there.

SCHOOL WAS OUT FOR SPRING BREAK AND I HAD TIME to see my mother on a weekday morning. I wanted to know why she had lost a second job just a few weeks after getting it.

We met at Ships, a 1950s-style coffee shop in Westwood Village. There were built-in toasters at every table. The place smelled of burnt toast. I found my mother in a booth by the front window overlooking Wilshire Boulevard. Rays of sunlight slanted across her table through the venetian blinds. She waved me over and I took a seat across from her.

Her expression looked flat, her cheeks looked puffy. But it was her unfocused, too-wide eyes that were the giveaway. Not a good sign.

"What happened, Mom?" I asked gently.

Her reply sounded sadly familiar. "He knew about me." She looked baffled. "He knew about my car accident."

"What do you mean?"

"I was typing a letter for him, and it was right there."

I knew she'd had a small car accident a few weeks before. There were no injuries; it was just a dented rear bumper she'd gotten scraping against a cement column in an underground parking garage. "Mom, that letter wasn't about you. You barely damaged your car."

"I'm sure it was about me. I recognized the details." With her eyes, she implored me to understand.

Here was my intelligent mother, explaining nonsense like it was fact. It was the telescope story again. "They" got our phone number using a telescope from their hiding place in our backyard. "They" were back.

A waitress came to our table to take our order. She looked as uninterested in what she was doing as we were in ordering food. She repeated the order I gave her, tucked her pencil behind an ear, and was gone.

"I'm sure the other secretaries had something to do with it," my mother confided. "They didn't like me."

I had noticed the other secretaries weren't friendly. Maybe my mother had asked them too many questions. She couldn't even concentrate on a book; how could she type legal documents and file important papers in the right folders? Half of an entire wall in that room had been lined with file cabinets.

My mother told me more about what happened. This apparently wasn't the first letter she'd had to type that mentioned her car accident. "I decided to talk to James about it this time." She went on to tell me how she knocked at her boss's door, went in, and asked about it. He didn't know what she meant.

"It was right there!" she insisted. "I read it to him."

She was fired the next morning.

We shook our heads. For different reasons.

"Do you see this? My cheek is paralyzed. Right here." She pointed to an area by her mouth.

"I don't see anything."

"And my upper lip is getting paralyzed. On the right side too."

"Your face looks normal to me."

She leaned in to give me a better look, then dropped back into her seat. "And my eyes are bugging."

I hated to admit it, but her eyes did look too big. "Maybe your eyes *are* different, Mom."

"And I'm forgetting things. I get home from the market and see I already have what I went there to get. There are duplicates all over the kitchen." She sighed, looking grateful to have someone to tell. "I'm losing my short-term memory. These are side effects from the medication."

My stomach sank with a pitch of nausea; my chest felt tight. Around us, chatter continued and dishes clinked, a car horn blared outside the window, a hissing bus left a bus stop—normal sounds of the day—while I sat with my mother, hearing the worst news I could imagine. Her medication wasn't stopping her illness, and, worse, it was hurting her.

"I'm worried, Mom." What else could I say?

We sat quietly for a long while.

Finally, I found words. It was a daring thought. "Can you ask your psychiatrist to take you off the medication?"

"I asked. He won't let me." She looked into my eyes and the walls around us throbbed with the fatal danger of that truth.

COLLEGE ENTRANCE EXAMS CAME ON SCHEDULE, AND my score on the math portion of the SAT kept me from following in my father's footsteps to Yale or to any other East Coast Ivy League. Snowy streets and the tantalizing smell of hot pretzels at sidewalk stands outside the Rockefeller Center in Manhattan were not in my future.

The University of California seemed my best bet, and UC Santa Cruz was at the top of my list. The school was unconventional, with narrative evaluations instead of grades and science classes with names like "Bugs." It was in the redwoods near the ocean, and San Francisco was a ninety-minute drive. But I wasn't ready to leave William, who couldn't afford college and was staying in LA for now. I checked the box for UC Santa Barbara, two hours away.

By this time, Jill had become more to me than I could have expected. Teasingly, she introduced herself to people as my wicked stepmother. She signed her name in birthday and Valentine's Day cards with WSM—Wicked Stepmother. She called me her daughter when we ran into friends of hers at the market or the art museum. We bought bright bouquets of flowers in the flower mart at the Central Market in downtown LA and came home to arrange them in vases together. She gave me a flyer she found for a writing contest and encouraged me to enter it. She enrolled me in a class at a jazz dance studio. At the end of the school year, she told me to invite my school friends over for a make-your-own-pita-sandwich swim party. No one had ever taken an interest in me like this before. It felt good.

William was my date for the senior prom, which was held in late May at the Century Plaza Hotel on Avenue of the Stars. We would meet my friend Susan and her date, Carl, at the prom after a romantic dinner at The Mandarin, a Chinese restaurant a few blocks from the house. Jill wanted me to wear the long black dress I'd worn to their wedding a few years before. I had to admit there were cigarette burn holes in it, and I didn't tell her how they'd gotten there. I'd hung out drinking with Vincent and his friends at the garage the night of their wedding and didn't care if hot ashes fell on the skirt. She had a solution for covering the holes. We went to the fabric store and bought pink butterfly appliqués to sew over them.

In June, graduation was a showy ceremony on the groomed front lawn of Beverly Hills High, with a parade of long white gowns and bouquets of long-stemmed red roses for every girl. Our chairs faced an audience of parents who sat dreaming dreams their kids didn't know how to have yet. My dad, Jill, and Vicki sat near the front row. My mother and brother took seats at the back. I went to them first when the ceremony was over.

My mother hugged me tight. "I'm so happy for you. Congratulations!" With wet eyes, she handed me a card I would take home to read and put in a box of mementos that would stay sealed for many years.

After goodbyes to them, I left with my father, Jill, and Vicki to go to a garden patio restaurant in Venice. I sat in the back seat of my dad's car feeling a terrible mix of happiness and relief—high school was over—and sadness for my mother, who I knew was on her way home to nothing. A quiet house, another empty afternoon. My divided loyalties hurt. I was leaving the nest, and the mother bird was nowhere in sight.

Two friends on their way to San Diego give me a ride home at the end of summer school at UC Santa Cruz in August. They plan to take the coastal route, a ten-hour drive. I don't love the idea. I'm ready to get home: I want a hot shower in the privacy of my own bathroom and a night in my double bed with the painted flowers on the headboard. I want the dust of the last eight weeks to settle. But it's their car.

Susan is at school in Utah already. I'll see William tomorrow for the first time in weeks. My mother is gone. She's not there to call.

When I finally arrive, Jill answers the door with a ready smile, my father a few paces behind her.

"Sue!" she gasps. "What happened to you?!" She has to be talking about my weight. I've gained something like ten pounds.

I want to shout at her, "My mother just died!" But I don't. I just pick up my suitcase and push past her and my dad, who looks concerned.

"Hi, honey," he murmurs as I pass him. "It's good to see you."

Upstairs, I close the door to my room, drop onto the bed, and dissolve in tears. A few years ago, my father offered me a home if I wanted one. But that was only a Band-Aid, and I'm still bleeding.

Chapter 26

The Channel Islands took shape in the distance off the coast outside of Santa Barbara, appearing near the horizon line like a mirage. After our drive to my new home in the off-campus dorm, my father helped me haul two suitcases and my new electric typewriter into the elevator. We would make a second trip to his car for my books, records, and stereo.

Students chatted in the crowded elevator about their summers and people they knew who were here again this year, while newbies like me stood awkwardly, watching the floor numbers above the elevator doors slowly climb. My roommate, Wendy, was a mechanical engineering major from a small town near Sacramento.

When I was filling out my college application, my father had suggested I rethink my choice of psychology as a major. He thought I might be choosing that path because of my exposure to it over the years. Something else might be a better fit for me. I worried that he could be right. Did I want to spend my life dealing with people with problems? I changed my major from psychology to music and abandoned my dream of becoming an art therapist. Maybe I could learn to compose music and score films someday instead.

The second I opened the door to my dorm room I knew my roommate had gotten there before me. The bed near the door was an avalanche of huge black plastic bags holding what looked like a closet full of clothes on hangers. Shoeboxes stuffed with high school photos she would make into a collage on her bulletin board that week covered her desk, and an electric sewing machine sat next to them. There wasn't a typewriter in sight. She had no stereo or books either, just a TV.

"It's okay," I told my dad with a shrug. "I get the window side."

Two high-walled desks positioned back to back divided the room in half. My father put my suitcases by the bed on the side by the window. I set my typewriter on the desk and slid the window open as wide as it would go, inhaling the cool ocean air.

"Nice pool." My father was looking out the window and admiring the swimming pool on a patio six floors down. I would never swim in that pool or hang out with the bikini-clad blondes tanning themselves around it. I focused instead on the dark blue line past a grassy field on the other side of a two-lane road. The ocean was walking distance from the dorm.

Just then, my roommate barreled in, huffing and grumbling and smelling like salty peanuts she must have been eating in the car. She dropped a huge armload of black plastic bags on top of the sliding pile on her bed.

My father held out a hand and gave her his charming smile, ignoring the sweat dripping down her forehead. "I'm Roger Sherman."

Wendy begrudgingly grasped his hand by the fingers

and gave it a limp shake. "Hullo." She tossed me a nervous glance.

"I'm Suzanne."

She muttered hello and swiped at her bangs. "More stuff in the car!" With that introduction, she was gone.

I had a feeling someone in charge had played fifty-two-card pickup with the roommate compatibility form I had carefully filled out. I looked to my father for sympathy, but he skated right on—"Where do you want me to put your stereo?"

Soon we were standing in the parking lot by his car, saying goodbye. My father put both hands on my shoulders and looked into my eyes. "You're about to start some of the best years of your life." His eyes were teary. He held me close and rocked me gently. "My baby girl."

With a heavy heart and a smile for him, I waved goodbye as my father drove away, leaving me alone to face the rest of my life. College may have been the best years of his life, but I was pretty sure they weren't going to be mine.

A FRIEND OR TWO SURFACED IN THE NEXT FEW weeks. Kate was a creative writing major a year ahead of me with her own room three floors up. She wore overalls and had short hair, which didn't faze me but raised eyebrows around the dorm. She assured me she was straight, something I understood almost as much as I understood what it meant for me.

Kate sang alto in the school choir. When she heard I was a music major and that I sang, she suggested I audition for the choir. She waited outside in the hall for me when I did and was the first to congratulate me when I placed in the soprano section.

As far as my roommate and I were concerned, however, it was clear that we had no place to connect. She slammed the window shut the second I left the room. Masses of fabric overflowed from her desk onto the floor. She was sewing a quilt to enter in the state fair the next summer. A foil-embossed poster of Starsky and Hutch was pinned to the wall over her bed. A Bowie poster was pinned on my side. Wendy and I were from the North and South Poles, perfect opposites who would quickly discover the best way to coexist: She would use headphones with her TV, I would use headphones with my stereo, and we would avoid talking entirely. I didn't like it, but I knew how to do this.

On my eighteenth birthday in October, alone, I walked across the big grassy field behind my dorm, the rocky Santa Ynez Mountains in view, to reflect on the past year. High school at Beverly had turned out to be my best year.

I fingered the silver yin-yang medallion hanging around my neck, which William and I had had made by a jeweler in Westwood Village. We'd ceremoniously broken it in half on the cut the jeweler had made in it so we could each wear a half while we were apart. We were romantics who wanted to believe we were two halves that became whole together.

Sitting in the empty field without him, I hoped we were more than two broken parts.

IN NOVEMBER, THE THANKSGIVING HOLIDAY TOOK ME home for my first visit back to LA since leaving for school. I had no plan to see my mother; the long weekend at my dad's would be full.

Jill picked me up at the Greyhound station, ready with her long list of tasks on a yellow legal pad. New gold candlesticks had to be placed in polished candleholders. A linen tablecloth and gold-flecked table runner needed to come down from a cupboard along with polished silver serving platters kept shiny in Saran Wrap. I would set the dining table with holiday silverware and put wine glasses at the tip of each knife point. I would help make two turkey stuffings—one with chestnuts, a second with oysters. There were two kinds of pie: pumpkin for me and my dad, pecan for Jill's side of the family. Roasting the turkey was Jill's project. My father's was to bring in wood for the fireplace from the garage, mix drinks for Jill's dad, and open red and white wines to serve with dinner.

Another Thanksgiving tradition came the next day. After a final cleanup and plates of leftovers for lunch, it was time to sit outside by the pool for the annual dinner review with Jill. Sipping iced tea with lemon in tall glasses, we compared this year's turkey to last year's. We considered the two stuffings and the pies and rated her mother's cranberry sauce and green beans. We didn't mention my sister arriving two hours late, as usual. Jill seemed happy about her recent choice to keep Lynne's place set at the table but to let her eat there alone while the rest of us retired to the living room after dessert for Jill's annual tradition of playing "Alice's Restaurant," by Arlo Guthrie. This new approach meant that Lynne's lateness hadn't put as much of a pall on things, and my father and Jill hadn't quietly argued in the kitchen over Lynne sitting alone at the table to eat her dinner and pie or whether she could bring the pie into the living room with her.

When the Thanksgiving dinner review was done, I took the moment to tell Jill about my concert in December and invite her and my dad to it. It would be my first concert with the chorus; we were going to sing Handel's "Messiah" at a historic church downtown.

Jill's response was quick—"Oh no, we can't do that."

I acted like it was okay, which in ways, it was. My mother planned to come. "Okay," I said. "I'll see you for two weeks in December anyway, at Christmas break."

Jill dropped her spoon into her glass with a clatter. "I don't know that you can do that. We may be going away for Christmas."

"We"? Had I heard her right? I was clearly not included in that equation.

"But I don't have anywhere else to go," I said. "The dorm will be closed."

She stood up with her empty glass. "I'll have to talk with your father about this. I need to get dinner ready now."

With that, she left me by the pool with my bitter tea.

I was starting to understand. Last night, she had asked for the house key back. I had gone out to the car to get something and come in using my key. It was before dinner, and my dad was having drinks with her folks in the living room. Jill had taken me aside in the entry hall. Speaking in a whisper, she'd said, "You have to stop using your house key. You need to knock like everyone else. You don't live here anymore."

I didn't understand. I thought we were family. She called me her daughter. I had clothes in the closet and books on the shelves. Was her time card punched out, her wifely duty done?

Not sure what else to do, I'd agreed to give my key back.

I'm sure my father never knew about that one. I'd like to think he wouldn't have allowed it to happen.

It was like a game of musical chairs. The music had ended, and I had lost my seat.

IN SANTA BARBARA AGAIN, A WEEK OF HARD RAINS came. On study breaks I stood at my dorm room window watching cyclists fly along the bike path through the grassy field beyond the pool patio, their rain ponchos waving in the wind like yellow sails.

Choir rehearsed twice a week, on Tuesdays and Fridays. We practiced humming exercises, ran through the tongue trill and two-octave-glide warm-ups, and sang measures over and over, working with the four sections to get the choral blend just right. We sounded good.

On the day of the concert, I gathered with the other singers backstage at the old brick church downtown. My mother was driving up; William was already there, staying with me in a motel for the weekend. They both had the address of the church. I would see them soon.

Some of the singers were sucking lemon slices in the last minutes before the show to keep their voices clear. Kate offered me a slice, but I had to say no. I was too busy trying to quiet the butterflies in my stomach.

As we filed onstage to take our places in the stands, I scanned the audience for my mother. There she was in the center, three rows up. Lynne sat next to her, slunk down in her seat with a sour face. She must have driven up with my mother to keep her company. I hadn't expected to see her. But I knew my mother wanted to be there. She had performed the "Messiah" in college herself; she knew my part. And she looked radiant watching me cross the stage.

I was singing for her tonight. She was the reason for it all.

On the conductor's cue, the joyous chorus of voices filled the building like choruses had done for the last 200 years. "Hallelujah! Hallelujah! Ha-lay-ay-lu-yah!"

Our harmonies rang into the eaves.

After the show, I hurried to the lobby to find William and my mother. William and I hugged hello.

"You were great!" he said.

I thanked him and asked if he'd seen my mom. He hadn't. Had she left already?

I checked the bathroom, I ran out to the parking lot. And there she was, in the driver's seat of her car, Lynne glowering at her side.

My mother rolled down her window and reached out with a hand. "You were wonderful! Absolutely beautiful."

"Let's *go*!" Lynne barked.

"Thank you, Mom." I took her hand in both of mine and squeezed it. "Would you like to see where I live before you go? It won't take long. It's only twenty minutes from here."

Lynne wasn't having it. "*No!*" She glared at me. Her agreement to come on the drive to Santa Barbara was done; this had to be over.

"We have to go," my mother said. And with her eyes she added, *I'm sorry*. Or maybe she said, *Help*.

I touched her shoulder. "Thank you for coming, Mom. I really appreciate it." There was nothing else I could do. I watched the car leave the parking lot and disappear up the street on its way to the highway.

Two weeks before I start school at UC Santa Cruz I have an appointment to see Bob. It's been a few years, and there's something I really need to talk with him about.

On the day of the appointment, he opens his office door with a smile. His salt-and-pepper hair and beard are neatly trimmed, his blue eyes are twinkling. I smell the woods or something else outdoorsy and delicious on his pullover sweater when we hug. "It's good to see you, Sue!" he exclaims, and waves me inside.

The office looks the same. Books are propped on his desk between white marble bookends shaped like sailboats. I recognize his ivory push-button phone.

How will this meeting go? Sitting across from him in our

chairs, I'm reminded of the first time we met, six years and a lifetime ago. I'm nervous.

"So," he says. "Your father tells me you're transferring to UC Santa Cruz. My son went there. I think you'll like Santa Cruz."

"I do." I can barely look into his eyes. Then, without knowing how else to say it, I blurt the news. "My mother killed herself."

Bob gasps. He folds over, covering his face with his hands.

I tell him how she died, without mentioning the second shot, a detail that may haunt me forever. He's shaking his head.

After a few moments, he looks up, meeting my eyes. It's the Bob I used to know. Or is it? "I need to tell you something," he says.

I can't imagine what he'll say.

"Sue, your mother called me a few months ago to ask for an appointment with me."

I'm still taking that in when he adds the punch: "I couldn't do it."

My mother wanted to see Bob? I try to imagine why. Maybe she thought he would help her get off that medication. Her psychiatrist wouldn't do it. She must have been desperate. And Bob refused to see her. I can't believe it. If he had agreed to see her, she might still be alive.

I almost feel sick. What bad timing. I need Bob's help today. I need him to be my savior again. "It's okay," I lie.

"I'm so sorry."

We sit for a few moments in a terrible silence.

"How are you doing?" He sits up straighter in his chair, rearranges himself. It's time to get back to work.

"I don't know." That was a big curveball he just threw.

"How is your father?"

I shrug. "I don't know. My brother moved in with them."

"How old is he now? About sixteen?"

"Yeah, he'll be a senior in high school. He's staying in the back office, sleeping on a couch. They're planning to buy him a cot."

"Don't you still have a bedroom there? Can he use that?"

"I think Jill doesn't want a boy upstairs sharing a bathroom with her daughter."

I appreciate Bob's frown about that one.

I can hear the desk clock ticking. Our fifty minutes are precious. Bob is the only one who may be able to help me. "I need to talk to you about something, Bob."

"Please do."

The words I've held on to for so long tumble out. "I'm afraid I may be getting what my mother had."

There's the Bob I know. He leans forward in his chair. "Tell me more."

Feeling embarrassed to say it, I describe what inspired my call to him a few days ago. "A man in the car behind me was staring at me."

"How do you know that?"

"I saw him in my rearview mirror when we were at a red light."

"What was unusual about it?"

"It sounds dumb."

"It's not dumb."

"He looked scary. And he was staring at me the whole time we sat there. I turned fast at the corner as soon as the light changed so he couldn't follow me."

"Okay."

The next part is harder to admit, but I have to tell him if I want his help.

"I have these terrible fears, and they're getting worse. Like at my dad's, I'm afraid to go out to the garage to do the laundry. I stand at the back door for about five minutes trying to get the guts to go. Then I run out to the garage and do the laundry as fast as I can, and then run back to the house."

"What are you afraid of out there?"

This is the hardest part to admit. "I'm afraid a man's hiding behind the barbecue." Bob doesn't laugh, which I appreciate. "The barbecue is brick," I add, "and it's big. It would be easy to hide behind."

"Why would a man hide behind the barbecue?"

"I don't know."

"What do you think he wants?"

"To kill me."

"What makes you think that?"

"I don't know."

"What will happen if that man sees you?"

I'm twisting my hands together, ashamed of what I'm about to say and helpless to change it. "He'll jump out and stab me. Or strangle me. Sometimes he shoots me. It all happens really fast." It's such a relief to have told someone, to have told Bob, I'm almost trembling.

His gaze is fixed on me. After a few moments of sitting without speaking, he says, "Sue, it's possible someone's hiding out there. That could happen. But it probably won't. You need to remember this. It's possible *but not* probable. *Do you see what I mean?"*

I'm listening.

"As often as you need to, when you're afraid of something you think could happen, ask yourself if it's possible or probable. You'll know the answer."

"I don't know if I'll know."

"You will know." Then he says what I may have come to him to hear. I've told him my terrible secret, and Bob doesn't think I'm getting what my mother had. "People with an illness like your mother's can't distinguish between possible and probable, but you can. I know you can."

His next words make me cry. "You're going to be okay."

With every cell in my body, I hope he's right.

Chapter 27

Isla Vista, or IV as the locals call it, is a sleepy beachside community bordering the north side of the UC Santa Barbara campus. The town found its place on the cultural map after the burning of the Bank of America building there in an anti-war demonstration in 1970. A plaque outside commemorates the event these eight years later.

Times were different then. When I arrived in the late '70s, the seaside town was still a hippie hangout and surfer's settlement, with weather-beaten houses and loose dogs with bandanas tied around their necks wandering in the streets. Tanned, shirtless surfers rode their bikes to the beach with a board tucked under an arm, or kicked back with a cold beer on porches in the afternoons if the surf wasn't good. I liked to walk to IV from my dorm to poke around the health food store, an oversized barn smelling of decayed wood and aging produce, to buy fig bars from the bulk bin. Sometimes I looked for new arrivals at the used record store. No matter what I did in that town, I felt free. No one expected me home for dinner, no one asked questions about what I did today and how did music theory class go.

In January, William moved up, with a plan to apply to the UC as soon as he could get financial aid. He rented a ramshackle two-bedroom with two loser guys, one of them a greasy-haired kook who lived on Pringles and slept with an unlit flare on the edge of his bed "for protection." The other guy was a macho Italian dude from Queens with a noisy black Corvette. He had his own room. William shared a room with the Pringles guy.

Money was tight, but William and I traded records for cash at the used record store and he gave blood for money at the plasmapheresis center every few weeks. I sometimes snuck sandwiches for him from the dorm cafeteria, walking out of the room with two of them tucked into my sleeves. We were getting by, and it was working.

Nothing bothered my good-natured boyfriend, and I liked that. Two Vietnamese refugee families with a herd of noisy kids and a pile of used bikes moved in next door to him and William never complained.

"They've had a hell of a time," was all he said when I said something about the racket.

When Macho Dude knocked a hole in the bathroom shower wall trying to repair a leaky faucet and the sky showed through, William shrugged. "The guy's got a lot of hubris," he said.

I had to look the word up.

JILL SENT LETTERS TO ME AT SCHOOL NOW AND THEN, and so did my stepsister. Vicki complained that it was lonely at home without me. We'd had some fun together. I would always remember the time she was playing a record in her room I thought I recognized. It was *Sgt. Pepper's Lonely Hearts Club Band*—but that wasn't the Beatles singing it. I went to ask her who it was.

"It's Peter Frampton," she said. "I like it so much better than the Beatles version."

Version?! Our five-year age difference was showing. But usually it didn't, or it didn't matter. One year, for Jill's birthday, she helped me write fortunes to put in cookies we bought at Twin Dragon and make a treasure hunt; we greeted Jill at the front door as a couple of Chinese men, with center parts in our hair and pencil mustaches drawn in, and handed her the basket of fortune cookies. The treasure hunt led to the dining room, where a hot dinner from Twin Dragon waited.

My stepmother wrote to give a cheery wrap-up on her latest happenings. She was on the Christmas decorations committee for the City of Beverly Hills, in charge of creating the glittery banners that would be stretched across Wilshire Boulevard at every corner through Beverly Hills from Thanksgiving to New Year's.

One day, she sent a letter that put a fire under my butt, and not in the way she intended. She sent a clipping from the *Los Angeles Times* with a photo of a popular fashion model, Cheryl Tiegs, posing in a swimsuit. "Cheryl Tiegs is 5'10" and weighs 118 pounds," the caption read. "She used to weigh as much as 150 pounds." At the top of the page, in big underlined capital letters, Jill had written, "THIS COULD BE YOU!"

What a laugh. I weighed 180, thirty pounds more than the supermodel did at her highest. But the underlined words were the biggest insult.

I showed the letter to Kate. "You should come with me to an author reading this Friday," she said. She was seeing Susie Orbach, author of the book *Fat Is a Feminist Issue.*

I went to that author reading and had my mind blown.

Some of what I heard wasn't new: Diets don't work. But fat could serve a purpose? That was new. Orbach said that emotional eating could have a good reason. I liked the idea that I may not have been doing anything wrong all those years, when I overate for comfort living with my mother, or when I tried to fill up on crumbs living with a stepmother who didn't have enough love to spare for me and with a father who couldn't take the time. I had taken care of myself the only way I knew how. And it was okay.

Then came the pivotal question: Did comfort eating still serve me? If my answer was no, my eating habits would likely change and excess weight would fall off easily, like it had for the author.

I read the book that night. Realizing I was free at last to live differently, I decided to change my eating habits.

I dropped fifteen pounds in three months.

Before spring break in April I wrote a "let me be me" letter to my dad and stepmother. I told them I didn't want to hear, "How can you eat a whole container of yogurt? I can only eat half." (My dad.) I didn't want a review of my weight the second I walked in the door. (My stepmother.) And I never wanted to be compared to anyone thinner than me again or told, "This could be you."

My father called. With Jill on the line too, in his even, lawyerly tone, he said, "Thanks for your letter, Suze. I want to wish you well going forward."

Jill didn't say a word.

A month later, my dad called again. This time he had news about my mother, and it wasn't good. She had quit her medication without her doctor's consent and was in the Westwood Hospital.

Oh no.

He told me the story. After school, David had found her sitting on the living room couch, unresponsive, staring straight ahead. She hadn't moved a muscle when he called her name. He'd phoned our father, who'd hurried over from the office and found her in the same position, stiff as a statue. An ambulance had come. The medics had called her "catatonic."

"But she's back on her medication now," my father said. "She's going to be fine."

Fine? Really?

I knew why my mother had quit her medication. She was stuck between a rock and a hard place. She had asked her doctor to take her off Thorazine and he wouldn't. The medication was hurting her, even paralyzing part of her face, and she was still feeling anxious and depressed, and sometimes suffering from delusions and hallucinations. "Imagine that you could never take the blindfold off," she had said to me once, so long ago.

There was no point telling my father any of that. It was simply a sad truth, and he couldn't change that truth. "Thanks for calling, Dad," I said. "Let me know how things go."

That night, kids in the cafeteria chattered and laughed like their only worry was homework. I tried to act like everything was okay when all I could think about was my mother at the Westwood Hospital, having to take pills she knew were hurting her.

MEMORIAL DAY WAS COMING. KATE ASKED ME TO keep her company on the drive to LA, where she was going for the three-day weekend to see a friend. I said sure, why not. We could stop by my mom's house on Monday before heading back to school. I had told Kate about my mother; she wanted to meet her.

The moment my mother opened the door for us, I knew depression was hitting her hard. Her eyes were saucers, eerily vacant; her shoulders were slumped. She seemed so small in my arms when I hugged her hello. I introduced Kate. She said a strange hello to my friend—polite and flat, without expression.

She led us to the dining room, where we sat at the table in the muted light, the lacy floor-length drapes hanging over both windows.

I asked if David was home.

"David is backpacking with school friends this weekend," she said.

"Good for him," I said, and I turned the topic to Kate, hoping to give them something to talk about. "Mom, Kate's a creative writing major."

"Oh." She gave Kate a weak smile.

I suggested Kate tell her about the writing program at UCSB. Kate described the program—she was in her third year in it. I watched my mother try to listen, her gaze drifting from Kate to the wall beside her or maybe to somewhere out of sight beyond that.

Manojit came home, and he stopped by the dining room to say hi.

"Hey, good to see you again," I said eagerly and introduced my friend, happy for the distraction.

After they said hello, he went to his room and our strained conversation stumbled on.

I had planned to tell my mother I would be going to UC Santa Cruz for six weeks this summer and might apply to the creative writing major and transfer there. But she seemed so down that day that I decided to wait and tell her when I called on her birthday in a few days. I was pretty sure she wouldn't like to hear that I would be moving farther away.

I looked for something else to say.

"Finals start this Wednesday," I managed. "Then school's out! I can't wait."

My mother gave a desultory nod.

If I had known this was the moment I'd once wondered if I'd ever face—our last goodbye—I imagine I would have done things differently. But I didn't recognize the look in her eyes.

"Well, Mom." I stood to signal to Kate that it was time to go. "We have a long drive ahead of us."

My mother smiled for the first time since we arrived. No more pressure to be social. Kate looked relieved too.

We followed my mother into the entry hall, where Kate opened the front door. Sunlight spilled in. It was a beautiful, warm day outside.

"Good to meet you, Mrs. Sherman," she said. "I'll see you at the car, Suzanne." And Kate was out the door like she couldn't leave fast enough.

I faced my mother in the entry hall. She looked child-like, barefoot and listless, her arms hanging limply at her sides. She wrapped them around me and pressed her cheek to my chest. I held her close.

"I love you," she said, and her eyes were wet when she looked up at me. She knew her plans for tomorrow. This was our last goodbye.

"I love you too, Mom." I hoped she knew I meant it.

After climbing into Kate's car, I glanced back at the house. The front door was already closed. Feeling helpless and unfinished like I often did with my mother, I snapped the seat belt across my lap. "Let's go."

KATE STEERED US THROUGH SANTA MONICA AND turned north at the Pacific Coast Highway. Through Malibu and Zuma Beach, the midday sun lit the great expanse of blue to our left like a welcome invitation. Cloud shadows deepened the blue at the horizon line.

I pulled an 8-track tape out of a box in the front seat and put it into the player. "Can I turn the music up?"

"Go for it," Kate said.

I turned up the volume and rolled down my window.

Ah! The glorious, whipping wind. The gloom I carried from my mother's house lifted on it to burst into thunderous, glittering white froth at the shore. I rested an arm on the car door and drew waves in the air with my hand—up, down, up, down—inhaling the salty sea air, sighing with the release.

Change was coming. I would be in Santa Cruz soon. Finally, I would live somewhere that was right for me, near the mountains and the trees. Maybe I would become a writer. William could move up from Santa Barbara if he wanted. I was done compromising my needs to hang on to his love or anyone else's.

I leaned out the passenger window and raised my arms to the sky. "Two more weeks!" I shouted. The rest of my life was about to begin.

Epilogue

A suicide can turn your world upside down. Even though the criminalization of suicide is long outdated, the grief of suicide-loss survivors is often buried or ignored, silenced by the stigma that still surrounds it. My experience of the silence around the topic and the ignored grief is not unusual.

Historically, suicide was considered an irrational act, an offense against God, even a moral failure. To this day, death by suicide can be difficult—even impossible—to talk about in families of suicide-loss survivors, and compassion is often hard to come by.

Thankfully, the term "commit suicide" has gone out of common use, replaced with "died by suicide" or "took their own life." Still, within families of suicide loss survivors, suicide can be a death rarely mentioned if it's mentioned at all.

The same is true for mental illness. The stigma remains, even though, at the time of this writing, it is estimated that nearly sixty million adults in the United States—about one in four—experience mental illness. In 2024, deaths by suicide were reported at a rate of 14.7 per 100,000. Put the two together—suicide and mental illness—and the stifling silence around them becomes deafening.

I WAS PRACTICED IN NOT THINKING OR TALKING about what you have read in the pages of this book. And then two pivotal events happened in the first years after my mother's death.

For seven years, I stayed on the watchtower, scouting for signs that I might be getting what she had. To manage my fears, I tried out Bob's suggestion with some success—ask yourself if something you fear happening is possible or probable.

On my twenty-sixth birthday, when I passed the then-recognized usual age of onset of schizophrenia symptom-free, I climbed down from the watchtower and looked around. I was in my first year in an MFA program, writing a one-act play about three siblings whose mentally ill mother died by suicide. One had written a letter to the other two telling them that if she were to get the illness their mother had, she would end her life too. She wanted them to know she'd written this letter when she was well and thinking clearly.

The day after my twenty-sixth birthday, I put the unfinished play in a drawer, opened the phone book, and called Suicide Prevention.

I wanted help. I needed to talk to other people who had lost a parent or other loved one to suicide. I hoped for camaraderie and support.

The woman who answered the Suicide Prevention hotline told me suicide-loss survivors had meetings around the city. I could find one near where I lived.

The meeting was helpful, and disturbing. Grief is different when it's new, and it was new for most of the people there. Their pain was raw. I decided I didn't belong there.

Going to the meeting a few times, however, helped me realize there was something important I needed to do. I was done tempting forever with the unresolved: My mother still didn't have a headstone on her grave. My conflict-avoidant father, a man who'd been suppressing his grief and guilt over his ex-wife's death since the day she died, had let this go by. For eight years.

I called him that Sunday and told him I had something serious to ask.

"Yeeeessss?" he said.

I took a deep breath, vowing to myself to hold on to my courage. "Dad, it's been eight years since Mom died. We have to put a headstone on her grave."

I could hear his breath through the phone line.

"I'll be home at Christmas," I continued. "David's coming out from New York. Lynne's already in LA. Can we go to the cemetery and do this?"

Where did his mind go then? Eight years? Already? He couldn't push the darkness away any longer. "Let's do it," he said finally.

That simple.

A WEEK BEFORE CHRISTMAS, I FLEW TO LOS ANGELES. My brother would arrive the next day. My dad met me at the gate at LAX, his shirt collar open, no briefcase in hand, just a smile and two arms opened wide for me.

The next weekend, the sun was warm when he drove the three of us to the cemetery in the valley. No one spoke about what we were doing. We drove to the valley like we were in a car together all the time. (We never were.) My sister was chatty, asking about my hair color—I had honey and darker browns woven in for a tortoiseshell effect. My brother regaled us with a tale about a piano recital he'd given dressed in a coat with tails. My father loved hearing about that.

I imagine all of our stomachs turned over when the car made a left into the cemetery parking lot.

At the funeral parlor, we were sent to an office to look at catalogs of gravestones. I had worried the staff there would say something about how long ago my mother had died, but no one mentioned it.

David and Lynne sat on the couch in the office, waiting it out, while my dad and I sat at a big table turning glossy catalog pages. He looked dazed by the task—out of his body, I would call it now. I turned page after page of gravestones, going through them quickly. None were right until I came to one with birds and flowers bordering a blank area for text. I showed it to my family, sure that I had found it. Everyone agreed.

Next came the hardest part. We had to write the words that would literally be etched in stone. We went to the car for privacy.

In the parking lot, the sun streamed hot through our opened car windows. This was the San Fernando Valley in December.

"We need three lines," I started, interrupting a strained silence. "The first two can be for her name and dates. The third can be for whatever we want to say about her."

My dad was happy to be given a plan. He reached over the seat to hand me a yellow legal pad and one of his silver Cross pens.

We tossed around ideas, including "Forever in Peace." I thought "forever" sounded too final, so Over. But it was the best one we'd come up with. I suggested a variation—"Ever with Peace"—and they liked it.

Great. Done.

My father went inside to finish the paperwork while the three of us sat in silence. He came back with bad news. Her gravestone wouldn't be ready for two weeks. I would be in San Francisco by then, David would be in New York, Lynne would be in the South Bay. We might never come here again.

"Why don't we go to Mom's grave now?" I suggested. "We're all here."

They liked the idea.

My dad drove with a cemetery brochure in his hand, my mother's section number written on it. He parked when he found the section, and we scattered in four directions, searching for a small square of metal lying flush with the lawn. All of us looking for Mom.

The blue sky seemed indifferent as I walked, avoiding stepping on flat gravestones. I remembered the day of the funeral. We had sat in the shade of a tree. A clue! Today that tree would be my North Star.

I spotted a tree up ahead on a gentle slope. Getting closer, I could see a grave marker peeking out from the grass. I bent close to read the numbers on the plastic-covered metal.

"Found it!" I shouted.

The others hurried over.

We stood in a close circle around the metal marker at our feet. A sob burst from my brother, and ready arms reached out to console him and each other. It was the first time we'd ever had a connection like this, the first time we'd shared our profound sadness over this loss together.

I remembered again the day my mother had called us to her room to tell us she had changed her will—that she wanted to be buried, not cremated. I had never known why.

Now I did.

FIVE YEARS LATER, OCTOBER BROUGHT MY THIRTY-first birthday.

I had seen this day coming for years, the last day my mother had imagined for me. She had beamed with love thinking of this day as we put the monkey candles into a cupboard on my thirteenth birthday. "We can use these again when you turn thirty-one," she had said. "We'll just switch the order around!"

Now there wouldn't be a single day she had dreamed of for me. My mother would be gone for the rest of my life.

At four o'clock I left my office to walk the two blocks to the San Francisco Bay for some private time. My heart felt heavy; I didn't like seeing my shadow on the sidewalk.

A foghorn wailed from somewhere across the water—sonorous and mournful. I found a spot by the railing on the empty cement promenade between the street and the seawater. No one was around.

A breeze teased my hair as I pushed back tears with the palm of a hand and closed my eyes. I didn't want to cry—not on my birthday, not today. In my mind, I said, *Here I am, Mom. I'm thirty-one.*

I told her my news. My first book was due to a publisher in three weeks. I lived in Oakland with a sweetheart. David had moved back to California in July. He lived near me and ran his own business as a municipal recycling consultant. He'd gotten married one month ago; the woman was wonderful. Lynne had moved to live near us recently, too. She had a job working the phones in customer service.

I wanted to tell my mother more, but tears were trying to come.

I opened my eyes.

And that's when it happened. Right in front of me, only ten feet away, a bouquet of long-stemmed roses bobbed on the seawater, their petals a deep ruby red.

I looked to the left. There was no one. I looked to the right. No one. I counted twelve roses and watched them dip and dance on the wind-kissed waves. One rose began to drift from the others, then a few more strayed slightly. None went far. The shape of the bouquet remained intact.

When I first heard the news of my mother's suicide, I had said it was inevitable. But this moment wasn't inevitable. This moment was hard-won. My mother was with me in spirit. She had brought this gift today to prove it. She had brought another gift too, a gift that would last long after these roses rode the steel-blue waves into the cold, dark night. By her gift on this day, my mother was showing me that life can't always continue, but love never dies.

Love is forever. Love is transcendent. Love knows the story.

And I'm still listening.

If you or someone you know is grieving a suicide, you can find support at Alliance of Hope (allianceofhope.org) and the American Foundation for Suicide Prevention (afsp.org).

For ongoing mental health support, contact the National Alliance on Mental Illness (nami.org, 1-800-950-NAMI) and the SAMHSA Helpline (1-800-662-HELP).

If you or someone you know needs immediate support, call or text 988 (Suicide & Crisis Lifeline).

Acknowledgments

Gratitude is not reserved for the living.

These acknowledgments include my profound gratitude for my mother, whose life is bared in these pages. I felt an almost palpable connection with her every time I wrote of her and felt her absence again when I finished the book. I am grateful for our time together in these pages and for the chance to set the record straight and share about who she really was and what happened. Exposing my father's many dimensions was hard sometimes; it reminded me of the importance of compassion.

I am also grateful to my brother and sister. We walked different paths on our shared journey. May kindness to ourselves always lead our way.

I thank my trusted friend, sister-writer Susan Hagen, an early reader who saw me with clear eyes and an open heart when the clouded waters of my life flowed fast and unfiltered. Her understanding gave me courage to visit the tenderest places, where language is the ladder to the light.

Much gratitude also goes to other early readers—Paula Girolo, Dan Munz, Roberta Teller—a few of the friends who generously shared their time and thoughts. I needed practice being seen and I treasure their support and encouragement.

And to Shannon Rose, who stood by me from the start: I say thank you forever.

About the Author

© *Kate Nagle Photography*

Suzanne Sherman is a memoir editor, coach, consultant, and author. Since 1996 she has taught memoir writing at colleges, online, and in workshops. She has also spoken at the California Writers Club, National Association of Memoir Writers, and Story Circle Network. Her other books are *Lesbian and Gay Marriage: Private Commitments, Public Ceremonies* (Temple University Press) and *Girlhood in America: Personal Stories 1910–2010* (SZS Publishing). Suzanne lives in Northern California.